AF255727

"What a necessary book this is! The writing *is* on the wall, and how people of faith read, resist, and rewrite it is of great urgency. Drawing on biblical and historical inspiration and his own experiences of activism and community, Eric Martin deftly breaks open ideas with humility and courage. In these pages we meet comrades for the journey, and their collective wisdom will illuminate how we move forward together."

—Amanda Daloisio, co-managing editor, *The Catholic Worker*

"In this book, Eric Martin evokes memories of Merton and the Berrigans as he looks for a public Catholicism responsive to our present-day polarization. This well-written narrative essay covers recent events, alternates between action and contemplation, and offers moral and spiritual commentary. The writing engages the reader with eyewitness authenticity, and the interviews with activists are moving. The message rings true: white supremacy has no legitimate voice in our politics."

—Roger Haight, SJ, visiting professor of theology,
Union Theological Seminary

"Eric Martin is one of the most prophetic figures of his generation. He is an heir of the Berrigan brothers and Dorothy Day—a deeply spiritual Catholic who is incarnational in praxis. *The Writing on the Wall* is a lament for a nation whose heart is bent toward fascism and a prophecy against religious leaders who seek civility over justice."

—Osagyefo Sekou, pastor, Valley and Mountain Fellowship

"Eric Martin's *The Writing on the Wall* takes readers to the front lines in Charlottesville in order to pull back the curtain on the tangled histories of hate that led to that day. Deeply reported, thoroughly revolutionary, and theologically attuned to the crisis in American politics and religion, this book is a collective psalm for our times."

—Kaya Oakes, author of *The Defiant Middle*

"Few books you read this year will be as provocative as Eric Martin's *The Writing on the Wall*. To 'provoke' is a 'calling forth' to form a church of divine inbreaking, 'grace with feet,' and a radical discipleship so foreign to our current status quo. It is a call to an embodied active love that refuses to be a place for 'sheltered piety.' Like the folding of a thousand paper cranes, is it about peace or fighting white supremacy? Yes."

—Gregory Boyle, founder, Homeboy Industries

The Writing on the Wall

The Writing on the Wall

Signs of Faith against Fascism

ERIC MARTIN

CASCADE *Books* · Eugene, Oregon

THE WRITING ON THE WALL
Signs of Faith against Fascism

Cascade Books
An Imprint of Wipf and Stock Publishers
199 W. 8th Ave., Suite 3
Eugene, OR 97401

www.wipfandstock.com

PAPERBACK ISBN: 978-1-6667-5909-9
HARDCOVER ISBN: 978-1-6667-5910-5
EBOOK ISBN: 978-1-6667-5911-2

Cataloguing-in-Publication data:

Names: Martin, Eric, author.

Title: The writing on the wall : signs of faith against fascism / Eric Martin.

Description: Eugene, OR : Cascade Books, 2023.

Identifiers: ISBN 978-1-6667-5909-9 (paperback) | ISBN 978-1-6667-5910-5 (hardcover) | ISBN 978-1-6667-5911-2 (ebook)

Subjects: LCSH: Unite the Right Rally (2017: Charlottesville (Va.)). | Social change—Religious aspects—Christianity. | Christian sociology.

Classification: F234.C47 M25 2023 (print) | F234.C47 (ebook)

Sections of this book came from articles previously published in The Flood Magazine, Sojourners, Political Theology Network, and The Bias Magazine.

Special thanks to the artists who gave permission to use their works, including Lindsey Leahy, Ramona Martinez (http://ramonamartinez.net), Sarah Fuller (http://sarahfullerart.com), N. O. Bonzo (http://nobonzo.com), Ben Wildflower (http://benwildflower.com), and Claire Payton & Bunmi Collins (https://www.stickynotecreative.com/), as well as the Archives and Special Collections, St. Catherine University, St. Paul, Minnesota, for permission to use a piece by Ade Bethune.

100% of author proceeds will go to survivors of Unite the Right attacks on August 11 and 12, 2017, distributed by Congregate Charlottesville.

Dedicated to many I won't name,
in deep love and gratitude.
Y'all know who you are.

"The two Confederate statues located in downtown Charlottesville have been vandalized for the second time in a week . . . The Stonewall Jackson statue appears to have been hardest hit. The noses on the two angelic icons on the base of the statue appear to have been knocked off . . . while the sword in the hand of the male angel symbol appears to have been broken. The Robert E. Lee statue has an eagle symbol at the base, and its beak is no longer there.

Legal analyst [so and so] says this is a very serious offense."

—Local news report, 2019

"1619"
"Freedom"
"Black Lives Matter"
"Native Land"

—Robert E. Lee statue, Charlottesville

Table of Contents

List of Illustrations and Photographs x
Introduction: Unite the Rite xi

PART I: Relocating Religious Leaders

Ch. 1: Of Charlottesville, Anti-Klan Reverends, & Gospel Specificity 3
Ch. 2: Of Open-Hearted Heresy, Pseudo-Anti-racisms,
    & the MAGAsterium 23
Ch. 3: Of Confederate Idols, the King's Wall,
    & an Ungovernable God of Graffiti 46

Interlude: An Interview with Rabbi Mordechai Liebling 67

PART II: Considering Ivory Virtues: Civility & Nonviolence

Ch. 4: Of Middle Fingers, Biblical Beheadings, & Anti-Civility 77
Ch. 5: Of Nazi-Slaying, Nonviolence, and the Mad Messiah 95

Interlude: An Interview with Dr. Jalane Schmidt 114

PART III: To Love and to Pray in a Fascist Creep

Ch. 6: Of Enemy-Love, Vengeance Psalms, and Flaming Nostrils 127
Ch. 7: Of Sacred Offensives, Destructive Prayer,
    & Our Lady of Anti-Fascism 143

Coda: The Writings on the Walls 163

Acknowledgments 169
Bibliography 171

List of Illustrations and Photographs

Figure 1. *Johnny Reb, 1909*, Ramona Martinez 1

Figure 2. *Protestor Mary*, Sarah Fuller 12

Figure 3. *Miraculous Metal*, Ben Wildflower 33

Figure 4. *Swords into Plowshares*, Bunmi Collins and Claire Payton 64

Figure 5. *Mary Punching Beast*, Ben Wildflower 75

Figure 6. Photo taken by author 79

Figure 7. *Against the Fascist Creep*, N. O. Bonzo 89

Figure 8. *My House Is a House of Prayer*, Ade Bethune 107

Figure 9. *Jonah*, Sarah Fuller 125

Figure 10. *Our Lady of Anti-fascism*, Ramona Martinez 158

Figure 11. Photo taken by Ramona Martinez 160

Figure 12. Photo #1 of Heather Heyer Way, taken by Lindsey Leahy 163

Figure 13. Photo #2 of Heather Heyer Way, taken by Lindsey Leahy 164

Figure 14. Photo #3 of Heather Heyer Way, taken by Lindsey Leahy 167

Introduction: Unite the Rite

In Charlottesville, at the corner of Fourth and Water, in the downtown shopping district, I was suddenly overwhelmed with the realization that these were human bodies among the blood and glass on the street. I won't detail the scene except to say this brokenness and death revealed a predictable snapshot of rising fascism, which is to say a portrait of hell. The whole national illusion of unity and shared existence was shown to be a vapid dream, and standing there would wake anyone from its slumber.

The day's brutality remains with those who experienced it, deep in the bone and marrow. The town's name became a reference point for a white riot, for swastikas and Confederate flags, for vicious and racist beatings, for a president who refused to condemn the Klan in an uncomplicated manner, for bodies flying in the air, for murder. The place where we lived, the life within that space and among a vivid community that labored and grew something impossible together, got reduced to a symbol for the new forms of an ancient bloodthirst down in the roots of our nation. People continue to bear that legacy in their bodies, their wounds, their traumas, and their memories.

What happened in Charlottesville on August 11 and 12, 2017, during Unite the Right might have become the flashpoint of white supremacist terrorism and the fascist creep, but it was just one manifestation of a nationwide movement animated by well-financed organizational and cultural momentum. Its image arises too in places as disparate as Portland, Austin, Richmond, and Berkeley. From Los Angeles to Boston, groups bent on accelerating social breakdown or murdering their demographic enemies have been coming further into the open since Trump's 2016 presidential run. But they're found in small towns and rural spaces too, like Fredericksburg, Virginia, and Shasta County, California. Across the country, people are organizing more aggressively for violence against people of color, Jews,

LGBTQ folk, women, Muslims, and immigrants. Which is to say, we live in a land of Charlottesvilles. That hellish intersection is a national crossroads.

I cannot help but connect Fourth and Water in Charlottesville to Fourth and Walnut in Louisville, Kentucky, as the Trappist monk Thomas Merton experienced it in 1958. Having lived in a cloistered monastery for almost two decades, he had absorbed a narrative that his removed life as a professional religious was above the calling of the typical city dweller. But on a trip into town, he experienced a dissolution of the supposed boundaries between the holy, monastic men and the profane commoners. At the site that now bears a municipal marker quoting his epiphany, he reflected:

> In Louisville, at the corner of Fourth and Walnut, in the center of the shopping district, I was suddenly overwhelmed with the realization that I loved all those people, that they were mine and I theirs, that we could not be alien to one another even though we were total strangers. It was like waking from a dream of separateness . . .
>
> This sense of liberation from an illusory difference was such a relief and such a joy to me that I almost laughed out loud. And I suppose my happiness could have taken form in the words: "Thank God, thank God that I *am* like other people, that I am only a human among others" . . .
>
> I have the immense joy of being *human*, a member of a race in which God became incarnate. As if the sorrows and stupidities of the human condition could overwhelm me, now I realize what we all are. And if only everybody could realize this! But it cannot be explained. There is no way of telling people that they are all walking around shining like the sun.[1]

Merton's vision, beautiful as it is profound, has inspired generations behind him, becoming canon in the Catholic Left and "progressive" Christianity more generally. But I found it offered little of use on the streets of my town, watching them try to keep Heather Heyer alive just feet away in that narrow street lined by brick walls. Merton may have encountered a deep love for everyone, but all I saw in front of me was love's negation, the cold and calculated result of accelerating thousands of pounds of metal at

---

1. Merton, *Conjectures of a Guilty Bystander*, 156–57.

top speed into a group of humans. Where Merton thanked God for others, here was the refusal to accept them, the insistence on seeing others as demographic competition, on keeping the strangers alien and codifying separateness. I felt immense dissonance reflecting on the Christian story that God became incarnate in this mess and mash of flesh I saw in the gutter. It couldn't be explained. These people were all walking around shining like the sun just moments before.

Fourth and Walnut had nothing to say that could be heard over the screaming and wailing at Fourth and Water. I found that I needed something else to think through the creep of fascism, in its visceral and grisly reality, something even the best of my own white Catholic tradition might not have to offer. I would later learn that at the exact place of Merton's epiphany of unity, people set a Confederate flag on fire over a bourbon barrel just days after George Floyd was murdered and amid protests over the police killing of Breonna Taylor.[2] The very times seemed to challenge, even defy, Merton's unifying epiphany right where it occurred.

This book grew from that disjuncture, that gap between what wisdom seemed available in my religious tradition and what actions and philosophies seemed required in the present political emergencies. It doesn't present a comprehensive philosophy of fascism or anti-fascism, a history behind white power groups or how they have been resisted, or even an in-depth view into the struggle in Charlottesville to live and love in defiance of what came to be called "The Summer of Hate."[3] It simply reflects questions, scriptural analyses, thought experiments, interviews, research, and stories. I offer it in hope that people of faith might find something that connects their religious commitments to their moral concerns and instinct for community in the face of growing fascist momentum.

For religious students who've been fed tepid repetitions of credal piety and irrelevant sermons that have nothing to do with the uprisings around

---

2. "Protesters take to the streets again."

3. Helpful books of these kinds can be found in Mark Bray's *Antifa: An Anti-fascist Handbook*, Devin Zane Shaw's *Philosophy of Antifascism: Punching Nazis and Fighting White Supremacy*, Kathleen Bellew's *Bring the War Home: The White Power Movement and Paramilitary America*, and Hilary Moore and James Tracy's *No Fascist USA! The John Brown Anti-Klan Committee and Lessons for Today's Movement*, among others.

the world, I hope it opens a small window into a much larger theological space with rebellious traditions as old as fascism, colonialism, and even the enslavement of the ancient Israelites. It offers people of all ages a way to see divine paths in the many forms of resistance to Nazism, the Klan, Confederate culture, and their offspring. And for those already involved or immersed, especially to my Catholic Worker communities and various friends of subversive orthodoxies,[4] I expect you might find some idea of your own recycled here that will help more of us along the way.

George Orwell observed in 1944 that the term fascism was invoked so much as to be meaningless. "I have heard it applied to farmers," he said, "shopkeepers, Social Credit, corporal punishment, fox-hunting, bull-fighting, the 1922 Committee, the 1941 Committee, Kipling, Gandhi, Chiang Kai-Shek, homosexuality, Priestley's broadcasts, Youth Hostels, astrology, women, dogs and I do not know what else."[5] The same overuse broadly continues in the twenty-first century, from media outlets calling Obama and George W. Bush fascists to Rush Limbaugh likening feminists to Nazis and media outlets labeling *anti*-fascists "fascists." Relying on public discourse to clarify the term's meaning would stretch it beyond any reference point.

The understanding of fascism used here starts with that of historian Robert Paxton, who insists that since there is no foundational fascist manifesto or consistent doctrine across examples of fascism, it's best understood according to how it functions rather than what it states. "Fascism is a system of political authority and social order intended to reinforce the unity, energy, and purity of communities in which liberal democracy stands accused of producing division and decline," he says.[6] The imagery is always that of rising, a people who have been wronged ascending like a phoenix from ashes, reborn and claiming again its inherent nobility that had been diluted or stained by a lesser and invasive (or domestic yet traitorous) subpopulation. Fascist narratives decried that democracy's penchant for (in theory) welcoming all equally to governmental control leads inevitably to social decline, victimizing those who once sat atop the social hierarchy and creating a supposed crisis that can't be solved using traditional means. If

4. All gratitude to Robert Inchausti for the phrase. See his *Subversive Orthodoxy*.

5. Orwell, *As I Please*, 113.

6. Paxton, "Five Stages of Fascism," 21.

the primary group is to reclaim its stature as masters, a "national chieftan who alone is capable of incarnating the group's historical destiny" is given leeway to use violent methods against outsiders.[7] Because this violence is redemptive, it attains a kind of aesthetic beauty that draws the group not only to reluctant tolerance of it but also a level of appreciation and at times even awe. Violence against intrusive outsiders—whether they be Jews, queer people, immigrants, or any other—becomes salvific.

This general narrative encapsulates what Paxton calls the mobilizing passions of fascism. But he warns against collapsing it into its most public faces of evil. It depends on a sustaining culture that only exists because of the habits and lives of a critical mass of the broader population:

> Conventional images of fascism . . . focus on moments of high drama in the fascist itinerary—the March on Rome, the Reichstag fire, *Kristallnacht*—and omit the solid texture of everyday experience and the complicity of ordinary people in the establishment and functioning of fascist regimes. Fascist movements could never grow without the help of ordinary people, even conventionally good people. Fascists could never attain power without the acquiescence or even active assent of the traditional elites—heads of state, party leaders, high government officials . . . The excesses of fascism in power also required wide complicity among members of the establishment: magistrates, police officials, army officers, businessmen. To understand fully how fascist regimes worked, we must dig down to the level of ordinary people and examine the banal choices they made in their daily routines. Making such choices meant accepting an apparent lesser evil or averting the eyes from some excesses that seemed not too damaging in the short term, even acceptable piecemeal, but which cumulatively added up to monstrous end results.[8]

Due to this everydayness of fascism, it can become difficult for many to recognize it in real time. Like a chameleon, it takes on the hue and garb of its surroundings. (This helps explain why, for example, anti-Semitism is integral to Germany's fascism but was absent from Italy's for the first sixteen years.[9]) Fascism in Japan or Spain will look different than in Brazil or Britain, he says, because each people's narrative of what makes them a

7. Paxton, *Anatomy of Fascism*, 219.

8. Paxton, *Anatomy of Fascism*, 13–14.

9. For a treatment of Jewish life in Italy under Mussolini, see Sarfatti, *Jews in Mussolini's Italy*.

special people of destiny depends on localized stereotypes and enemies. "An authentically popular fascism in the United States," he says, more to the point of this book, "would be pious and anti-Black," appearing far more religious in nature than that of European iterations.[10]

Fascism has risen in its more spectacular forms before in the US. The American Nazi Party is the most famous example, but during World War II there were also the Silver Shirts ("S.S."), a group inspired by Hitler that grew to over 15,000 people and tried to overthrow the San Diego government,[11] the German American Bund of 25,000 pro-Hitler Nazis that held a 1939 rally with 20,000 people in Madison Square Garden,[12] and the Christian Front of New York and Boston, made up of Catholics who aimed to "install in the United States a temporary dictatorship that would eliminate Communists and Jews" and was given "political cover, theological leadership, and ecclesiastic approval" by priests.[13]

But the roots of fascism go deeper in American history, just as American history sinks further into the roots of fascism. Paxton argues that while the story usually begins with Benito Mussolini in Italy, it should rightly go back to the previous century and across the Atlantic. Afraid of Black Americans being able to vote and exercise freedom in the Reconstruction era, the KKK formed itself into a militia to return things to the old social order. "The Klan constituted an alternate civic authority, parallel to the legal state," he notes, using organized violence while dressed in uniforms to advance the white race. "The first version of the Klan in the defeated American South was a remarkable preview of the way fascist movements were to function in interwar Europe," Paxton observes. "It is arguable, at least, that fascism (understood functionally) was born in the late 1860s in the American South."[14] Its genesis in this case is not so much in Italy or Munich but Pulaski, Tennessee.

Paxton's suggestion is hardly new, as Hitler himself called the US "the one state" with the kind of racist laws that Germany would emulate in the Nuremberg Laws. Legal scholar James Whitman says in *Hitler's American Model* that at a key 1934 meeting that developed the anti-Jewish laws, "the

10. Paxton, "Five Stages of Fascism," 22–3.

11. For a Jewish response to the group, see Atwood, "'This List Is Not Complete,'" 142–45.

12. See Marshall Curry's 2017 documentary *A Night at the Garden*.

13. Gallagher, *Nazis of Copley Square*, 2.

14. Paxton, "Five Stages of Fascism," 12.

most radical Nazis present were the most ardent champions of the lessons that American approaches held for Germany."[15] The highest-ranking Nazi politicians, judges, and legal scholars held multiple meetings examining how the United States committed genocide against Natives and set up a legal system of enslavement and segregation against Black people. When Whitman asks, "Is the South fascist?" he finds it sufficient to answer that the story of the Third Reich can't be told without American white supremacy providing "some of the working materials" for Nazism and notes that "it was not outlandish for them to think of their program of the early 1930s as a more thoroughgoing and rigorous realization of American approaches toward Blacks, Asians, Native Americans, Filipinos, Puerto Ricans, and others."[16]

The Klan behind the culture that captured Hitler's attention was not a small band of vigilantes but at its height grew to between four and six million people and included in its ranks governors, Congress members, police chiefs, and even a Supreme Court justice. (And though no evidence exists that President Wilson was a member, his close friend wrote the book that launched the second Klan and he publicly praised the movie that came from it, making *The Birth of a Nation* the first film ever shown at the White House and helping the KKK eventually reach a membership of roughly five percent of the national population.) A Klan historian notes that the group's program was supported by millions more, "possibly even a majority of Americans," and as a result it "seemed ordinary and respectable to contemporaries. At many of its events, elected officials spoke."[17] While it had plenty of rural people of poorer classes, it's important to remember that even from the beginning it was a group that defied the stereotype of the backwards, uncivilized yokel. A resident of the small town where it was born recalled that the early Klan "was composed of the nicest and most cultured young men in the town and country, thus the origin of the club's name is Greek." Another said that "the very conception of the Ku-Klux was amid influences elevating and refining, and its charter members were gentlemen of education and refined tastes."[18]

15. Whitman, *Hitler's American Model*, 2.
16. Whitman, *Hitler's American Model*, 145, 161.
17. Gordon, *Second Coming of the Klan*, 3.
18. Parsons, *Ku-Klux*, 31.

But as Orwell said, there are many ways of defining fascism. Politician, poet, and early postcolonial theorist Aimé Césaire stated in his landmark *Discourses on Colonialism* that fascism is just European colonialism brought home. For example, before the Nazi genocide against the Jews was Germany's 1904–1907 genocide against the Herero and Nama peoples in present-day Namibia, using cruel medical experiments, concentration camps, mass starvation, torture, and rape (if people didn't die by disease or exhaustion). They shipped Herero skulls back to Germany for race scientists to "prove" the inferiority of Africans, and those who survived were forced into slavery—all methods that would be re-employed in the Holocaust. Césaire noted that politicians who were lauded for resisting European fascism were likewise celebrated for colonial rule, revealing the hypocrisy of the continent's morals and civility. He also highlighted a staple of fascism by pointing out the willful amnesia of those who benefit from its inequities, a trait all too relevant in the United States today:

> Before the arrival of the French in their country, the Vietnamese were people of an old culture, exquisite and refined. To recall this fact upsets the digestion of the Banque d'Indochine. Start the forgetting machine!
>
> These Madagascans who are being tortured today, less than a century ago were poets, artists, administrators? Shhhhh! Keep your lips buttoned! And silence falls, silence as deep as a safe![19]

While Paxton pushed the birth of fascism past Mussolini to the rise of the Klan, Césaire's vision goes even further, marking it at least as early as European expansion and the first slave ships. The notions work together rather than compete, particularly in US history where the slave ships make a straight line to the Klan. And it takes only minimal imagination to harmonize this picture with others that widen the focus even more, like that of Penny Nakatsu. She gave her understanding of fascism in the US at the Black Panther Party's United Front Against Fascism conference in Oakland in 1969, including the imprisonment of Japanese Americans during World War II in the definition. "I'm speaking of the incarceration of more than 110,000 people, human beings, for the crime of having yellow faces, of having Asian names," she said. "I will not call them relocation camps. I will not

19. Césaire, *Discourse on Colonialism*, 52.

call them detention camps . . . I come from a generation of children born in concentration camps," she insisted, invoking the name usually reserved for places like Auschwitz or Dachau.[20]

My students usually ask whether Nakatsu identifies *fascism* or something *fascistic*. This question arises all over fascism studies. Was Franco's Spain fascism per se, or a murderous and authoritarian government that closely resembled fascism without fitting all its criteria? The question also appears in discussions about today's political landscape in the US. Do the sometimes-tight and sometimes-loose coalitions of white nationalists, Confederates, Nazis, white-supremacist street gangs like Rise Above Movement, white "identitarians," and what has been called the "alt-right" constitute an actual fascist movement, or is it "merely" a bloc of groups working together for a white ethno-state? Countless articles and talking heads have chimed in on whether Donald Trump is a fascist, including Paxton (who insisted for four years that he was not, only to change his mind after the Capitol riot[21]).

What these questions highlight again is the word's malleability. They seem helpful if the goal is forming a precise, shared line of demarcation between fascism and near-fascism, but they sound utterly irrelevant if protecting vulnerable people from fascist and fascistic violence is the focus. What does it matter to the Basque farmers struggling to avoid falling bombs whether Franco is slightly on this side or that of the dividing line? What's the difference if Milo Yiannopoulos is outright or nearly fascist to an immigrant without documentation who is about to be doxxed by him in a public speech, endangering their life?

The definition from anti-fascist journalist Talia Lavin helps in this regard. Lavin calls fascism "the words and actions of those who espouse a politics of genocide, who seek to destroy and harm members of marginalized groups, who openly or covertly align themselves with past and present fascistic movements, and who agitate for or commit acts of violence against the minorities they despise."[22] For those concerned with protecting people in peril, the struggle against fascism will resist white supremacist or anti-trans violence, for example, even if it doesn't come adorned with

20. Nakatsu, "Speech at the United Front against Fascism," 271.

21. For his early, negative assessment of the link between Trump and fascism, see Paxton, "American Duce"; for his later, positive assessment, see Paxton, "I've Hesitated to Call Donald Trump a Fascist."

22. Lavin, "On the Uses and Manifestations of Antifascism," 1.

white hoods, swastika armbands, or fascist membership cards. The word's uncertain boundaries shouldn't act as a grace for those toeing the line but demand that we resist any who approach it. As Lavin puts it, "antifascism exists in relation to fascism as antimatter does to matter—its opposite, and, hopefully, its equal." If people do violence at the edge of fascism's definition, antifascists will have to meet them there.

Yet conveniently, many of the groups animated by Trump's 2016 presidential run rendered the debates moot by adopting the most overt symbols of fascism. Alt-right leader Richard Spencer wasted no time in leading a room of Hitler salutes in a public, recorded forum in the nation's capital just after the election, shouting "Hail, Trump!" after referring to the press with the same German word the Nazis used for them. Yiannopoulos sang to his friends while they gave him Hitler salutes. The Discord servers used by Unite the Right planners were published by anti-fascist media outlet Unicorn Riot, revealing ample Nazi imagery of all kinds. Some of them would carry fascist symbols into public in Charlottesville, shouting Nazi slogans like "Blood and Soil" or sporting a Hitler shirt, a swastika flag or tattoo. We don't need to wring our hands about whether or not these movements are fascist when they have adopted fascist symbols, historical figures, chants, and aims as their inspiration, often openly. We do not need to debate whether or not Trump is consciously acting in a fascist manner if we focus instead on how he has *functioned*—purposefully or not—to embolden and inspire groups acting in its name and manner.

Fascism is here in the open today. Unite the Right in Charlottesville in 2017 and in the Capitol riot of 2021 are its most visible manifestations, but it rises across the nation in overt and more hidden ways for those paying attention. And, as Paxton predicted for the United States, its intensification has everything to do with religion.

I remember the crosses. Symbols of all kinds paraded through Charlottesville on flags and shirts and armbands, but among them were crosses.

The head of the Traditionalist Worker Party, a now-disbanded street gang operating under the guise of a "white rights" group, displayed a cross on the helmet he wore in preparation for brawling. Others carried shields bearing crosses, as if they were the medieval crusaders so many of them post on their social media. One of the designs was specifically modeled after the St. Andrew's Cross, flown by the League of the South, a white separatist group itching for an independent (and, unsurprisingly, white) South. A variation of the flag was split, half Confederate flag, half cross, the arms blending seamlessly from one cross to the next.

Regarding my own church, evidence suggests that far more Catholics showed up on the wrong side of the Unite the Right riot than the right one. This certainly couldn't be said of Jews or Buddhists or Muslims. Catholics crossed state lines to join the various assortments of neo-Nazis, alt-righters, and the Klan, but it seems nobody who worked at the Catholic parish less than a block down the street bothered to make the trek to protect those at risk. There were more Catholics allied with the League of the South, literally blending the Cross of Christ with the Confederate flag, than there to oppose them. And they interpreted the event as a liturgical one, playing on the name Unite the Right to dub it Unite the Rite.

This suggests a massive cultural problem in the church, made all the more visible when Unicorn Riot published the Discord chats. Among the planning for violence in Charlottesville and chat rooms called "Swastika," "Waffen-SS," and "Fascist Bootcamp" are others set aside for Bible study, prayer groups, and several solely for Catholics, including one exploring what "extra ecclesiam nulla salus" (outside the church there is no salvation) means. Among the predictable racism and anti-LGBTQ rhetoric in the most extreme forms, are anti-Semitic prayers, celebrations for members that have been confirmed into the church or accepted into the Knights of Columbus, pictures featuring rosaries on guns reserved for "our enemies," and conversations about combining monasticism with the neo-Nazi group Atomwaffen or the merits of Augustine and Chesterton. One image that stands out is an icon of Christ hanging on a wooden swastika instead of a cross, his body contorted to match the disfigured rood, revealing just how much the Third Reich and the Second Coming are intertwined in the worldview of these thousands of users in the Christian spaces with over half a million posts.

In a deep dive into online white supremacist groups, including a chapter on religious fascists, Talia Lavin addresses the common idea that people exchanging hate on the internet pose no real threat in the physical world. "The thing about hate, though, is it metastasizes," Lavin writes. "The thing about channels that are filled, twenty-four hours a day, with stochastic violence—testosterone-filled megaphones shouting for blood—is that sooner or later, someone is going to take them up on it. From Robert Bowers [who killed eleven people in a Pittsburgh synagogue] to Anders Breivik [who self-identifies as a Nazi and killed seventy-seven people in Norway] to Brenton Tarrant [who killed fifty-one people in Christchurch, New Zealand mosques], racist networks have proven over and over again that the steady dissemination of murderous propaganda leaves a trail of blood behind it."[23]

This Christian presence in fascist spaces isn't unique just to online chats or a weekend in Charlottesville. More fascist groups today than not come with a Christian wing or are driven centrally by Christians, as Paxton suggested would be the case in the US. The January 6 Capitol riot had people in overt fascist imagery—including a "Camp Auschwitz" hoodie and Confederate flags—blended in with prayer sessions, large crosses within sight of the hanging noose just outside the building, and a picture of Jesus with a MAGA hat on. The woman who stole Nancy Pelosi's laptop once they overtook the police has a Twitter account plastered with Bible verses and two pictures of (a very white) Jesus up top, along with a portrait of herself giving a Hitler salute.[24] (The Christian presence in the riot was so large that it was referred to in the media as "a Christian revolt."[25]) In Portland alone the Proud Boys, who have a subgroup called The Catholic Proud Boys,[26] work closely with street brawlers who call themselves Patriot Prayer, led by a man who appears sometimes wearing a "John 3:16" shirt. One of the main Proud Boys there was arrested for pulling out a sizeable revolver and pointing it directly at anti-fascists just feet away during a protest, all while wearing multiple weapons hanging from his body armor that bore a patch with three Christian crosses on it.

Examples of Christofascism from the last six years abound to the point of exhaustion. In 2019 a devout Catholic in Atomwaffen, a neo-Nazi group with an offshoot store run by someone calling themselves "Catholic-waffen," murdered a gay, Jewish teen after setting up a fake date in Orange County. Another neo-Nazi group, The Base, was started by a Catholic who advertised it as "the most hardcore collection of pro-white individuals in the world" and made the group's first public statement, "Führer, you were only the beginning. We will finish what you started." (Seven members were

<hr>

23. Lavin, *Culture Warlords*, 130.

24. Evans, "Woman Accused of Stealing Nancy Pelosi's Laptop Appears in Video Making Nazi Salute."

25. Boorstein, "Capitol Attack Was a Kind of Christian Revolt."

26. As their Twitter account has been suspended, see Kitts, "Proud Boys, Nationalism, and Religion," 12–32.

arrested in 2020 for planning an attack on a rally in Richmond and plotting to kill Antifa members and media in Georgia. Three of them brought more than 1,600 rounds of ammunition and a homemade machine gun.[27]) Another from the Catholic Discord server was revealed by Anti-fascist Action Nebraska to be statewide field director for the governor of Nebraska, running a team of twenty-four people and encouraging his fellow Nazis to start working for Republican politicians.[28] ("It's easy, boys," he said. "Let's take this whole apparatus over.") The creator of America First Political Action Conference, which hosts federal and state-level Republicans in an attempt to mainstream his Nazism, wears his Catholicism on his sleeve between publicly invoking Hitler and talking wistfully about the Holocaust. From alt-right architect Steve Bannon working in Trump's administration to anonymous foot soldiers bragging online about putting Nazi recruitment materials on college campus walls, Christians are not just part of the fascist creep but constitutive of its populace and ideology.

"Are there any Christians against fascism?" a student asked me on the first day of class in 2022, full of hope. The question stuck with me. Of course there are many, but the uncertainty itself was telling. The lack (but not complete absence) of an organized, public opposition to fascism today by people of faith threatens to cede the massive potential in the churches to those many who are blessing the fascist creep with their gods, their sacraments, their cultural capital. It runs the risk of prodding young people who are thirsty for meaningful engagement in justice work that takes seriously their faith lives and the moral emergencies all around them into paralysis or resignation. I hear from dozens of students every semester various forms of the same message: *I want to be righteous in this time of encroaching evils, but I'm not sure how. What do I do?* Stagnant churches are declaring themselves worthless to these people with waking consciences. And as the fascist creep turns into a march that promises to accelerate with or without Trump, feigned neutrality is an ecclesial crime.

Even though I was studying theology at the time, I found precious few resources to speak to what happened at Fourth and Water in Charlottesville

27. Kelly, "From a Catholic Prep School to Nazism."

28. Antifa Nebraska, "Bennett Bressman, Nebraska Governor's Field Director"; Osberg, "GOP Governor Had White Nationalist on Payroll."

from within my faith tradition. I remember going to Mass the following morning, in a daze and grappling to comprehend what just erupted in our town, and the priest said absolutely nothing to even acknowledge the historic attack. The liturgy went forward as if in a vacuum. Like so many of my students, I sank further into frustration and anger with Christian culture.

Yet there was no need for defeatism. Answers might have evaded me but patchwork paths forward presented themselves all around, from within communities of faith and without. This book hopes to help build, in however small a way, an already-growing culture of revolutionary Christian care that sets itself against fascism and fascists, echoing the pockets of insurrectionary love I found along the way. It's more fragments of an anti-fascist faith than systematic theology. More a collection of anarchist antiphons than a complete psalter. It's a modest gathering of what I found from radical traditions, including biblical and militant (or both), that can speak meaningfully to what we encountered at Fourth and Water.

If too many churches have taken no stance, we can still find people of faith insisting with hands held that we can't let fascists fill any more graves. This book merely seeks to share a piece of their stories, outlooks, and spiritualities, along with those with no religion who nevertheless have much to teach Christians about love, justice, and solidarity. These chapters are an invitation to respond to their testimonies with something more than words.

Part I. Relocating Religious Leaders

Poem and letterpress block print by Ramona Martinez, Charlottesville, 2020.

Johnny Reb, 1909, Ramona Martinez

1

Of Charlottesville, Anti-Klan Reverends, & Gospel Specificity

> *Where this flower blooms*
> *There is beauty in shortcomings.*
> *No real expectation to be perfect,*
> *Blooming in the trenches,*
> *That's above average after all.*
> *Surviving.*
>
> —ZYAHNA BRYANT[1]

"I SWEAR THEY WANT a Jewish Confederacy," a bearded man with a Confederate tie confided softly to his neighbor, leaning in conspiratorially. "And if we aren't careful, that's exactly what they'll get."

That was the first comment I heard from him during that city council meeting in February of 2017. Local high schooler Zyahna Bryant had pushed the idea of removing the prominent Robert E. Lee statue downtown and renaming Lee Park all the way to a vote that night. I was new to Charlottesville and had never seen anything like the scene that played out that night. Adults screamed at councilors as they voted in a room with even the standing room in the back filled. Police had to intervene when what looked like a fifty-year-old businessman threatened to take a Black high school student outside and beat him. An elderly woman dressed in Civil War–era

---

1. Bryant, *Reclaim*, 70. For more on Bryant, who brought the issue of Confederate statues in Charlottesville to public attention, see https://zybryant.com/.

clothes laughed mockingly when the Black vice-mayor said "You are not my enemy, I am not yours" to the crowd in an attempt to calm them. When a councilor explained her vote to remove the statue by invoking Isaiah 58 and its call to "loose the chains of injustice," a man red in the face bellowed "Keep Scripture in the church!" and "Burn the Bible!" And after the 3–2 vote to remove the statue, the anger was so palpable that citizens who had supported removal needed escorts out so no one assaulted them. Somewhat dazed, I jotted in my notes what Confederates of all kinds would make clear in their words and actions: "This is about so much more than a statue."

When the news spread that Charlottesville would be moving its Robert E. Lee and Stonewall Jackson statues to museums, more overt white supremacists inside and out of Charlottesville took note, leading to what became known as the Summer of Hate in 2017. The Loyal White Knights of the KKK from North Carolina came in full regalia on July 8. Locals teamed up with more prominent racists like Richard Spencer and David Duke to plan the Unite the Right event that would be held on August 12. Flash mobs of torch-wielding white supremacists appeared several times at night in front of the Lee statue, aesthetically invoking the same Klan that once held meetings in the courtroom only blocks away.

Many citizens resisted, including religious people. Christians of different denominations, Buddhists, Muslims, Jews, Catholic Workers, and various faith communities and individuals driven by their religious commitments gathered to oppose the emerging alliance of the Klan, neo-Nazis, the alt-right, and Trump supporters. A new group called Congregate Charlottesville was the main conduit for this organizing, created by Brittany Caine-Conley, a.k.a. Smash the Patriarchy, who became a central figure in town and was better known simply as Reverend Smash.

True to her name, Smash did not aim to reform or denounce or shake her fist at injustice. She wanted to smash it all—patriarchy and white supremacy and heteronormativity and Christian supersessionism. She often wore a black hat around town with the word LOVE encompassing the entire front side, and she meant that too. She believes that in certain situations to smash is to love, and to love is to smash. She became a spiritual leader in the city, a public lover whose theology, way, and witness offer a different path than the one that civic and religious institutions made available.

When the Ku Klux Klan decided to rally in downtown Charlottesville, replete with anti-Semitic signs quoting the gospels of John and Luke and "White power!" chants, she didn't shrug her shoulders and mutter something about the First Amendment as so many authorities in town encouraged citizens to do. She mobilized with fellow United Church of Christ pastor Seth Wispelwey, calling on clergy to show up with their bodies against the demonstration. They came out and opposed the KKK as a people of faith, joining the crowd of a thousand who showed up blowing vuvuzelas to drown out the Klan's messages. They moved out of the church building and onto the streets. And when local white nationalists began planning the Unite the Right riot, she and Wispelwey put out a national call for a thousand clergy to do it again.

A thousand clergy would not come. In fact, many in the town itself not only refused to join Congregate Charlottesville but argued that she was wrong to confront anyone and would bear responsibility for violence if clergy opposed the rioters planning to come armed with guns and cars and shields and clubs and mace. Recognizing the absurdity of these claims, she proceeded anyway.

There are many Christians who don't want to get involved in the revolution until they see in it a sign from heaven, that is, a religious sign. But they're not going to see more than what they're seeing, just as [the Pharisees] couldn't see any more than what Jesus was doing, which was freeing the oppressed and announcing the good news to the poor.

—*"Young Nicaraguan" in Solentiname*[2]

Hundreds of people had come for the clergy trainings to prepare for Unite the Right. The night before the "rally," many joined from out of town as pastors invited the group forward for blessings of safety. But the next morning at a 6 AM sunrise service, significantly fewer people came up for a similar altar call. And when the service ended, and Smash and Seth called on the

---

2. Cardenal, *Gospel in Solentiname Vol. 2*, 217.

clergy group to assemble, numbers had dwindled to forty or so people. I recognized only a handful of locals who had been to the trainings. We felt a great gratitude to the people in that room who had come from afar to risk, as Congregate Charlottesville's call to clergy described it, "an extremely high potential for physical violence and brutality."[3] We also felt an equally great weight at the realization that we would have to ad-lib in a dangerous situation with a new gathering that hadn't been in the same room before.

Looking around that church basement, it was clear that the initial plan to assemble a group of primarily white people had failed. We were largely a whole host of vulnerable people in that room, the exact ones that the alt-right groups openly fantasize about conquering or killing: rabbis with yarmulkes, Black pastors, women, queer and trans folk. In the corner sat public intellectual Cornel West dressed in his signature suit, and I would later see white nationalists single him out with special vitriol. Those least likely to be brutalized were largely absent.

Theological differences arose immediately when Smash and Seth shared the plan with the out-of-towners, many of whom bristled at the idea of blocking the park, risking arrest, and civil disobedience. One pastor said that her congregation could never see such a thing as a Christian act. Another pastor who had built a name by presenting as radical informed our local leaders that their plan was, in fact, territorial and colonial. To block the Klan and their friends from the park would be to exhibit a similar mindset as those we came to oppose, and this person would not join in such an action. It would be more Christian to let them have their "rally."

Smash and the other leaders responded with more restraint than should be expected when told they were acting like Nazis while trying to nonviolently disrupt Nazi organizing at the risk of their lives. By the time we left our numbers had thinned once again, with those who felt uneasy with direct action splitting off to a permitted area to pray. The rest of us assembled two-by-two. I walked arm-in-arm with a Muslim woman in a solemn procession from the church to the park bearing the now-infamous Robert E. Lee statue. I marveled that while several white Christians departed for safer quarters, she could face people who wanted her dead on racial and religious grounds.

When we arrived, we lined up single file facing the park that was already heavily barricaded with makeshift police fencing. White supremacists marched in, battalion by battalion, chests puffed and mouths running.

3. Caine-Conley and Wispelwey, "Call to Clergy and Faith Leaders."

They yelled horrible things, attacking with their words before their fists and sticks and cars. A militia stood outside the metal fencing, protecting the Klan and neo-Nazis and facing us only feet away with their armor and guns. We knew from those who infiltrated their communications that many entering the park were concealing guns and brass knuckles behind their body armor and shields. Mace cannisters hung from tactical belts. Anyone could see that these people did not come for a rally or to honor a statue. They came heavily armed to assault, maim, and kill—all of which they would do.

Tasked with getting fellow Catholics to join the clergy group, I found myself nearly empty-handed as the date approached. Out of the hundreds of people I emailed with Congregate Charlottesville's call to action, only one came—not a local, not anyone from the parish sitting less than a block from the planned site of the riot, but my friend Katie, who drove all the way from Cincinnati after work on Friday.

Two days before Unite the Right, I visited the person in charge of justice ministries at the parish in town most likely to respond. When I asked how we could get people to join the clergy group, she told me about a prayer session the night before. The parish held a vigil to reflect on and pray for the divisions in Charlottesville as a way to prepare for Saturday. They gathered, they fell silent, they lit candles, they placed the situation before God, and they went home. I pressed her on whether that satisfied them or if anyone would join us in two days, and she relayed a telling detail. After the proceedings had ended and everyone shuffled out, the last two people turned to each other and one said, "It feels so good to have *done* something." The other agreed, and with that, they left.

Smash hadn't fallen into leadership by accident but had a specific understanding of Scripture, Jesus, God, and church that made it inevitable. She was, as the rapper Lupe Fiasco once said about her, "church on the move" for a reason. Her ordination papers,[4] submitted just weeks before

---

4. All quotes in the following section are from Caine-Conley, "God's Insistence."

the KKK rally in July that preceded the Unite the Right riot, provide a clear understanding of her viewpoint precisely as the crisis point approached, revealing the thought that animated her response to the largest overt white supremacist gathering in modern US history.

Rather than theology, Smash prefers theopoetics, which she describes as opting for imagination, mystery, and "embodied experiences of the divine" instead of looking for systematic understandings of God based on logic. Rather than dogma, she looks to explore the voice she hears calling her to "Madly follow a parabolic messiah who deconstructed the conventional structures of society and religion, always gazing with a hope beyond hope at God's dream." Embedded in this call are three foundations that frame her theopoetics: deconstruction as the hermeneutics of God's kindom, Jesus as parable and parabler, and the absolute future of God's dream.

Smash draws on the theologian John Caputo's notion of deconstruction, referring to the opening of earthly realities to their animating energies, or, to use Caputo's language, to the vocative reality entering into the existential. These two realities speak to the difference between a nation's justice system and justice itself, or between specific democratic institutions and the essence of democracy. Smash uses this concept to argue that a Christian's call is to participate in ushering Jesus (the vocative realm) into the church (the existential realm), even if historical communities inevitably fail to fully enflesh the spirit of the Gospels. Caputo argues that when Christians look to the heavens to pray to Jesus, they might more easily find him in the streets, trying to get warm on a steam grate. The way Smash draws upon Caputo here reveals much about the way she understands divinity. "To Caputo's portrait of Jesus as the homeless person or undocumented immigrant," she says, "I would add the drag queen, the young Syrian, the tattooed bartender and every other face that has ever been on the margins of the Christian empire."

Jesus, for Smash, is opposed to the status quo as a result of being himself an inbreaking of the deeper reality that earthly societies sometimes try to organize around. "Jesus called and still calls his followers out of current constructions and realities, toward the transformative, upside-down, ugly, radical, and sometimes chaotic kin-dom of God." But to be called out of these constructions leaves people in a state of bewilderment, pointing toward a future, a world, and a way of being that no one can possibly understand in full. Christians must embrace this precisely as *risk*, she argues. Deconstruction is the name for how Jesus-as-event breaks through the church-as-institution.

Her second foundation is that of Jesus as parable and parabler. She argues that parables perform the opposite function of myth. Myth creates understandings of worlds. Parables subvert that understanding, opening "space for something entirely new and unexpected to happen." Take for example the parable of the mustard seed. It's typically understood to mean that the tiniest of seeds will grow into a great tree, like the cedar of Lebanon. Smash points out that the mustard seed in fact grows into something more like a shrub, an invasive plant that pops up and disrupts the vegetation in haphazard ways. (This is in line with biblical scholars John Donahue and Daniel Harrington, who say of the parable, "The point is that the kingdom is both hardy and intrusive."[5]) This is "starkly juxtaposed to the imperial power of a kingdom that would be similar to a mighty cedar," she states. "Jesus deconstructs our assumptions about the kin-dom of God." It's not big or intimidatingly strong. It's unpredictable, spreading outward instead of towering over, and it defies expectations.

Likewise, the parable of the good Samaritan undermines our expectations of who responds well to God's call. Jesus tells of a man who was beaten by robbers and left on the side of the road. While a priest and a man from a religiously respectable tribe pass by the man in the ditch, it's the Samaritan, seen as an untrustworthy foreigner, who cares for the man with his time, money, and attention. "The outsiders are in and the insiders are out," Smash says of the parable. "That's the radical, parabolic claim of the Gospel." To translate the idea of the Samaritan today, she says, "My Samaritan would be a gender queer, mixed-race teenager who has had an abortion and can't speak English." Her point is not, as she so often says, to win "the woke Olympics," but to get to the heart of what the biblical text means today. People in the twenty-first-century US don't encounter Samaritans, but Smash can drive home the unpopularity of Samaritans at the time by drawing on outcasts here and now.

These examples help uncover Jesus not just as an issuer of parables but as a parable himself. He deconstructs myths and expectations of what a messiah would be and do, entering the world unexpectedly as a lowly person and exiting it by state execution. When Christians look for the inbreaking of Jesus today, then, they have to look outside the church structures, Smash argues. Jesus shows up parabolically rather than institutionally, civilly, or comfortably. He comes in ways that upset dogma and doctrine, in manners that frustrate the orthodox. He comes in subversive ways that

5. Donahue and Harrington, *The Gospel of Mark*, 151.

look more like failure than success, more untidy than shiny, ugly and smelly rather than presentably.

Her third foundation is what she calls the absolute future of God's dream. Rather than viewing the future as a continuation of the present, perhaps with developments but by and large in keeping with the norms and assumptions of the now, Smash looks to an "absolute future" instituted by God. This reframing, she says, "shatters the horizon of all our expectations and conceived possibilities." This is God's dream, and it entails an open journey rather than a well-mapped navigation on a ready-made path. People on the journey don't know where it leads. Smash's theopoetics center around this journey because the space between our reality and God's dream is so vast it's impossible to know the way forward. Her framework focuses on *becoming*, on the coming of God's vision that always surpasses our own ability to comprehend. "Our religion centers around the most outstanding shattering of a foreseeable future: When God showed up as a poor, homeless man, who spoke in riddles and hung out with local untouchables. If we wish to follow this God, we too must be radical spiritual sojourners, getting lost on a mangled path that leads to God knows where."

Because God showed up as "weak, powerless, and mad," the only way toward God's dream is to become so ourselves. "God's kin-dom is a completely mad, strategic reversal of power and powerlessness, strength and weakness. Jesus, as the provocateur of the kin-dom, deconstructs everything we know about being reasonable, powerful, strong human beings, pointing us to a future of God's dream that we can't quite comprehend but desire with our whole selves." For Smash, Jesus embodies a reign of kinship that deconstructs reason, power, and strength toward something beautifully beyond our comprehension.

When the clergy line decided to block one of the two entrances to the park during Unite the Right so that what was becoming a small army couldn't keep assembling, we climbed a short set of stairs and linked arms in two rows. Half of us faced the street where the various white nationalist groups came in battalions to the park as the morning inched towards the scheduled start time. The other half, including me, faced those who had already gathered in the park to make sure we kept eyes on them since they were armed and aggressive. I don't remember how much time passed before I suddenly saw a group of them start entering single file to my right, coming right through our line which had apparently broken.

Some of us in the back line weren't too happy about this. Neither, apparently, were the other anti-fascists below. Not every group knew each other, and a few of them started to think we were guarding the fascists instead of trying to deny them the park. We rearranged ourselves, some of us moving from the back to the front so we would hold the line when the next group came.

It's hard to describe what it's like to know that armed Nazis with swastikas and Confederate flags are coming, intent on getting to the precise point that you are blocking, and that you've committed to nonviolence, to what Smash calls absorbing violence like Jesus rather than dealing it. My left arm was wrapped at the elbow with her right, and Seth was on her other side. We had made clear to each other when we switched from the back row that we would not let anyone through. We had nothing to guard us, no shield or mace or gun. The only arms we bore were each other's.

But, by the logic of grace, more would appear. A small group toting red flags approached and asked if we wanted them to form a line in front of us so they could take the brunt of whatever group came next. Maybe they assumed we would buckle again, or maybe they feared for our safety. Either way, I will always remember their offer. We knew that those who infiltrated the alt-right's communications found plenty of evidence that these people planned and coordinated violence. We knew there would be blood, as there was the night before and would be again just moments later. And here this little band offered to be the shield we lacked.

I looked more closely at their flag and saw that it said "IWW." I thought of Dorothy Day, who was once with the Wobblies, the Industrial Workers of the World. (And, I would later learn, one of them was a Catholic Worker from out of state.) Beneath their letters read, "AN INJURY TO ONE IS AN INJURY TO ALL." The priests from the Catholic church around the corner might not have come, but at least the spirit of Dorothy managed to appear in the form of her old union.

The Jesus who came as parabler and parable was also, to Smash, a protestor. In a sermon about Jesus' procession into Jerusalem shortly before his killing,[6] she noted that on Passover Jews flocked to Jerusalem to celebrate their liberation from Egypt centuries before. Pontius Pilate also processed into the city with his military in order to deter possible unrest, as became tradition for governors wary of Jews. Zechariah's vision of a king who would ride into Jerusalem on a donkey instead of soldiers (9:9–10) radically undercut the pomp and self-glorification of the emperor and those working for him. Jesus' act of riding in humbly was a *protest* against Roman imperialism and ornate displays of power, she emphasized. This was one of the particular kinds of parables Jesus embodied, making a highly public and political statement on the streets of the central city in the region. Reverend Smash creatively appropriated this Jesus to the present moment in her preaching:

FIGURE 2

Jesus is holding up protest signs that say . . .
No more war, we want peace!
Take from the rich and give to the poor!
Weakness is greater than strength!
Down with the status quo!
Long live the outcasts!
Set the captives free!
Losers are the real winners!
Your laws are not just!
I am the way, love is the way!

Protestor Mary, Sarah Fuller

6. Caine-Conley, "Procession of Protest."

Here the act of protest, occupying the streets with signs against the violence of rulers, is divine, holy, godly. To resist and oppose is what Jesus did, what the living God still does. "Can you imagine Pontius Pilate's disgust and anger," Smash mused, "when he caught wind of Jesus' unruly, provocative act of resistance?" How far this vision is from the parish where people felt a sense of accomplishment in the face of a white terrorist gathering without ever entering the public square or getting in any attacker's way.

Salvation for Smash does not come in the form of a messiah who bid his followers to let neo-Nazis descend upon the neighborhoods of vulnerable people after retreating to a room far away to pray. Her Jesus did not come with shrugged shoulders, a copy of the First Amendment in his right hand, and a quizzical look on his face that says, *Look, I don't like the KKK either but we have to respect their right to genocidal speech.* Her Jesus is a savior knee-deep in the messiness, rebelling against the powerful for the threatened. She summons a messiah rebelling against white supremacy and white supremacists, condemning the foamy caricature of Jesus that prematurely fills in the kenotic spaces into which Christians are called. The god, the christ, and the church that would blame the violence of neo-Nazis and MAGA crowds on those who, like Smash, confront them bears no resemblance to the gospel stories of a God that she draws upon at the end of the same sermon in a stirring call:

> So let us shout and protest together! Let us protest whatever stands
> in the way of God's dream of justice rolling down like water. We
> will not be silenced!
> Hosanna! Shut it down!
> Hosanna! Give peace a chance!
> Hosanna! Equality now!
> Hosanna! No Justice, no peace!
> Hosanna! Black Lives Matter!
> Hosanna! Power to the people!
> Hosanna! Now is the time to make justice a reality for all God's
> children!
> Hosanna! Let it be so. Amen.

When Smash and Seth sought someone to train Congregate Charlottesville in nonviolent resistance leading up to Unite the Right, they called on

Reverend Osagyefo Uhuru Sekou. Every week we met under his guidance in a local church to worship, prepare our consciences, and ready our bodies to absorb whatever might come their way.

It's easy to get swept up in the moment with Sekou. His preaching can produce an emotional reaction, a sense of being grasped by the Spirit. I already knew that, in addition to having gone to jail for prophetic Christian actions and spending decades organizing, he was also a professional musician, singing gospel songs and movement music. The fact that he has a message, a theology, and a weighted past can get overlooked. But when he entered the church on the first day and spoke of a Jesus from radically *below*—the guy born, as he would repeat every week, to an unimportant family in an unimportant people in an unimportant part of an empire—he wasn't simply inspiring us but reconfiguring our theological understandings. This new framework meant that he didn't issue the normal kind of Christian altar call, asking people to "give their lives to Jesus," whatever that might mean, but invited a willingness to give up our lives for our neighbors under threat, in whom we can see Jesus' face.

These weren't just cheap platitudes. Sekou made clear every week that the group was signing up for something that may prove fatal, that no one should join unless ready for that sacrifice. As the community was still trying to piece together the Right's plans and gauge how dangerous they were, one of the clergy pulled Sekou aside and asked what he could share. "This isn't a normal protest with normal stakes," he replied ominously. "It's not a matter of whether they'll try to murder someone but whether they'll succeed." On the last day of training the group wrote notes that would be delivered to loved ones in case of death, a somber experience that some thought overly dramatic at the time. But in hindsight, after one of the Nazis killed Heather Heyer and the scope of their plans for violence—including plans to run people over with a car—had been increasingly laid bare, the solemnity of that altar call and the severity of the kind of discipleship Sekou called us to seem all the starker. The soil and rasp and laughter in his voice were coupled with a powerful embodiment of Bonhoeffer's reminder that "When Christ calls someone, he bids them come and die."

Sekou made clear he wouldn't ask us to do anything he wouldn't do himself. For those of us wary of churches and leaders, we could recognize in his preaching not emotional manipulation but spiritual preparation. Some of us had never stood when a reverend called us to stand, but we trusted him because like Smash and Seth he echoed the call already issued by our neighbors—to use our bodies in a concrete struggle. That was wholly and holy enough.

Sekou's background informed his theology as well as the spirit of the clergy's resistance against Unite the Right. He grew up in the little town of Zent in the Arkansas Delta, with, as he tells it, eleven houses and thirty-five people. His grandpa, who helped his grandmother raise him, had survived the 1919 Elaine race massacre, in which whites fired into a church, eventually murdering hundreds of Black people organizing for an end to exploitative wages. (The only people prosecuted afterwards were Black.[7]) He began preaching at age twenty-three for the Black Pentecostal Church of God in Christ, a church that started in part to combat lynching.

During the Rodney King uprisings in 1992 he was a student at the University of Tennessee-Knoxville and invited Kwame Ture to speak. He had previously met Ture, who coined the term "Black Power" when he was known as Stokely Carmichael in 1966, through the All-African People's Revolutionary Party. Sekou was looking for a political home and found one in Ture's party. They had a study system, and he read deeply of Marx, Lenin, Palestinian history, Guinea-Bissau's liberation struggle, Maoism, and freedom fighters across the continent of Africa. "I'd hold his bags and he'd tell me stories," he said of Ture, who was "giving me that sixties stuff." Ture gave him his current name of Osagyefo Uhuru Sekou. When I asked why, he said, "Well, if you're going to be a revolutionary, you need a revolutionary name."[8]

After George W. Bush's reelection in 2004, Sekou started the Clergy and Laity Concerned About Iraq at Riverside Church, continuing the legacy of the group concerned with Vietnam that was co-founded in the early 1970s by, among others, Rabbi Abraham Joshua Heschel and Daniel Berrigan. During this time, civil rights icon Diane Nash, who organized the second wave of the freedom rides, introduced him to James Lawson; the man who once trained Dr. King in nonviolence now had Sekou learning under him.

The next year Sekou moved to Paris, following the footsteps of James Baldwin when he left Jim Crow America in 1948 for a decade in France.

7. See for example, Uenuma, "Massacre of Black Sharecroppers."

8. Sekou, phone interview.

Lecturing on nonviolence, wearing a black scarf, hat, and pants because "that was Baldwin's attire when he first arrived in Paris," and digging into French existentialism, he "wrestled with what it meant to be a Black preacher with an artist's heart and a love for Sophia." In November of 2005, Sekou found himself marching with *La Devoir Collectif de la Mémoir*, a group of mostly Arab and African hip-hop artists and activists, who had invited him to speak at a rally when a young African man died after being chased by police. They set fire to cars and Sekou marched with them while chanting, "*Fraternité! Liberté! Égalité!*" Rather than condemning the group for property destruction, he noted that "burning cars were the burning concerns of those who lived on the night side of a society."[9]

In 2006 he worked in New Orleans in the aftermath of Hurricane Katrina, founding and acting as the executive director of the Interfaith Worker Justice Center. From there he became the senior minister at a church in South Jamaica, Queens, where LGBTQ communities became a central concern. "I lost the vote for a pastorage in 2009," he said, "because congregants and elites opposed my position on gay marriage—a positive one."[10]

In 2010 he went to Haiti after an earthquake that decimated the country, spending his days digging latrines among human excrement. The house he stayed in may have been left standing, "But god, you spared nothing else. Port-au-Prince is flattened." His time there challenged his faith, he would later recall. The destruction and misery were coupled with the community coming together to rebuild and his experience of getting water from the well for bathing. "There is something deeply theological, god, about shoveling shit and going to the well . . . Words like solidarity and comrade seem cheap and arcane to me now, only sacrifice, covenant and accompaniment suffice." Confronting reality with integrity meant accusing God for the mass suffering. "I am angry with you, god . . . We are rebuilding the shit and filth, but you are hiding. Haiti is not a test of our faith but a test of your grace. Show yourself."[11]

Shortly after, he became editor-in-chief of *Spare Change News*, a street paper working against homelessness, followed by a position with the Fellowship of Reconciliation. In 2013, after George Zimmerman murdered Trayvon Martin, Sekou again grappled with the injustice plain for all to see.

9. Sekou, "Prophet in Exile."

10. Philadelphia Gay News, "Rev. Osagyefo Uhuru Sekou—Ally to All."

11. Sekou, "Dear God."

No matter the verdict on Zimmerman, he promised, "if ambers like the cityscape or jubilation erupts, there will be at least one riot—in my soul." [12]

Like the biblical witnesses of the psalmists and prophets, Sekou has space in his conception of and relationship with God for accusations and challenges, naming a mode of hope that is inseparable from holding the Creator to the covenant. His theology is, as Gustavo Gutiérrez conceptualized it, a second step. "The pastoral activity of the Church does not flow as a conclusion from theological premises," Gutiérrez wrote. "Theology does not produce pastoral activity; rather it reflects up on it." [13] Sekou fits this mold, writing in light of his experiences with liberation movements, not issuing teachings and setting up boundaries to their activities from above but speaking from within his work among them.

When Darren Wilson of the Ferguson police killed Michael Brown, Sekou joined local organizers and marched in the streets, getting arrested multiple times. Ferguson was, he declared in 2015, "America's Nazareth." Jesus, the one born among a people deemed unimportant, under occupation and brutality, could be glimpsed in an underbelly like that neighborhood, getting born among the people in that struggle. "If Black Lives Matter is the Word, Ferguson is the Word made flesh," he asserted, discarding orthodoxy for a hermeneutic vivified by the blight and blood of what Matthew's Jesus called the least of these. "Can we see the religious sensibilities at work in the life of these movements?" he asked, in a question that most mainstream churches have answered negatively. [14]

This theological outlook, for Sekou, went back further than Michael Brown's killing. In 2017 he republished his 2001 *Urbansouls: Reflections on Youth, Religion, and Hip-Hop Culture*. In it he crafts a theology rooted in young people of color. No attempts to do so had reached academic circles, he said, because of "the lack of value attributed to poor Black and Brown youth voices in the academy." [15] This is to the university's detriment, as hip-hop artists are in fact "para-theologians," issuers of the Word beyond the boundaries erected by the official gatekeepers, people outside the church who channel theological insights for artistic, activist, and intellectual aims. Hip-hop, for Sekou, is a critical theology of existence, a spiritual outlet for voices as theologically unassuming as the woodworking Palestinian

12. Sekou, "There Will Be at Least One Riot."
13. Gutiérrez, *Theology of Liberation*, 9.
14. Wilkes, "Living in the End Times: An Interview with Rev. Osagyefo Sekou."
15. Sekou, *Urbansouls*, 6.

oppressed since infancy by the Roman Empire. In these voices lies what he calls the "redemption of the church," an expression of hope that speaks to more people than suits and degrees ever could.

For Sekou, hip-hop isn't just music but the substance of "urban psalms." He looks to Grandmaster Flash and the Furious Five's "The Message" as an example, where he finds not just a complaint about metropolitan injustice but a religious cry from the heart of one's spirit about life in 1982 New York: "Don't push me 'cause I'm close to the edge / I'm trying not to lose my head / It's like a jungle sometimes / It makes me wonder how I keep from going under." From Easy-E to Mary J. Blige, from Biggie Smalls and N.W.A. to KRS-One and Lauryn Hill, Sekou finds mature and largely untapped theological expression in these urban psalmists. A sample of his exegesis on Tupac, whom he calls "my generation's Malcolm X," gives voice to his framework:

> Tupac provides postmodern appropriations of the Black Christian ontological yearnings, which have been hopeful against hopelessness. "God can you save me?" can be heard on more than a few of Tupac's songs. "How many brothers fell victim to the streets? Rest in peace, young n-gg-, there's a heaven for a G', be a lie if I told ya that I never thought of death . . ." Repose within quietude over a slow groove, this ode creeps at the velocity of funeral procession set off by a gospel offing. Ebony bodies plunging lifeless on black pavement while "Life Goes On" is a moral issue. "Only God Can Judge Me," "Hail Mary," and "Blasphemy" are urban psalms sermonizing a Tupacian theory of morality.[16]

Sekou's concern isn't to reconcile how hip-hop artists relate to academic theology. He's more interested in hearing how they understand their own circumstances and what they tell listeners about the eternal from their own earthly situation. But this is a far distance from those who usually pass for official theologians, and this habit of seeking divine insight from people on the ground would continue during his time in Ferguson. "I take my orders from 23-year-old queer women," he stated. "They don't need to get saved. The church needs to get saved."[17]

Lazy critiques label this kind of talk empty virtue signaling, but the place from which Sekou does his religious wrestling places him with those

---

16. Sekou, *Urbansouls*. For other treatments of Tupac as a theologian or prophet, see Gafney, *Womanist Midrash*, 82; and Grimes, "'But Do the Lord Care?'" 326–52.

17. Van Gelder, "Rev. Sekou on Today's Civil Rights Leaders."

seeking to secure the kind of physical salvation that the psalmists and prophets would tether to the spiritual. Like Smash, he highlights the blunt geography of theology, asserting that where we physically stand dictates what theological insights become accessible to us. From the removed study, disengaged professionals might see movements like Black Lives Matter as disruptive of a flawed but overall beneficent system, something to be quashed with sensitive language.[18] From the trench, it can look like salvation. That's why when Sekou reflects on the founders of Black Lives Matter, Alicia Garza, Opal Tometi, and Patrisse Cullors, he says "I call them the Holy Trinity."[19] Uprisings might look dangerous to one's power from a certain position, but from another, godly. What may sound blasphemous from one space may sound revelatory in another. "When we're in the streets protesting," he says, "that's a little taste of heaven."

This notion implies that God's dream appears amid active oppression. Heaven arises and uprises in the face of hell, opposing it. We don't find it dwelling in some neutral existence, barricaded behind an altar or floating above the fray, but in active rejection of that which would negate it. "The gospel is not a neutral term,"[20] he wrote when discussing Ferguson. Until the completion of history in the Christian framework, when the kin-dom comes, those who are committed to its fruition can only locate it and partake in its flowering by entering the messy and sometimes ugly struggle against evil and hatred.

Sekou made sure we were people of song. He'd come down the aisle to start the nonviolence trainings, belting *All in Charlottesville*, and we'd respond, *I'm gonna let it shine*. Sometimes it would be, *Oooh, freedom* or *Over my head*, inviting our response. Whatever the words, when he entered that space he lifted us up along with his voice, expecting us to call back, to lift each other.

18. For an in-depth treatment of this phenomenon, see chapter 2 of Cone, *The Cross and the Lynching Tree*, 30–64, where he examines why Reinhold Niebuhr, the preeminent American theologian in the mid-twentieth century, couldn't connect the crucifixion with the lynching of Black Americans. Cone suggests it is in part because Niebuhr never left his office at Union Theological Seminary to walk several blocks east and learn the concerns of Black Harlem residents.

19. Obie, "For Activist Rev. Sekou, 'The Revolution Has Come.'"

20. Dockter, "Gospel is Not a Neutral Term."

A heaviness hung over the town that whole summer as white nationalists held planning sessions in the open air downtown, prompting some to
gather and disrupt their meetings. I remember arriving on my bike once
after being summoned to find a small crowd already singing an anti-fascist
psalm in their faces. "Fuck white supremacy," seemed to be the only lyr-
ics, and they danced under the moonlight, preventing fascists from having
conversations, ready to repeat the phrase as long as the riot planners stayed
there trying to organize.

The coalescing culture of resistance in Charlottesville sustained people
in efforts to upset the Unite the Right organizing, but everybody involved
felt the immovable mood of foreboding those weeks and months. So when
Sekou came singing freedom songs, inviting us into the words and traditions of so many who had fought before, it shone a modest light of hope
into the dark days. We had the sense that people had faced worse, and, as
St. Augustine said, sang but kept going. Many of us who were white took up
these hymns from Black traditions for the first time, with a palpable sense
of their desperate hope and rooted faith. With rumors of small-scale war
thrown about, we didn't hear freedom in the air until invited to sing the
words, willing them into existence.

The nonviolence trainings were also faith services, the faith services
were also conscientization sessions. There were no hard distinctions between communal prayer, lessons in the theology of Walter Wink, and
practicing sniper fire drills or how to protect your vital organs in a human
chain if the police attack. It imbued political preparations with the divine
and infused the holy with what Seth Wispelwey called "gospel specificity,"
affixing worship to the earthy needs of those endangered by the Klan, the
alt-right, the MAGA crowd. Becoming people of faith was inseparable from
becoming anti-fascist in that community. To fail to become political in that
situation, to not engage the polis as it faced a looming terrorist attack, was
to advertise one's religious irrelevance.

When I reflect on the absence of officials from my Catholic church
in Congregate Charlottesville, I'm reminded that the theologian Wolfhart
Pannenberg said religions die when their light fails. Unlike Protestants,
Buddhists, Jews, Muslims, and atheists, no Catholic clerics came to any
of the services or contacted Smash, Sekou, or Seth at all. A living spark
flared up in that church every week that was entirely missing in the town's
Catholic culture, as its people could not connect their God, their salvation,
their cross, or their Scriptures with opposing the Nazis. It was as if their call

came not from Jesus but the concordat Pope Pius XII signed with Hitler, assuring him the church wouldn't get in the way of his genocide as long as they could go about their business. Jews still didn't matter enough to local Catholic officials to get involved.

> *Because the church is the community that participates in Jesus Christ's liberating work in history, it can never endorse "law and order" that causes suffering. To do so is to say yes to structures of oppression. Because the church has received the gospel-hint and has accepted what that means for human existence, the church must be a revolutionary community, breaking laws that destroy persons.*
>
> —James Cone[21]

The very meaning of church, then, can't help but be challenged, changed, opened. Who was my church? And who was church to my neighbors in need? Who connected the biblical stories to the vital issues of life and death in concrete reality? Who knew the dignity of humans, who acted for life, who understood the preferential option for the poor and oppressed, who acted eucharistically by being willing to be broken without even having an ecclesial structure to catechize them with such ideas? How can it be that my anarchist and socialist neighbors who had no religion, or even hated it, could better embody the ideas of solidarity and justice that Catholics enshrine in teachings from on high, while those on high would not?

All I know is that in those trainings the line between the political and religious grew so blurry as to dissolve altogether. The people standing by my side were church—grace with feet. And when August 12 arrived and we marched to the park to face whatever the day held, it was anti-fascists I'd never met before standing behind the clergy that started singing hymns with us in our guerrilla worship service in the street. This was an anti-fascist church-on-the-go, with Black Lives Matter and Antifa and Anarchist People of Color and Jews and Muslims and Buddhists and so many

---

21. Cone, *A Black Theology of Liberation*, 130.

unaffiliated protestors assembled as the not-so-mystical body of the anti-Klan Christ, our only wall being the police barrier between all of us and the alt-right. I could not then and cannot now help but wonder what the words "my church" mean after something like this.

unaffiliated protestors assembled as the not-so-mystical body of the anti-Klan Christ, our only wall being the police barrier between all of us and the alt-right. I could not then and cannot now help but wonder what the words "my church" mean after something like this.

2

Of Open-Hearted Heresy, Pseudo-Anti-racisms, & the MAGAsterium

*The Catholic Church has a knee on the neck of Black people
and people of color. If what I'm saying is unsettling, good, you
are listening. Listen! Listen, the church, the Body of Christ,
the people have taken to the streets crying out, "Enough is
enough!" . . . Do we join them in solidarity or do we hold them
in contempt?*

—BISHOP FERNAND CHERI[1]

WHILE REVERENDS SMASH AND Sekou offered one kind of witness the day
of Unite the Right, my local bishop gave another when he echoed what has
become a notorious talking point of Donald Trump's.

The town was confronted by people wearing Hitler shirts and MAGA
hats, bearing swastika tattoos and Confederate flags. They chanted slurs,
beating their shields and mocking queer people and Jews, just three hundred
feet from the synagogue they had threatened to burn. After they attacked
a group of anti-fascists in the streets with flags, sticks, shields, mace, and
fists, the city and then the state declared a state of emergency and cleared
the park. The clergy regrouped at a local café to plan for new circumstances.

The café had room to mill about, and as the majority of the group
came from out of town, many of us got to know each other amid these

---

1. Cheri, "Let the Church Roll On."

strange circumstances. But the room fell to a surreal hush as the TV showed Donald Trump about to address what we just witnessed. "We condemn in the strongest possible terms this egregious display of hatred, bigotry, and violence—" he began his sentence. I can still see clearly the way the person in front of me jerked his head in rage and hear the sound of simultaneous anger that came out of everyone's mouth when Trump finished his thought by adding, "on many sides, on many sides."

No one there expected much from Trump, who was one of the main inspirations for the rioters that day, but this comment planted a ridiculous notion in the minds of millions of viewers. On one side was a group who had been planning to attack Charlottesville residents and on the other, a group who came to defend them. On one side were neo-Nazis and on the other, Jews. On one side were neo-Confederates and the KKK and on the other, Black, Indigenous, Latinx, and Asian peoples. On one side was an alt-right group who wanted to subjugate women and annihilate LGBTQ communities and on the other, women and queer activists. One side came explicitly having discussed murdering someone with a car, and would soon do so, while the other came ready to put their lives on the line defending their neighbors and friends.

Trump's political interest in conflating everyone's responsibility for violence rendered his comments unsurprising, but I was dismayed to learn that just hours later my local Catholic bishop mimicked his pseudo-logic. Bishop DiLorenzo of Richmond released a short statement that day:

> In the last 24 hours, hatred and violence have been on display in the City of Charlottesville. I earnestly pray for peace. I invoke the prayer of St. Francis who prayed "Lord make me an instrument of thy peace. Where there is hatred, let me sow love; where there is injury, pardon." I pray that those men and women on both sides can talk and seek solutions to their differences respectfully. The love of Jesus Christ is the most powerful weapon against hatred. Only the light of Christ can quench the torches of hatred and violence. Let us pray for peace.[2]

I think back on that strange moment in the café with the clergy. Not long after this, a woman ran up to the few of us outside, panting for air, crying that someone had just run over community defenders two blocks away, asking for our presence quickly. People had been walking up a narrow street that was earlier closed to traffic by police when a Nazi, who slept

2. DiLorenzo, "Statement on Events Occurring in Charlottesville."

with a portrait of Hitler by his bedside, plowed through them in his Dodge Challenger.[3]

In the wake of the murder of Heather Heyer, even Republicans tried to get Trump to amend his absurd both-sides statement. So I assumed, when I heard that the US bishops were preparing a document on racism, inspired in part by the planned riot in Charlottesville, that they too would improve on the Richmond bishop's statement that parroted Trump's rhetoric and condemn white supremacy. But I and so many other Catholics would be sorely disappointed in 2018 when they released *Open Wide Our Hearts.*

The bishops' Committee on Cultural Diversity and Anti-Racism Committee were the primary crafters of this new letter, the fourth focusing on race in the USCCB's history, though it gained the support of the bishops as a conference.[4] Only three members voted against adopting it, for reasons unspecified. These three remind us that in a group of hundreds of bishops, a document with their collective approval is a compromise between people who are more radical and more retrograde, more anti-racist and more racist. This document reveals less about each individual bishop's views on race than what they teach as a body.

This chapter focuses on some of the letter's shortcomings that reveal the distance between anti-racist activists and the bishops as well as the harmful race education Catholics receive from their magisterium. I opt for this approach because there isn't enough space even to explore all its unhelpful aspects, let alone give a comprehensive report on its contents (which can be found elsewhere). Further, I agree with Catholic theologian Bryan Massingale when he writes that *Open Wide Our Hearts* is "so inadequate as to be virtually useless."[5] The letter seems sufficiently appalling

---

3. For pictures of the murderer's bedroom, including the portrait of Hitler, the copy of *Mein Kampf,* and the Nazi flag hanging just by his bed, see Emily Gorcenski's website *How Hate Sleeps*: https://howhatesleeps.com.

4. They released *Discrimination and the Christian Conscience* in 1958 in response to the *Brown v. Board of Education* case, *The National Race Crisis* in 1968 after the assassination of Dr. King, itself coming on the heels of the long, hot summer of 1967, and *Brothers and Sisters to Us* in 1979 amid a reinvigorated far-right scene and violent white pushback against busing designed to desegregate schools. For an analysis of these documents, see Massingale, *Racial Justice and the Catholic Church,* 50–69.

5. Munch, "Worship of a False God." Massingale is not alone in his opinion. Dan

to warrant a strictly combative reading, redirecting people of faith to look elsewhere for leadership on race issues.

The problems begin with the very definition of their topic. Racism, they say, is "when—either consciously or unconsciously—a person holds that his or her own race or ethnicity is superior, and therefore judges persons of other races or ethnicities as inferior and unworthy of equal regard."[6] Doing so is a violation of justice and is therefore sinful, it reads, much like when Cain killed Abel. While the recognition that racism is cultural, structural, or systemic occasionally appears, such as when they acknowledge that the prison and police systems can be racist, their dominant understanding is interpersonal. It is an "attitude" that "leads individuals or groups to exclude," they write, or "a person ignor[ing] the fundamental truth" that we are all made in God's image. Both the diagnosis and the remedy rely on an incomplete perception of racism as residing primarily in the human heart.[7]

The very title, *Open Wide Our Hearts*, indicates this direction, suggesting that the antidote to racism is found in hearts that no longer remain closed. But this neglects reality, the way racism gets codified into law and entrenched in culture such that it no longer depends on bigoted people acting with malice. No matter how many wide-open hearts work in the Department of Education or public school offices, for example, white students will receive far more funding than students of color until policy changes. The working definition of racism simply has to involve structural and cultural racism, the ways it gets organized into social practices and protected by legal, judicial, medical, residential, and other institutions. This letter fails to do so.

And who are these racist people with closed hearts? Strangely, readers get no clear answer. While some specific examples of racism are listed, the perpetrators of things like hiring discrimination, racial profiling, harassment of Muslims, "xenophobic rhetoric," and racist education inequality are left mysteriously unnamed. That white people benefit from racist systems goes unmentioned, as does the fact that the vast majority

Horan, another Catholic theologian, argued the letter "has effectively proven to be a *worthless statement*" (Horan, "When Will the US Bishops Address the Evil?").

6. US Conference of Catholic Bishops, *Open Wide Our Hearts*, 3.

7. US Conference of Catholic Bishops, *Open Wide Our Hearts*, 5.

of the "extreme nationalist ideologies" that the bishops refer to are white supremacist groups that the FBI has declared the biggest domestic threat in the nation.[8] A reader in need of basic knowledge on racism, though, could easily conclude that no particular group is any more guilty than others of this sin.

Racism's perpetrators are cloaked behind a convenient use of the passive voice and agent-less crimes throughout this letter. Readers find that African Americans "face discrimination," that "there is" a fear of Muslims, and that Hispanics "have been referred to" by derogatory names and there have been 550 cases of them "being lynched."[9] But the bishops provide no details about who is behind all this. When they use active voice, the subject is curiously disembodied. "Racial profiling targets" Hispanics and African Americans. "Extreme nationalist ideologies" feed public discourse with a hatred of outsiders. "Racism comes in the form of the sin of omission" when people and groups fail to work for justice.

This all points to a serious problem with the bishops' letter—its *vagueness*. It professes the need to get specific about the issue but ignores its own advice. One will look in vain for the phrases "white supremacy," "white nationalism," "white terrorism," "white bigotry," "white advantage," "white privilege," or any other kind of unambiguous indication that it's a particular kind of race that both benefits systematically in society and has without interruption in US history enacted what the bishops call racism. Their dependence on the word "racism" belies a skittish evasion of precise language that runs throughout the letter. It wholly lacks the kind of gospel specificity called for by Seth Wispelwey in Charlottesville.

This vague cloud of unknowing is also theological. In the very first paragraph of the letter, the bishops draw on 1 John and 1 Corinthians as well as quotes from Popes Benedict and Francis to argue that the Trinity calls people to unity with God and each other. Just as God relates to us as a parent, the Spirit calls on the Church to share that unifying love with the world, the same unity with God that Christ enacted on the cross. But

8. For example, FBI director Christopher Wray said in 2021 that white supremacists comprise "the biggest chunk of our domestic terrorism portfolio" and adds that they "have been responsible for the most lethal attacks over the last decade" ("FBI chief calls Capitol attack 'domestic terrorism' and defends US intelligence," *The Guardian*, March 2, 2021, https://www/theguardian.com/us-news/2021/mar/02/fbi-christopher-wray-capitol-attack-domestic-terrorism). Even conservative outlets like *Business Insider* and *Forbes* report the same.

9. US Conference of Catholic Bishops, *Open Wide Our Hearts*, 16.

"racism," despite Christ's already complete victory over sin and death, infects our country nonetheless.

Their first footnote in the document cites a passage from Pope Benedict's 2005 *Deus Caritas Est*, which argues that uniting with God in love "makes us a 'we' which transcends our divisions and makes us one, until in the end God is 'all in all.'" Planted in the second sentence of this letter, the idea is lofty but unearned. Readers are inexplicably floating away from Earth—Unite the Right, the church's history of enslavement and genocide, and all the flesh and blood that gives weight to the problem of "racism"—transported from the immediate to the heavenly.

Someone living in the US might wonder, for example, what the bishops think about the most ubiquitous racial claim in the country: Black Lives Matter. An antiracist document would naturally address this movement but the letter has already ascended too high to deal with details on the ground. Catholic journalist Olga Segura notes that *Open Wide Our Hearts'* failure to acknowledge or even use the words Black Lives Matter misses an opportunity to draw upon a movement that has resources and an infrastructure already combating white supremacy, thus limiting their effectiveness.[10] But even before questions of tactics arise, those of relevance come to mind as the bishops deliberately ignore the most visible entrance into conversations about race today. Their silence on the movement and issue suggests much about the bishops' willingness to come down from the heavens.

Reflecting from these heights makes little sense when standing at Fourth and Water in Charlottesville, where a neo-Nazi plowed through people organized against white supremacy. The idea that anything "transcends our divisions" in the face of Ferguson, Standing Rock, Portland, Richmond, Detroit, Sacramento, Kenosha, and elsewhere implies a cheap, fictitious unity. This letter revels in abstraction, retreating into the embrace of a removed God, whenever it for a moment provides readers with anything concrete or historical. There is no lingering look at what "racism" actually entails down below, where people live. Their unwillingness to engage Black Lives Matter shows that the 1968 diagnosis of the Black Catholic

---

10. Segura, "Do US bishops really believe black lives matter?" Segura has pointed out elsewhere that the letter was not implemented even minimally in many dioceses, reflecting a tepid attempt by the bishops to place importance on spreading awareness in the church of racial justice (https://www.americamagazine.org/faith/2019/11/21/i-reached-out-every-us-diocese-here-are-ones-implementing-2018-pastoral-letter). Her book, *Birth of a Movement: Black Lives Matter and the Catholic Church*, helps lay out the church's relationship to racial justice today.

Clergy Caucus remains true today; too many whites in the hierarchy are too used to leading and not psychologically prepared to support and learn from Black communities.[11]

A Black student was pulled from his graduation procession on July 28 and told to remove his face mask, displaying the words Black Lives Matter, before being allowed to march in the ceremony with the rest of his classmates from York Catholic High School.

—Sam Ruland, *York Daily Record*, August 3, 2020[12]

The second section, which aims for justice in the tradition of the prophet Micah, continues this problem. The nature of justice flows from God's triune nature, they say (already departing from Micah), which instills in a people made in that image a desire for community. But because Adam and Eve gave into temptation, all are inclined to sin, as seen today with the perpetuation of racism. To move toward justice, we must hear and know the stories of those who suffer its consequences. They again frame this section by invoking Pope Benedict, who defines the human "as a spiritual being" and says human relations take place on the spiritual plane.

Combining this immaterial understanding of humans with the original sin myth as a historical explanation for racism leaves the reader floating away again, far from the bleeding bodies of Michael Brown and Breonna Taylor. When the bishops speak again in language that obscures agency for "the history of the injustices done to so many," it seems that only an archetype of humanity is to blame. And because none of us spiritual beings are immune to sin, this implies again that *everyone* is complicit in the problem at hand. No one, it seems, need feel more responsibility than others in this narrative, which takes place more in the garden of Eden than the streets of Ferguson.

11. Black Catholic Clergy Caucus, "Statement," 230–32.
12. Ruland, "Student Stopped from Wearing 'Black Lives Matter' Mask."

This ahistorical account of racism allows for the curious solution of "further catechesis" rather than anti-racist education, organizing, and action.[13] It assumes that the antidote, rather than the problem itself, flows from church teaching. Given the explanation, appearing in the very same paragraph, that racism persists because people and institutions fail to acknowledge its presence, neglect history, and fail to atone for their sins, this document begs the question of whether the bishops grasp the implications of their own words.

They point out that "As Christians, we are called to listen and know the stories of our brothers and sisters." This attention to voices that are presumed to be from below is a deeply necessary prelude to antiracist work. But the bishops could learn much from Catholic theologian Natalia Imperatori-Lee's observation that thinking in and about the church too often "focus[es] on grand unifying narratives of the one, holy, catholic, and apostolic church, leaving the details of how that church functions in the lives of the people of God as an afterthought."[14] The bodily lives of actual people cannot be subsumed in the hovering stories ecclesial authorities are prone to tell about the church without sacrificing relevance and meaningful engagement with those already working for racial justice.

One such rhetorical evasion has a noteworthy story behind it. The bishops say that "the re-appearance of symbols of hatred, such as nooses and swastikas in public spaces, is a tragic indicator of rising racial and ethnic animus." The symbols (which seem to be manifesting on their own in this phrasing, a kind of white supremacy *ex nihilo*) of course represent a history of white societies trying to slaughter all the Jews, enslave Black people, and hang them on ropes along with Latinx and Indigenous Americans. This missing data seems relevant in a document on racism.

But also significant is how this inclusion of swastikas and nooses came to appear in the document. Bishop Anthony Taylor of Little Rock submitted an amendment that would condemn swastikas, nooses, and Confederate flags. Such a basic step should be perfunctory, simply a beginning point to get on to more pervasive forms of white supremacy.

13. US Conference of Catholic Bishops, *Open Wide Our Hearts*, 10.

14. Imperatori-Lee, *Cuéntame*, 134.

But—astonishingly—the bishops voted not to condemn these symbols of genocide, slavery, torture, and murder.

This vote shows most starkly where the USCCB is on race: unwilling to condemn a swastika, a noose, or to even mention a Confederate flag. They explained this by arguing that swastikas and nooses were already "widely recognized signs of hatred."[15] This provides little clarity, however. Just because something is considered hateful does not mean it should not be condemned. It seems, in fact, that it makes it all the easier to condemn. And if these symbols are "re-appearing"—in another example of the bishops' passive voice that fails to name which race has imbued them with histories of hatred and who might be placing them in the public square again—then perhaps they aren't so widely recognized as negative.

The bishops overestimate how many people assume these symbols are objectionable and underestimate the need to condemn them, as a sample of incidents just at Catholic high schools between 2016 and 2022 attests. Students from several high schools, including the Catholic Junipero Serra High School in San Juan Capistrano, appeared in a photo online giving a Hitler salute by a large swastika made out of beer cups. At St. Teresa's Academy, a Kansas City all-girls Catholic high school, students posted a picture of a swastika at a party where they were playing Nazis vs. Jews beer pong. Fellow students said the school never shared that the symbol at issue was a swastika, and one reported that the administration's response was "the same punishment one of my peers received for bringing an e-cigarette to class." In Modesto, California, at Central Catholic High, students made a video showing a noose while they shouted a racist slur and "You must die!" at a specific Black student, fired a gun, and then sent the video to that student. They were later charged with making terrorist threats, criminal conspiracy, and committing a hate crime. A lacrosse player for Cleveland's Lake Catholic High showed up with a swastika on his leg while players and adults, including a school official, spewed anti-Semitic slurs. An Oakland Catholic High student posted a photo with hand-drawn swastikas on her shirt and a German flag painted on her forehead. Two rabbis, joined by the Pittsburgh bishop, said in response, "The swastika is an image that can only be condemned." Two years later, in *Open Wide Our Hearts*, the US bishops disagreed.[16]

15. Segura and O'Loughlin, "U.S. bishops Adopt New Anti-Racism Letter."

16. See Economou, "Former Newport Beach"; Moxley, "St. Teresa's"; NBC Bay Area Staff, "Modesto Police"; Brown, "Two Teens Charged"; Tabachnick, "Catholic Students";

As for the Confederate flag, "some still claim it as a sign of heritage," the bishops argued in an impressive evasion of precisely what they claim is important to do when opposing racism. They state repeatedly that people and groups must confront history if we're ever to move towards racial reconciliation. But refusing to even acknowledge the Confederate flag in a document on racism in the US for this reason indefensibly hand-waves the history of slavery, murderous opposition to civil rights, and violence like the 2015 massacre of Black churchgoers in Charleston as a nebulously benign "heritage." It's tempting to argue back by pointing out that Nazis could say the same of swastikas, claiming it as their heritage and therefore baselessly implying that it has nothing to do with hate, but such an example would fail to be useful because the bishops also chose not to condemn swastikas.

The Confederate flag somehow not representing white supremacy would be news to white supremacists. When planning for the Unite the Right riot in Charlottesville, Ray Azzmador of the primary neo-Nazi website Stormfront told his alt-right co-planners that his group would come with Confederate flags, some argued they should go with less obviously white supremacist symbols for better optics. The lead organizer disagreed, arguing it would be a great symbol for recruiting outsiders to their cause. (This came amid posts such as "Heil Hitler!" in the conversation.) "I want as many Confederate flags as possible," he wrote. Another in the conversation said the "fact that it's an internationally recognized symbol will help resonate with other WN [white nationalist] movements worldwide."[17]

People within the church can grasp the same logic. George Zimmerman, a Catholic who became famous for killing seventeen-year-old Trayvon Martin in 2012 and whose acquittal sparked the Black Lives Matter movement, made money afterwards by autographing Confederate flags. Two years later, white students at St. Anthony's Catholic high school on Long Island brought a Confederate flag to a game against a mostly Black school while some wore blackface and yelled a racist slur. Steve King, a Catholic former congressman from Iowa who is the most public white supremacist US politician in recent years, kept a Confederate flag on his desk. Racists within the church know the flag stands for anti-Blackness and white power.

"Lacrosse Player."

17. Information about the Discord chats used for planning Unite the Right, along with a searchable database, can be found at the anti-fascist media outlet Unicorn Riot. Schiano, "Charlottesville Violence Planned Over Discord Servers."

What exactly is the point, Catholics are left to wonder, of writing a letter on racism in response to the largest overtly white supremacist gathering in decades, if the letter can't come out clearly and passionately against the central symbols of white supremacy, symbols displayed in Charlottesville at Unite the Right and by Catholics in schools, social media accounts, and public offices?

A simple image redirects Christians to a far more successful catechesis in antiracist theology. Ben Wildflower modeled his "Miraculous Metal" after traditional Catholic "miraculous medals" portraying Mary standing atop the world, feet on a snake, beaming down blessings with her hands to those seeking preparation for grace. "O Mary, conceived without sin," reads the edge, "pray for us who have recourse to thee." Nuns would give these devotionals to Wildflower when he visited the grave of Mother Teresa, who dispersed them while she was alive.

FIGURE 3

Miraculous Metal, Ben Wildflower

Drones fall from the sky in Wildflower's rendition, a sign that he bothers to connect heaven with earth. Mary's rays of grace extended toward the world take the form of fire raining down from "DIY aerosol can flamethrowers," as he describes it,[18] setting a swastika and Confederate flag on fire. She treads on the serpent that not only recalls the tempter in Genesis but resembles the snake from the Don't Tread On Me flag that often accompanies racist militias and rallies. A broken gun nearby lies in two. "The demons of militarism and nationalism tremble," he writes. Around the perimeter, the original words are adapted to read, "O Mary, conceived without white supremacy, pray for us trying to dismantle this shit."

The original miraculous medal had twelve stars adorning its back, representing the twelve disciples. Wildflower has transposed them to the front to form the blessed mother's halo. Burning swastikas and Confederate flags, the art suggests that dismantling white supremacist systems is holy. *This is discipleship.*

The bishops might refuse to condemn the central symbols of Nazism and slavery, but the faithful can turn instead to the Mother of God who burns them. Her makeshift aerosol can invokes one of the best known images from the Unite the Right riot in Charlottesville, depicting Corey Long spraying flame at a Confederate flag in the hands of rioters during Unite the Right in self-defense.[19] Like Long, one can imagine this Mary getting immediately shot at by a Klan member and being jailed for disrupting the peace. Like Long, this Mary reveals a kind of God that is foreign to the bishops' letter on racism—one that names, confronts, opposes, and insists on dismantling white supremacy.

Wildflower concludes his description of Miraculous Metal simply: "Hail Mary."

The Second Vatican Council embraced Jews as "brothers and sisters" in their 1965 document *Nostra Aetate*, significantly altering the church's stance toward Judaism. But what kind of sibling will not, when given the chance, with nothing at stake but the raising of a hand, condemn the central symbol representing the slaughter of six million of their kin? What kind of family member refuses to condemn the same symbol that remains

18. See https://benwildflower.com/products/miraculous-metal-print.

19. To see the image, see St. Félix, "Image of Revolutionary Fire at Charlottesville."

a central rallying point of neo-Nazis organizing to finish what the Third Reich started? *Open Wide Our Hearts* came out only one month after a man driven by the "white genocide" myth murdered eleven Jews in the Tree of Life synagogue in Pittsburgh.[20] Why would the bishops not condemn this symbol that invariably functions to make genocide against Jews, their stated family, more likely?

"Brothers and sisters to us," claimed the US bishops in the title of their 1979 document on relations with Black Americans. But what kind of sibling refuses to condemn the two most prominent symbols of Black torture, enslavement, and murder in the American imagination? Brothers and sisters to us, they claim about Indigenous and Hispanic people. But what kind of sibling refuses to condemn the noose that was used to kill, in addition to thousands of Black people, many of their ancestors too? Not only does this language ignore the reality of genderqueer people, but what kind of family member do the bishops position white Christians to be with this choice?

To be black and Catholic, as I am, is to belong to an institution that you know has the theological resources to denounce the causes of your oppression, yet to doubt that such a word will arrive on time.

—DWAYNE DAVID PAUL[21]

The bishops do use the language of condemnation once in their letter, however. Shortly after referencing swastikas and nooses, they begin a paragraph saying, "We read the headlines that report the killing of unarmed African Americans by law enforcement officials." They do not elaborate or condemn this but move on to note the "disproportionate" percentage of people of color in jail. They note in a painstakingly passive voice that for "many of our fellow citizens, who have done nothing wrong, interactions with the police are often fraught with fear and even danger." Then they close

20. Santanam, "Synagogue Shooter Talked of Killing Jews."
21. Paul, "U.S. Catholic Bishops Must Choose."

out the paragraph with the most censorious language in the document: "At the same time, we reject harsh rhetoric that belittles and dehumanizes law enforcement personnel who labor to keep our communities safe. We also condemn violent attacks against police."

Given the way the paragraph is constructed, starting by pitting police and Black people against each other and ending by condemning violence against police, the implication seems to be that the bishops picture Black people attacking police in this scenario. While they don't condemn police killing unarmed Black people (or, notably, ever name one of these people who have been killed) they do condemn attacks on police and even reject (a word used only here) belittling them.

Condemning violence seems a good default position, but to do so in this selective manner disregards the killings they purport to be concerned about and sides with the police against Black people *in a document on racism*. It also collapses the vast power disparity between a group of people with the state's ammunition at its disposal—tanks, military equipment, and the entire legal system—and another that has always suffered the brunt of the state's domestic power. The official teaching from the US Catholic leaderships seems to be that a police officer's right not to be struggled against is more important than a Black person's life. In so doing, they side more strongly with the police over and against Black people in their vision of mutual hostilities. The document leans on a Blue Lives Matter ideology here without making it explicit.[22] When the Jesuit Mario Powell expressed anger at "banal and vanilla statements" issued by Catholic leaders who refuse to "jump up on the cross with black Americans," it's hard to imagine what could better fit the description.[23]

22. Because counter-sloganeering has effectively ruined clarity in public discourse about "x" Lives Matter, this phrase deserves attention. If "Blue Lives Matter" simply means that the people who are police officers matter, then Christians would of course affirm it and add that they are imbued with the sacred breath of God, just as all people are. But insofar as the phrase has been weaponized as a contradicting claim over and against "Black Lives Matter," so that it acts as a negative response to both the Movement for Black Lives and the assertion that Black Lives Matter as well as an erasure of Black people in their primary social movement's title (only to be replaced with the very category of people who have been recorded time and again brutalizing them), uncritically aligning with the Blue Lives Matter "movement" is at least implicitly siding against the main voice for Black communities today.

23. Powell, "How Long, O Lord?" For an account from his fellow Jesuit Patrick Saint-Jean on white supremacy and Black lives from within the church, see "After George Floyd's Suffocation."

The bishops tip their hand when they defend the police as those "who labor to keep our communities safe." Whose communities do they keep safe in the logic of this letter? Readers are just one sentence removed from hearing that police kill unarmed Black people, clarifying at least whose communities the bishops do *not* mean. This amounts to the bishops adding an extra layer of policing on an already over-policed people. No fighting back, the bishops say. Don't even name-call back. Tamir Rice's parents can open wide their hearts in response to a Cleveland police officer killing their twelve-year-old playing in a park, but it's official religious teaching that they can't say bad things about the man who put two bullets through that child's body. He was keeping "our" community safe.

This is analogous to a religious group two thousand years ago refusing to condemn those who killed children while hunting Mary, Joseph, and Jesus on the government's behalf and condemning Mary for "belittling" the powerful in the Magnificat. As one of my students said in frustration, people of color are statistically more likely to be shot by the state than find a bishop's document that will condemn their oppressors.

Open Wide Our Hearts points toward forgiveness. It quotes 1 John 1:9, which reads, "If we acknowledge our sins, [God] is faithful and just and will forgive our sins and cleanse us from every wrongdoing." This theme pervades the document. Forgiveness is mentioned nine times, and each assumes either that God forgives the church for its sins, subtly suggests that people of color ought to forgive the church if they are holy people, or assumes that asking for forgiveness is part of a formula that will result in reconciliation with "all who have been harmed" by the church's racism. But while they talk nebulously about "repairing" wrongs, they don't discuss reparations.

James Cone, the founder of Black liberation theology, laid out a clear and concise rationale for why white Christians should pay reparations. In 2014, an interviewer said to him, "Most whites want mercy and forgiveness but not justice and reparations. How does the Cross inform the issue of justice and reparations?" He answered,

> Well, the Cross, as I said, is God taking the side of the victim. It's a symbol of that. God making ultimate identification with the powerless. Now, if the powerful in our society—the white people—if

they want to become Christians, they have to give up that power and become identified with the powerless if they're going to be a Christian. You can't be identified with the powerful and also be a Christian at the same time. That's a contradiction in terms.

Now, how do I know that you're really identifying with the victim? Well, if you're identifying with the victim, you . . . have to pay back that which you took. You just don't say, "Please, forgive me now." The only way in which your forgiveness can be authentic, your reception of it can be authentic, your repentance can be authentic, is that you give back that which you took. And white people took a lot from Black people.

Consider also the view of Rabbi Abraham Joshua Heschel. Responding to a story by Simon Wiesenthal, in which a dying Nazi asked him, a Jew in Auschwitz, to forgive him for murdering Jewish adults and children, Heschel reflected on the boundaries of forgiveness:

> No one can forgive crimes committed against other people. It is therefore preposterous to assume that anybody alive can extend forgiveness for the suffering of any one of the six million people who perished.
>
> According to Jewish tradition, even God can only forgive sins committed against God, not against humans.[24]

Given these insights from Cone and Heschel, it is instructive to read how the bishops handle their account of Father Augustus Tolton, the first Black priest in the US. After escaping slavery, the letter says, Tolton had to find a seminary in Rome that would accept him when all US seminaries rejected him. On his return from Italy, readers learn, nebulously, that "he faced much discrimination and racism." No perpetrators are specified aside from one person identified as "a brother priest who was white" who "made public and ugly statements urging the white people of the city not to go to Fr. Tolton's parish." (Notably, this constitutes half of the times the word "white" is mentioned in the body of the letter.) Tolton's own words, not included by the bishops, make clear that the problem was more than just one person, when he told the archbishop of Baltimore that white priests resented the "n----r priest" and while they "rejoiced at my arrival, now they wish I were away because too many white people come down to my church from other parishes."[25]

---

24. Wiesenthal, *Sunflower*, 171, with de-gendered language.

25. Tolton's letter is quoted in Davis, *Black Catholics in the United States*, 156–57.

His reaction to this persecution, they say, was to "exhibit the love of Christ, forgiving what was done to him and continuing to serve others." While this didn't solve the problem and (as the vague wording states) "things got so bad" that he had to move towns, "he served the faithful until his death." They conclude by waxing, "Fr. Tolton often spoke of how the Church had taught him to always 'pray and forgive my persecutors.'"[26] Tolton, the reader is left to conclude, responded to racism by becoming a consummate servant and forgiving those who had wronged him.[27]

Because they present Tolton as one of the "holy men" who can point us forward in this racial crisis, their depiction of his story implies that Black, Indigenous, and Latinx people would also be made holy if they react to racism today by becoming consummate servants (to what kind of recipients, one wonders?) and forgiving those who have wronged them. This unstated suggestion allows the bishops to set boundaries around the proper responses that people of color have available to them when "things get bad" for them, and do so under the guise of simply telling the story of a saintly Black Catholic. It does precisely what Steve Biko criticized the apartheid church in South Africa for when he said, "It makes Christianity too much of a 'turn the other cheek' religion whilst addressing itself to a destitute people."[28] What it amounts to is using the life and legacy of an enslaved man who liberated himself only to face white supremacy in and enacted by the Catholic Church in order to police how people of color today ought to respond to the church's white supremacist past and present. The right response, they imply, is one that absolves the white consciences easily, serves white people, and releases them from that wrong.

This way of telling the story implies that the church doesn't need to "pay back that which you took," as James Cone said. It requires no acknowledging centuries of calls for reparations or that Congress had for decades failed to find a hearing for the H.R. 40 bill to establish a federal commission

26. US Conference of Catholic Bishops, *Open Wide Our Hearts*, 19.

27. The bishops' recommended first-grade lessons in their letter (which exist for each grade) listed on their website shows how this miseducation has real, practical consequences in forming young minds. There is no indication that students should learn to oppose or name white supremacy, that anything bad happened to Tolton at all aside from "some people" not liking him and "seminaries" not accepting him, nor is there any mention of white people in his story. The moral of the lesson seems to be merely that Black people should love God and serve the church. https://www.usccb.org/issues-and-action/human-life-and-dignity/racism/upload/grade-1-resource.pdf.

28. Biko, "The Church as Seen By a Young Layman," in *I Write What I Like*, 58.

to assess the impacts of slavery and recommend appropriate reparations. (The bill would be heard, but not pass, three years later.) The bishops don't grapple with how the church can make reparations for its crimes of enslaving people and looting their labor to build churches and universities. Their letter rightly brings up *Dum Diversas,* the 1452 document in which the pope allowed Spanish and Portuguese royalty to buy and sell Africans. But it doesn't say anything about how the church might try to start making amends for that crime, or the many others that greatly enriched the church on the backs of people of color. The only way the church's repentance can be authentic, says Cone, is by giving back that which has been taken. Even God, according to Heschel, can't forgive the wrong done.

Readers might wonder, then, about a particularly curious portion of *Open Wide Our Hearts.* In the most direct confession of sin in the letter, the bishops say:

> Therefore we, the Catholic bishops in the United States, acknowledge the many times when the Church has failed to live as Christ taught—to love our brothers and sisters. Acts of racism have been committed by leaders and members of the Catholic Church—by bishops, clergy, religious, and laity—and her institutions. We express deep sorrow and regret for them. We also acknowledge those instances when we have not done enough or stood by silently when grave acts of injustice were committed. We ask for forgiveness from all who have been harmed by these sins committed in the past or in the present.

Even if the wording again protects specific perpetrators with anonymity, this at least gestures toward responsibility and humility. Yet the bishops' will to absolution comes through in a footnote attached to the above quote. When they say they acknowledge "the many times when the Church has failed to live as Christ taught," they cite one of Augustine's sermons, in which he preaches, "The Church as a whole says: Forgive us our trespasses! Therefore, she has blemishes and wrinkles. But by means of confession the wrinkles are smoothed away and the blemishes washed clean. The Church stands in prayer in order to be purified by confession and, as long as men live on earth it will be so."[29]

It's hard to imagine claiming a cheaper grace. The footnote attempts to forgive the sins of the church because the bishops wrote a few sentences of "confession." In place of reparations for slavery, this paragraph is assumed

29. US Conference of Catholic Bishops, *Open Wide Our Hearts,* 22.

to suffice. This smooths the wrinkles (a peculiar description of instituting torture and slavery) and washes the blemishes clean on its own.

The letter fails to specify "the many times" the church didn't live in a Christ-like way, making the word "confess" hard to take seriously. The historian Shannen Dee Williams points out that the Catholic Church introduced slavery to what is now the territory of the United States in the 1500s, that it was "the largest corporate slaveholder in the Americas," and that it was a Catholic Supreme Court Justice Roger Taney, who ruled in 1857 that Black people had no rights that whites were bound to respect.[30] If the bishops seek forgiveness for these crimes, they should name them. Did they want clemency for the history of stealing Indigenous children from parents or shuffling priests accused of sexual abuse and rape to Indigenous communities and concealing the stories from the public?[31] It's hard to say, given their policy of dodging particulars. As Dr. Jonathan Cordero pointed out in a talk that detailed how Catholic missionaries in present-day California would rape Indigenous women while making them sing hymns and would hunt and kill women and children who escaped the missions, "An apology doesn't mean anything unless it first acknowledges the truth."[32]

While the bishops avoid these truths, they make it easy to learn of moments when those in the church ostensibly acted as racial heroes. One remarkably absurd example comes after they discuss some ways the US government oppressed Native Americans, which one might assume would lead to a confession of the Catholic Church's genocide against them through the mission system. Instead, the bishops say, "During this time there were missions that stood as a barrier to the abuse of indigenous peoples and provided a form of protection in a rapidly changing reality. Although not all encounters with missionaries were benign, a number of missionaries

30. Williams, "If Racial Justice and Peace Will Ever Be Attained."

31. See, for example, Schwing, "After Years of Sexual Abuse in Native Communities." This particular account includes a priest impregnating a sixteen-year-old Alaska Native girl, forcing her to get an abortion, and blaming her father for raping her. Her father landed up in prison as a result.

32. Cordero, "Challenging the Conventional Narrative." Someone like Cordero, with Ramaytush Ohlone/Chumash background and expertise in California Indian and Spanish relations during the mission period, could have helped the bishops avoid peddling a romantic myth and anchor their account in fact if they had reached out for consultation.

heroically defended Native Americans as they sought to bring the Good News of Christ to many who had yet to hear it."[33] Suddenly finding an appetite for specificity, they list supposed racial saints in the church like Jesuit Fr. Pierre-Jean de Smet, Franciscan Anselm Weber, and St. Junipero Serra. People like St. Kateri Tekakwitha, Nicholas William Black Elk Sr., and the martyrs of *La Florida* Missions were happy to be evangelized to, they say. "Many, but certainly not all, Native peoples accepted the Gospel willingly," they write in a brazen bit of gaslighting and a telling retreat back into evasive nonspecificity. This kind of emphasizing one's presumed virtues and minimizing one's racist sins in a letter urging readers to confront their own complicity with racism is, to put it lightly, dishonest and hypocritical.

The letter's problems abound. It devotes more citations to Popes John Paul II and Benedict than to all the people of color in US history. It reinscribes the very mentality that grounded the church's genocide against Native peoples by proposing evangelization to the world as a solution to racism. It views the church as a historical solution to racism rather than one of its primary historical actors and ideological bulwarks. It assumes in all its phrasing, including in the very title, that Catholics are white. And in this, the bishops repeat the same mistake Bryan Massingale points out is characteristic of US church history.[34] At every turn the bishops seem intent to not alienate this presumed white reader, coddling them rather than inviting them to face actual history and, as Massingale says, "*Sit in the discomfort.*"[35]

A treatment of race in a white supremacist society should not make white people comfortable, yet this letter does so. It is comforting for white people to talk about racism instead of white supremacy and frame the conversation in terms of Trinitarian love rather than rage at injustice. It is comforting for white people to occasionally reference the existence of systemic and cultural racism but operate overall as if the issue is (other) backwards individuals. It is comforting for whites to know that people of color get killed by police yet save true condemnations for threats to the largely white police force. It is comforting for white people to insist repeatedly that "all" races need conversion and to bury monstrous race crimes under

33. US Conference of Catholic Bishops, *Open Wide Our Hearts*, 12.

34. Massingale, *Racial Justice and the Catholic Church*, 81.

35. Massingale, "Assumptions of White Privilege."

vague phraseologies and specific examples of past virtue. It is comforting for white people to speak of race atrocities in a passive voice that erases the perpetrator and imply that these stories should end in saintly forgiveness against wrongdoers. It is comforting for white people to headline a list of groups who have been targeted for racial prejudice with—yes—the Irish and Italians. It is comforting for white people to speak of white supremacy in the past tense and mostly ignore systemic injustices people of color face today. And finally, it is comforting for white people to skip over reparations in the "reconciliation process" and claim that an abridged confession washes the racial slate clean.

Compare how the bishops use papal teachings here to the way Reverend Dr. Brandy Daniels, who is not Catholic, interprets the words of Pope Francis' encyclical *Fratelli Tutti* from her experience in Portland. She says "when Francis writes of the value of solidarity, which 'finds concrete expression in service, which can take a variety of forms in an effort to care for others,' and 'means thinking and acting in terms of community,' I immediate thought of the Snack Bloc, the National Lawyers Guild, the therapists who show up to community events and offer sliding scale and free services for people in the community." Tying anti-fascists to the good Samaritan, who stopped to help the person in need when even a religious official would not, she said, "I think of the folks who do jail support, providing food and warm beverages to protestors after they are released from jail." These people—despite the protestations that "Antifa are not, cannot be, good Samaritans"—model the kind of love Pope Francis and Jesus point to precisely by taking a side for the vulnerable person, Daniels insists. And in so doing, she identifies (and models, in front lines from Charlottesville to Portland) a different kind of way Catholic traditions can be interpreted in the present moment.[36]

Compare too the drastically opposing visions of an archbishop and a lay theologian on how to view movements against white supremacy. José Gomez, president of the United States Conference of Catholic Bishops and archbishop of Los Angeles, said in a speech that social justice movements are "pseudo-religions" that should be seen as "rivals" to Christianity. In response, Dr. Craig Ford argued that "Black Lives Matter and other justice movements are secular expressions of Jesus' presence among those who are

36. Daniels, "Antifa Activist as Good Samaritan?"

reviled and rejected."[37] Like Daniels, where the archbishop sees competition Ford sees divine inbreaking.

When the Catholic and then-congressman Steve King of Iowa publicly asked what was so offensive about white supremacy, his bishop recommended that he read *Open Wide Our Hearts* in response.[38] King had earned a reputation for being the most forthright racist in Congress. He retweeted a prominent British neo-Nazi and refused to apologize for it, forcing even House Speaker Paul Ryan to state that "Nazis have no place in our politics."[39] He had also sat for an interview with a notable fascist in Austria to discuss the great replacement theory, a paranoid staple of white supremacist ideology manufacturing fear about immigrants reproducing more than white people.[40] ("We can't restore our civilization with someone else's babies," he previously wrote on social media.[41]) King spoke so frankly of his bigotry that the founder of the flagship online platform for Nazism, *The Daily Stormer*, called him "our guy" and acknowledged that "Steve King is basically an open white nationalist at this point."[42] Anybody who saw the Iowan's work desk would have already known, as it sported a Confederate flag.

When his local prelate suggested that King read the bishops' letter on racism, he likely assumed it could counter King's ideology directly. But King would search in vain for an answer to his question about what's offensive about white supremacy, as the document never even mentions those words. Its aversion to naming what kind of racism plagues the nation renders it useless in educating Catholics like King, who could understandably finish reading it and conclude that the problem is *everyone*. (And therefore, functionally, no one.) King could even walk away strengthened with the knowledge that the US hierarchy as a body has still never explicitly condemned white supremacy.

37. Fraga, "Thousands Call for Gomez to Apologize."

38. White, "Iowa Bishop Calls King's Racist Rhetoric 'Totally Inappropriate.'"

39. Porter, "King Won't Apologize for Retweeting British Neo-Nazi."

40. Mathias and Robins-Early, "Rep. Steve King Goes Full White Nationalist."

41. Sharman, "Steve King: Republican Criticized by Own Party."

42. Marchin, "Cheney Calls GOP Representative Steve King's Comments 'Racist' and 'Abhorrent.'"

This letter is simply a spectacular failure if it can't forthrightly contradict and denounce Catholics who associate with, amplify, and get public praise from fascists and Nazis. Its impulse to missionize misses that in a world with Christians such as Reverends Smash and Sekou, the bishops themselves are mission territory. Like the reverends, many Catholics cannot conceive of a God who refuses to say Black Lives Matter, and in turn cannot take seriously a bureaucratic body that refuses to say the same. But the bishops can learn from other anti-fascists, including un-religious and even anti-religious activists. They too provide theological insight, including in the movement against Confederate statues so intimately linked with Unite the Right in Charlottesville.

3

Of Confederate Idols, the King's Wall, and an Ungovernable God of Graffiti

What does it mean that someone's personal identity is bound up in a racist Confederate monument, a monument to white supremacy? For me, the argument about re-contextualization has already been made. I think the best and most honest context for these monuments is white supremacy. Nothing says what these monuments really mean like a thousand white supremacists coming to defend them.

—Dr. Lisa Woolfork[1]

Vandalism in holy Scripture? Holy Scripture as vandalism?

Perhaps. Hints of a vandal God appeared in the confrontation between anti-racists and the city of Richmond in 2020. Residents had long struggled to remove the city's Confederate statues, which became increasingly marked with spray paint. Eventually, some were in a permanent state of graffiti. And on June 20, the Confederate Soldiers and Sailors Monument at Libby Hill Park bore three biblical references at the base of its hundred-foot-tall pedestal that propped up a Confederate soldier. Among political messages appeared a large JER 6:14, covering a whole side of a pedestal slab.

---

1. Jaffe, "Faith and Freedom on the March in Charlottesville." Woolfork is a professor of English at University of Virginia and a community organizer in Charlottesville with Black Lives Matter and other groups.

Just below it read ISAIAH 58. And below those, between BLM and JUSTICE signs, MICAH 6:8. Down the steps at the root of the statue, just outside the black metal gate surrounding it, lay the words BLACK LIVES ARE MADE IN THE IMAGE OF GOD on the tiled ground in yellow letters.

After neo-Confederates scrubbed off the biblical references, those from Jeremiah and Micah appeared prominently again, one sprawling across a whole side of the pedestal and several fifteen or so feet in the air. They remained in place when the city finally removed the towering Confederate soldier a few weeks later on July 8, mingling with words like GEORGE FLOYD, JUNE 19, and many reading BLM.

Just what were these biblical references doing graffitied on the statue's base and pillar? How to explain this seemingly odd juxtaposition of deface-ment and sacred Scripture?

The scene in Richmond was just one manifestation of a movement that has existed ever since the statues started going up[2] but had been sweeping the nation more dramatically for the last half-decade, escalating even more in the wake of George Floyd's murder. Statues were coming down by decree of city governments and concerned citizens alike, and many that remained were decorated with anti-racist messages. Only weeks earlier, Richmond residents tagged and tore down a statue of Confederate general Williams Carter Wickham. People in Birmingham, Alabama, toppled the memorial for Confederate Navy captain Charles Linn. In nearby Montgomery, citi-zens did the same to a Lee statue that had been moved in 1960 to the all-white Robert E. Lee High School that was opened in defiance of the *Brown v. Board of Education* decision. Doctoral history student Maya Little put red paint and her own blood on the bronze "Silent Sam" Confederate soldier on University of North Carolina's campus before people pulled it down in 2018. In DC, Boston, Philadelphia, Portland, Nashville, St. Paul, Freder-icksburg, Michigan, Indiana, Florida, Texas, New York, California, and all around the country, people and governments attacked, removed, protested, and told histories about white supremacist statues and monuments.

The movement was not at all confined to one country. In June of 2020 in Bristol, England, people pushed a statue of slave trader Edward Colston into the harbor. Days earlier Belgians in Antwerp set aflame a statue of King Leopold II, whose rule in the Congo was so vicious that even other Euro-pean colonialists condemned him, and covered his image with graffiti in

2. For example, see Cox, "Black Protesters Have Been Rallying Against Confederate Statues for Generations."

other cities. That same month, Waikato Tainui people secured the removal of colonial invader John Fane Charles Hamilton's statue in New Zealand, two years after it was covered in red paint and hit in the face repeatedly with a claw hammer. In São Paulo, Brazil, a group called Peripheral Revolution put tires around a statue of seventeenth-century colonizer Borba Gato and set them on fire in 2021. Across countries and continents, opposition to symbols of violent racism became a global conscientization process.

And it took another form in Richmond, curiously, with these biblical references sprayed on a celebration of Robert E. Lee. The passages were chosen well. Isaiah 58 is famous for its claim that God scorns performed pieties and demands loosing the bonds of injustice, breaking every yoke, and letting the oppressed go free. Micah asks what God requires of people but "to do justice, and to love kindness, and to walk humbly with your God?" Jeremiah shows God proclaiming that the unfaithful "have treated the wound of my people carelessly, saying, 'Peace, peace,' when there is no peace." Together they comprise ancient commands to enact justice for the oppressed, condemning present iniquities and providing a way forward. God's word, insisting on conversion toward the wounded and unfree, sprayed in the middle of a public, national battleground over symbols, history, idols.

Thus it was that the biblical prophets' names, along with those of George Floyd and Black Lives Matter, outlasted the Confederate soldier on his own monument.

The iconoclasts understood that Confederate statues are cultic sites. The now-famous Robert E. Lee statue in Charlottesville stood twenty-four feet tall from 1924 to 2022. For a century it loomed over onlookers, gloriously to some and menacingly to others. The bronze figure told no direct story, contrary to the insistent reprimands that these statues can't be altered because they're "history." Rather, it conveyed a myth, exalting the single man in whose arms laid the responsibility to enable the further enslavement of Black people. At the statue's unveiling, University of Virginia president Edwin Alderman, a eugenicist and white supremacist who had accepted money from the KKK—"faithfully yours," he signed off in his thank-you letter[3]—called Lee "stainless." One hundred cadets dressed in Confederate

3. Turnage, "KKK Once Gave UVa $1,000."

colors paraded through town for the event. In this worship, amnesia was virtue and history a heresy.

Alderman was a fitting man to speak at the inaugural ceremony for Lee's statue, as they shared the same disregard for Black people. He was on the record saying, "It is a solemn duty of the white man to see that the negro gets his chance in everything save social equality and political control . . . Social equality and political control would mean deterioration of the advanced group, and the South is serving the Nation when it says it shall not be so."[4] The university's library still bears his name to this day.

Christian ministers during and after the Confederacy preached a religion that conflated the biblical story with that of the white South. Records show sermons across the defeated region preaching that the Confederate soldier was the standard-bearer for Christian virtue and their army was the modern inheritor of God's favor, the new Israelites. (When we read these sermons together, students invariably highlight the sick irony of a culture bent on enslaving others claiming the divinely chosen status of an enslaved people.) George C. Harris in Mississippi preached that the white Southerner's sins were "washed away under the baptism of blood" during the noble fight to keep Black people chained, a sanctifying struggle in their religious imagination.[5] President John Tyler's son even published a *Confederate Catechism* in 1920 to indoctrinate children in the myth of Confederate sanctity.

Ministers likened Robert E. Lee to Moses, leading his people onward by the grace of God, and many exalted him as similar to Jesus Christ. Historian Charles Reagan Wilson wrote, "Laymen and preachers alike compared Lee's 1861 decision at Arlington to reject the offered command of federal forces with the temptations of Christ. Lee's temptations were money, power, and fame, which he abandoned for principle and honor. One minister described the time before Appomattox as 'the anguish-fraught hour of [the general's] Gethsemane.' Lee's postwar image as the sad but proud man seemed to epitomize the Man of Sorrows."[6] This comparison with Christ

4. Dye, "Why UVA Should Rename Alderman Library."

5. Wilson, *Baptized in Blood*, 44.

6. Wilson, *Baptized in Blood*, 48. Though many might find comparing an enslaver with Jesus comically absurd, theologian M. Shawn Copeland reminds us that what Lee represents is more widely divinized, even by those in respectable church positions: "Antiblack logics repressed the demands of conscience, obscured morality, and eclipsed ethics to induce authority and authorities to kneel before the racialized idol of whiteness. In an even more perilous, totalizing move, these authorities attempted to bleach and

went so far that some, like Reverend Henry A. White, preached that Lee was the "perfect man."[7] (Wilson noted with subtle connotation, "In an understatement, one minister commented that Lee was pure enough to have founded a religion."[8]) He thus bore the sufferings of white Southerners like "a true crown of thorns," an instrument used to torture Jesus before his execution, and therefore Lee was "not only their commander, but their Father."

In this upside-down version of Christianity, Jefferson Davis was—despite being very much alive—a martyr and Stonewall Jackson a warrior-prophet straight out of the Hebrew Bible. Rank-and-file Confederate soldiers were exemplars of Christian virtue, duty, and angelic discipleship. What they baptized was not war-making itself, since the devilish and anti-religious North also fought, but the struggle to maintain a system that stole Black labor in mechanized brutality, rape, family separation, and torture. That was holy, and to resist it was hellish, apostasy. This view was not held by the occasional extremist but nurtured over decades in mainstream white churches across the landscape, manufacturing a cult of Confederate worship, heralding Lee as a Christ figure.

We were tied firmly to posts by a Mr. Gwin, our overseer, who was ordered by Gen. Lee to strip us to the waist and give us fifty lashes each, excepting my sister, who received but twenty . . . [Robert E. Lee told him to] lay it on well . . . Not satisfied with simply lacerating our naked flesh, Gen. Lee then ordered the overseer to thoroughly wash our backs with brine, which was done.

—WESLEY NORRIS, FORMERLY ENSLAVED
AT LEE'S ARLINGTON HOUSE[9]

---

domesticate the Divine, to make over the Divine in their image and likeness. Thus, in adhering to the culture and customs of anti-blackness, ecclesial authorities, both episcopal and parochial, bound themselves to the idolatry of whiteness" (Copeland, "'African American Catholic Hymnal,'" 67–82).

7. Wilson, *Baptized in Blood*, 49.

8. Wilson, *Baptized in Blood*, 49.

9. In Blassingame, *Slave Testimony*, 467.

The most prominent symbols of this cult are the Confederate flags and statues punctuating the graveyards, courthouses, street corners, universities, and town squares of our nation, most especially those depicting Robert E. Lee. Charlottesville's twenty-four-foot statue was dwarfed by Richmond's bronze bust standing over sixty feet, which attracted over 100,000 people at its 1890 reveal, including fifteen thousand Confederate soldiers and fifty Confederate generals. But they can be found far beyond the South in places like New Jersey, New York, Ohio, Pennsylvania, Arizona, and Colorado. Lee even had an elementary school named after him in San Diego, California.

Alderman may have seen him as stainless and the Confederate preachers at the altar may have compared him to Christ, but W. E. B. Du Bois saw something else in Lee. He wrote in 1928 of "the inescapable truth that Robert E. Lee led a bloody war to perpetuate slavery" and that Lee was a man who "was asked to lead armies against human progress and Christian decency and did not dare refuse." Du Bois, who has an understanding not only more steeped in history than those who weaved a moral myth around Lee but also more theologically attuned, concluded his essay, "It is ridiculous to seek to excuse Robert Lee as the most formidable agency this nation ever raised to make 4 million human beings goods instead of men. Either he knew what slavery meant when he helped maim and murder thousands in its defense, or he did not. If he did not he was a fool. If he did, Robert Lee was a traitor and a rebel—not indeed to his country, but to humanity and humanity's God."[10]

It is Du Bois' vision that more and more people began to see clearly after Unite the Right's organizers chose Lee's visage to assemble around. (Not that it took hindsight to see. A Black Charlottesville resident understood what Lee's statue meant when it went up, observing, "The Southern white folks is on top."[11]) His legacy is leading armies to kill others so white people could keep enslaving Black people and looting their labor. That white Southerners made of him a messiah figure is just a reminder that strange gods bear strange fruit.

10. Du Bois, *Writings*, 1223.
11. Nelsen and Harold, *Charlottesville 2017*, 8.

The Richmond spray-painters could have conjured numerous other Bible passages, including any number from Daniel, a book populated with idols and their devotees. This collection of apocalyptic tales speaks strongly to the kind of idolatry found in Confederate culture. Composed in two different eras of crisis, Daniel is one of the most incendiary biblical texts, unabashedly hostile to oppressors and imperial domination. The first six chapters were likely written during the Babylonian exile, when many Jews were held captive in a foreign land after King Nebuchadnezzar destroyed Jerusalem and its temple in 587 BCE. The following six chapters were penned leading up to 165 BCE, when the whole collection found its final form, in response to the extreme persecution of Jews at the hands of Antiochus IV Epiphanes, Greek king of the Seleucid Empire.

The biblical scholar Lawrence Wills argues that Daniel's tales are "affirmations of the enduring worth, even superiority, of people who have lost their political power."[12] Hebrew Testament specialist Daniel Smith-Christopher argues that the book is fundamentally an anti-imperial text, noting that most modern assessments have "tended to overlook their potent socio-political power as stories of resistance to cultural and spiritual assimilation of a minority by a dominant foreign power."[13] (In a culture that places a premium on immigrants assimilating to "our" ways, the book's relevance to present politics therefore extends further than struggles over Confederate statues.) He also notes that while scholars have puzzled at the patchwork nature of the book of Daniel, which seems to have held together two sets of disparate tales composed centuries apart, one thing that unifies the texts as a whole is antagonism against authority, making any attempt today to understand Daniel require a "creative theology of confrontation."[14]

Smith-Christopher thinks Daniel is subversive, revolutionary, and even treasonous. Because the chapters return repeatedly to the theme of the abuse of a minority people, it summons its readers to the same sedition that would move a European to side with North Africans in the time of colonization, he says. He believes "the book of Daniel calls people of faith to just such a treason against the rule of the powerful."[15] The tales do not so

12. Kotzé, "Interpretation of Daniel 1: 8–16," 126.

13. Smith-Christopher, "Daniel," in *The New Interpreter's Bible*, 20.

14. Smith-Christopher, "Daniel," in *The New Interpreter's Bible*, 21.

15. Smith-Christopher, "Daniel," in *The New Interpreter's Bible*, 34.

much argue for as assume that its readers will "inevitably" be in opposition to the state and its "idolatrous patriotism." Perhaps this is why priest and theologian Christopher Rowland says the book has been "exegetical dynamite in its ability to support and inform struggles for change" in situations of political abuse and exploitation.[16] A text like this naturally lends itself to movements attacking white supremacist culture today.

Why does such a politically explosive book, latest of all in the Hebrew Testament, appear in the Bible at all? John J. Collins, a leader in Daniel studies, argues its stories are affirmations of a politically disenfranchised people's worth, and "there can be no doubt that ethnic pride was a major reason why the stories . . . were preserved."[17] The book's compilers, then, as well as those who formed the biblical canon, embraced the ethnic pride of oppressed peoples as part of God's sacred story with creation, constitutive of divine revelation. Jews were struggling to survive in political systems bent against them, and part of their resilience and survival tactics took the form of insisting that their lives mattered to God. Reading Daniel in an era when the simple assertion that Black Lives Matter caused a national crisis in which millions feel the need to rebut it with slogans like All Lives Matter or White Lives Matter, it's instructive to learn that the authors of Daniel and the compilers of the Bible felt no need to attach a "Babylonian Lives Matter" message to the texts. As an examination of Daniel's fifth chapter shows, such a concern is antithetical to its God.

King Belshazzar made a great festival for a thousand of his lords, and he was drinking wine in the presence of the thousand. Under the influence of the wine, Belshazzar commanded that they bring in the vessels of gold and silver that his father Nebuchadnezzar had taken out of the temple in Jerusalem, so that the king and his lords, his wives, and his concubines might drink from them. So they brought in the vessels of gold and silver that had been taken out of the temple, the house of God in Jerusalem, and the king and his lords, his wives, and his concubines drank from them. They drank

16. Rowland, "Book of Daniel and the Radical Critique of Empire," in Collins, *Book of Daniel*, 445.

17. Collins, *Daniel*, 44.

the wine and praised the gods of gold and silver, bronze, iron, wood, and stone.

The chapter's very first words invoke idolatry. Belshazzar's name—meaning "Bel, protect the king"—bodes ill for him. It points toward the end of this tale, in which a false god won't be able to protect the king. The setting is the night the Persians conquered the Babylonians in 539 BCE, though commentators uniformly point out this is not a reliable historical document. Whatever the accuracy, this story from the beginning is about more than an individual dying. It deals with the death of an empire.

The king and his guests guzzle wine, extending the book's theme of excess set out in the first four chapters. It also picks up the motif of abusing power, as Belshazzar uses the vessels his father stole from the house of Israel's God while conquering Jerusalem, as narrated in the first chapter. *The New Interpreter's Bible* says contemporary readers would have recognized the vessels as a symbol of the Jews' oppression in their Babylonian exile.[18] The scene is dense with tension from the outset, the rulers getting drunk with a sacred object, taken from a people forced into servitude on a foreign land, now under the reign of a tyrant whose very name spells idolatry.

And, with special resonance to those in the struggles around Confederate statues, they worshiped idols made of bronze and stone.

Immediately the fingers of a human hand appeared and began writing on the plaster of the wall of the royal palace, next to the lampstand. The king was watching the hand as it wrote. Then the king's face turned pale, and his thoughts terrified him. His limbs gave way, and his knees knocked together. The king cried aloud to bring in the enchanters, the Chaldeans, and the diviners; and the king said to the wise men of Babylon, "Whoever can read this writing and tell me its interpretation shall be clothed in purple, have a chain of gold around his neck, and rank third in the kingdom." Then all the king's wise men came in, but they could not read the writing or tell the king the interpretation. Then King Belshazzar became greatly terrified

18. Smith-Christopher, "Daniel," 81.

and his face turned pale, and his lords were perplexed.

A divine emissary, which we later learn was sent by God, wastes no time in indecision but arrives "immediately" after the worship of idols, during the royal revelry. The Aramaic word used for the hand refers specifically to what is below the wrist only, making this a disembodied agent, apparently floating. Collins notes that "the vision of a detached hand writing remains one of the most haunting images in literature."[19] Likewise, biblical scholar and translator Robert Alter says, "This sort of a spooky, quasimagical apparition is not characteristic of earlier biblical narrative."[20]

And just as the writing on Confederate statues horrifies and haunts their idolaters and the powerful today, so Belshazzar quaked upon seeing his wall vandalized. His "face turned pale" and his countenance changed, much like the rich young man in Mark's gospel when Jesus tells him the price of discipleship. Perhaps their faces both fall because they know their future is foretold, however inscrutably, and that in neither situation is it what they had hoped for. In fact, while his confusion may stem from simple drunkenness, Belshazzar's reaction suggests that he already knows the writing portends nothing good for him. His conscience, it seems, may be as heavy as the bronze images of his gods.

Alter inserts a comical note. He translates the king's bodily response in verse 6 as "the cords of his loins went slack," explaining in a footnote that "the loins are imagined in biblical usage as the seat of strength. This physical realization of the king's dismay is unusual and virtually satiric."[21] Which is to say in grander language, the king either pissed or crapped himself in fear of the hand and what it wrote. (Biblical languages scholar Thomas A. Howe explains more directly than Alter that the king most likely "soiled his pants."[22]) I think too of how this might relate to the frenzied, almost apoplectic responses to the vandalizing of the noble statues dedicated to the heroes of slavery. In Charlottesville the loins of some locals were so unsettled at the notion that someone might deface the statues that they parked their trucks nearby at night, armed, ready to assure that no one would commit sacrilege against the bronze gods of the white South.

19. Collins, *Daniel*, 246.
20. Alter, *Hebrew Bible*, 769.
21. Alter, *Hebrew Bible*, 769.
22. Howe, *Daniel in the Preterists' Den*, 160.

Yet unlike today's idolaters, Belshazzar senses there is something worth attending to in these words on the wall, something worth understanding. Even while drunk, he has the wherewithal to suspect that his own fate is tethered to their meaning. And at no point does it occur to him to cuff the hand that wrote them or perform great indignation over the sanctity of his property. Despite his flaws, his attention turns not towards retribution but seeking insight.

Notably, the king does not think to consult anyone outside his court when he tries to uncover the writing's meaning. He assumes that if there is truth to be found, wisdom to be dispensed, it will surely come from his inner circle, surely from the ruling class. His implicit assumption is that God's words can be read by the powerful. It is an assumption that proves incorrect.

The queen, when she heard the discussion of the king and his lords, came into the banqueting hall. The queen said, "O king, live forever! Do not let your thoughts terrify you or your face grow pale. There is a man in your kingdom who is endowed with a spirit of the holy gods. In the days of your father he was found to have enlightenment, understanding, and wisdom like the wisdom of the gods . . . Now let Daniel be called, and he will give the interpretation."

Then Daniel was brought in before the king. The king said to Daniel, "So you are Daniel, one of the exiles of Judah, whom my father the king brought from Judah? I have heard of you that a spirit of the gods is in you, and that enlightenment, understanding, and excellent wisdom are found in you. Now the wise men, the enchanters, have been brought in before me to read this writing and tell me its interpretation, but they were not able to give the interpretation of the matter . . . Now if you are able to read the writing and tell me its interpretation, you shall be clothed in purple, have a chain of gold around your neck, and rank third in the kingdom."

Then Daniel answered in the presence of the king, "Let your gifts be for yourself, or give your rewards to someone else!"

All the king's men prove unable to discern the graffiti, but his mother, Queen Amytis of Media, knows what her son has neglected to consider, that someone outside his court may know. She tells him to summon Daniel, as the king's father found him to be an expert in interpreting dreams and explaining riddles. (And here, Collins thinks the king needing to be educated by his mother about Daniel's existence implies a "frivolity" in his character for not knowing what's available to him. He did not pay attention to the existence of those beneath him.[23]) "Let Daniel be called," she advises, and the king agrees.

Belshazzar begins his encounter with the outsider by stating that Daniel is in exile from Judah, in a land not his own against his will. It's unclear whether this is an acknowledgment, a reminder, a warning, a mocking. Whatever the case, the only one who is oppressed, exploited, captive, is the only one who has "enlightenment, understanding, and excellent wisdom," in contrast to those over him. The scales of power have, for the moment, shifted by divine intervention.

This reversal becomes clearer when the king extends an offer that, notably, he never made available to captive Judah before he had existential need of one of them: to be like a Babylonian. *Help me*, the offer said, *and I will make you like me, one of us, the owners, the governors, the rulers.* Belshazzar offers purple robes symbolizing royal power as well as the rank of third in the kingdom. The offer amounts to assimilation into empire at the highest level, a stunning change of fate if taken.

Daniel, seeing it for what it is, immediately throws the offer back at the king. "Let your gifts be for yourself, or give your rewards to someone else!" He does not dignify the attempt to play power games. Not only has Belshazzar summoned one who is outside his people but also above the political maneuvering of the elite class. (Knowing what the words say already, Daniel also presumably understands that the king's power is fleeting, that despite the queen mother's greeting to her son the king will not in fact "live forever" but die before the sun rises.) *The New Interpreter's Bible* notes that Daniel's tone would be seen in the court as hostile. "Its presence here signals a serious turn in the polemics directed against the authorities."[24] Collins agrees, saying the "curtness of Daniel's response contrasts with the

---

23. Collins, *Daniel*, 218.
24. Smith-Christopher, "Daniel," 83.

gracious speech of the king that precedes it," establishing a "denunciatory tone."[25]

This shift in tone is central to the story and weighs heavily in its relation to anti-idolatry movements today. The word translated as "woe" in the mouth of Luke's Jesus means to denounce, meaning this new "denunciatory tone" is like the one Jesus took when he publicly admonished those abusing their power. *Woe to you, king!* Daniel says. *No flattery with offers of power-sharing or fine clothes, no dangling deals to move up in society by joining the idolatrous oppressors!*

Readers might wonder if this lack of will to power, this will against power, has something to do with why Daniel can read the words yet the others cannot. Like those who can see the writings on the imperial walls for what they are today, Daniel says no offer can tempt him to share in power at the price of righteousness. "You have exalted yourself against the Lord of heaven!" Daniel cries in verse 23, charging him with praising the wrong gods while getting drunk with ego and wine, filling the sacred vessels with his hubris. Like today's Daniels, he scorned ruling in order to reveal to the king his own pride and lack of foresight, in the very halls of royal power.

In fact, verse 23 invokes, nearly verbatim, Psalm 115:5–6 to deride and insult the king's statues. The psalm reads, "They have mouths, but do not speak; eyes, but do not see. They have ears but do not hear; noses, but do not smell." Commentators agree that both the psalmist's dig and Daniel's reference is meant to mock idols, highlighting how inert and dead they are. "You have praised the gods of silver and gold, of bronze, iron, wood, and stone, which do not see or hear or know," Daniel adds, "but the God in whose power is your very breath, and to whom belong all your ways, you have not honored." The king and his drunken court, he says, have dishonored the true God by opting for simulations.

Daniel's speech is a reprimand, a reminder that the king knew better. Or perhaps, that he had the opportunity to know better. In his devotion to gods who know nothing, he in turn knew nothing. The bronze gods, in this sense, are not neutral but active agents, affecting their disciples, imputing their lack. They pass their myths to new generations, new children.

Collins notes that the accusatory speech in verses 17–23 is not in the original text, written during the Babylonian captivity, but was a later addition to the story by redactors centuries later, designed to emphasize that

25. Collins, *Daniel*, 249.

God deals with this idolatrous king harshly.[26] So this breach in civility, this challenge to the powerful, was not a problem section of an ancient text that later editors had to stomach. They inserted it deliberately, long after the original was crafted, to use the earlier story to speak to the (then) present oppression under Antiochus IV Epiphanes.

Embedded in the history of this text, then, is a precedent, an invitation for readers to do likewise, to use Daniel's story to examine how similar power dynamics function today. If Daniel's denunciation of the king could be seen by the biblical crafters to speak to Antiochus centuries later, people today can with equal right point it toward Confederates to denounce their idols, their gluttonous excess and power grasping. This move to apply it to the present is seeded in the history of the Bible itself, which applies (and even changes) old stories to aid modern movements for justice. It is not too much to say that Daniel is an activist text, going beyond mere storytelling and entering the fray of political turmoil, siding with those below even if it demands updating Scripture.

"So from [God's] presence the hand was sent and this writing was inscribed. And this is the writing that was inscribed: MENE, MENE, TEKEL, *and* PARSIN. *This is the interpretation of the matter:* MENE: *God has numbered the days of your kingdom and brought it to an end;* TEKEL, *you have been weighed on the scales and found wanting;* PERES, *your kingdom is divided and given to the Medes and Persians."*

Then Belshazzar gave the command, and Daniel was clothed in purple, a chain of gold was put around his neck, and a proclamation was made concerning him that he should rank third in the kingdom.

That very night, Belshazzar, the Chaldean king, was killed.

Daniel reveals that the very God who Belshazzar neglected sent the hand. Collins calls it a "divine emissary." The question of whether the hand is literally God's or a human's is rendered moot by Daniel's words. Whoever this disembodied hand directly belongs to, it is on God's mission. *The hand*

26. Collins, *Daniel*, 249.

who tagged up your property was divinely sent, he tells the king. *This is God's graffiti marking up your state property. This vandalism is holy writ.*

No wonder he was terrified. His gods of bronze, which never challenged the powerful and had no concern for the exploited, hadn't prepared him to encounter this kind of disobedient, rebellious inbreaking of the divine in opposition to state power.

And then, Daniel interprets the writing on the wall. MENE, MENE, TEKEL, and PARSIN. *You have been weighed. You have been found wanting. Your kingdom is at an end.* The three assertions are brutal in their simplicity, their finality. Once again, the powerful one finds the tables turned. The one who is used to weighing others finds he has, unaware, been weighed. The king swiftly finds he is not at the top of the hierarchy of power but that he is dreadfully, even fatally vulnerable. He has been found to be too light, lacking in substance, less than. And his empire will be divided between others. In a matter of moments, the king has gone from guzzling wine in sacred vessels stolen from the house of God, robbed from the people he now exiles, hosting revelry in court, to being cast down and without power.

What is symbolic becomes physically manifest that night when the king is killed. ("Punishment is swift and severe with no chance for repentance," reads the New Revised Standard Version's footnote.[27]) The text is silent about who kills him, but the culprit is as obvious as it is disturbing to rulers. Just as the hand that tagged the king's wall was sent by God, so too the hand that took his life.

What to make of this God who sends emissaries to break human law by putting graffiti on state property and slaying the king? Two hands, each up to felonious business, violating the bounds of civility and the legal code. What to make of this decidedly unruly, ungovernable God? What to take from this radical reversal of fortunes, in which at first the king revels in drunken power while Daniel languishes with apparently no one in the court knowing who he is, while at the story's end Daniel is robed in power and the king is slain in his sleep?

This points toward a difficult question, an accompanying riddle. It's not so much that the king can't make out the letters on the wall as that he can make no sense of them. And yet, he does finally show himself capable of

27. *Harper Collins Study Bible, New Revised Standard Version,* 1180.

understanding when someone he considered beneath him translates. Daniel acts in good faith toward the king. In both his interpretation and his denunciation he reveals truth to the one holding him captive. He does not need to do this for his survival. We see elsewhere in the story that God will protect Daniel and his friends, even if it means rescue from a fiery furnace or lion's den. Daniel is not motivated by saving his own skin but something else.

I sense something of enemy-love in Daniel's actions. Rather than try to kill his adversary or celebrate his foretold doom, he treats Belshazzar humanly, as someone worthy of rebuke but also dignity, despite the lack of reciprocity. It was unfair of the king to expect a conversation with Daniel, one more act of lording his authority over an exiled captive. No one should expect Daniel to speak in a collected manner to his oppressor or meet him in the halls of power. It would be legitimate to reject the summons or spit on the king's floor instead of entering into dialogue.

Daniel shows one path enemy-love might take. Even foretelling his kingdom's destruction is a mercy, a grace. Loving someone can entail, or in some circumstances even require, revealing the consequences of their idolatry and exploitation, however dire. It can be an act of love to violate the charade of civility that would bracket the violence of empire, of one people acting as if they were supreme over another. To say no, to cry *woe!* in dens far more vicious than a lion's, is to speak a true word. The two hands of graffiti and death are sent from God in Daniel 5. So too, it seems, was the voice that refused the king's games, that proclaimed the end not just of the king but of the empire.

In November 1943, Vichy officials arrested twenty-three members of the French Resistance. The group, including eleven Jews, had been carrying out armed attacks on Nazi collaborators for the better part of the year. Most had fled Eastern Europe and were fighting for survival in a time of genocide. The Vichy government tortured and executed them all, twenty-two by firing squad and one, Olga Bancic, by beheading.

Not satisfied with merely killing them, Vichy officials printed out fifteen thousand copies of *L'affiche Rouge*, the Red Poster, and plastered them on public walls. It read at the top, "Liberators?" Beneath were ten faces and names of the executed, all foreign, some Jewish. The poster insinuated that the resistance was Jewish, criminal, foreign, and beneath true French patriots. "Liberation by the criminal army!" read the sign at the bottom.

The government did not have the last word. Strange scrawl materialized night after night, by hands belonging to unknown bodies, covering the posters in all caps, MORTS POUR LA FRANCE (THEY DIED FOR FRANCE), words reserved for French soldiers fallen in combat.

This too, in the face of anti-Semitic state lies, is the writing on the wall. Graffiti on the ruler's walls, inbreaking of truth, homage to the dead. To keep the civil order would have been to sanction sacrilege, to approve of the smearing of Jews because they were Jews, to murder reputations after bodies.

Unknown French dissidents knew better than to accept the civil order of the Nazis and their collaborators. They could read the writing on the wall. Some of them, with God-sent hands, wrote it as well.

A group in 2019 met at each statue in Charlottesville that celebrated white supremacy, led by pastors Isaac Collins and Phil Woodson, calling themselves "Swords to Plowshares." They gathered early, once a week at a different site, educating the community on the history behind the statue and its figure as well as saying prayers. A sample from their handout reads:

One: Why are you here so early in the morning?

Many: The Spirit has called us here to tell the truth: this statue is an idol to white supremacy. We have been gathered to reckon with the full history of Charlottesville's past, to assess the state of our present reality, and to cast a different vision for the future. We can't let this statue tell lies about our city anymore.

One: What future do you want for Charlottesville?

Many: We want a city without idols to white supremacy. We want to see swords turned into plowshares. We want to be free.

One: The Spirit is here. Will you accept the power to create the future you want to see?

Many: This is our community, and we do have power. We have power to plant seeds of justice. We are united, and we will create a Charlottesville without idols.

We can't let these statues tell lies anymore, the group professed. Their proclamation redirects complaints about statue removals "erasing history."

These statues lie. They are what is described as devilish and satanic in Scripture—deceivers. The assumption that they tell history has it backwards. They obscure, mis-tell, and propagandize about history. *The enslavers are glorious*, they say—*they were then and remain so today*. The drive to remove them stems from the desire not to banish history but finally take it seriously.

As Kelly Brown Douglass writes, the statues distort reality by omission as well, by who is not depicted, not remembered, or (as in the case of the Sacagawea statue in Charlottesville) misremembered as lesser-than or docile. "When Black people are included in the monuments depicting that period, they are typically portrayed as a subordinate part of the white narrative, if not as supplicants," she writes.[28] Noting that there are roughly 1,500 Confederate symbols in public spaces alone, seven times as many statues for Confederates than the "founding fathers," and about three times as many Jefferson Davis statues than those for Dr. King or Frederick Douglass, she argues that "Confederate monuments, with their outsized presence on the public square, have in fact become the prevailing symbols of social memory" in the US.

With their direct and indirect lies, the statues become something more—weapons. They are blunt instruments of brutality, forming a social story that teaches white supremacist myths to children and perpetuates ideas that undergird oppression and overt violence, as we saw in Charlottesville. People who defend them as bearers of history never accuse the US military of destroying history for removing the statue of Saddam Hussein in Baghdad or the early revolutionaries of erasing the past because they toppled the statue of King George III and made over 42,000 bullets with the material. (What, exactly, is their attachment to these particular statues then, one wonders?) These are rather celebrations of oppressors that act maliciously in the public imagination, normalizing the exaltation of villains to the point that most onlookers see nothing at all wrong with honoring the cause of slavery. The story they tell and the culture that narrates it have become canon, part of the national fabric that goes unquestioned. They cannot remain in a neighborly society.

That's why anti-racists with spray paint see something in the biblical passages from Micah and Jeremiah that speaks to this moment and these weapons. Idols are for transforming, not leaving alone, celebrating, or protecting as truth-tellers. (This is a kinder approach than that of Moses, who melted down the famed golden calf and made its idolaters drink the ashes

---

28. Douglas, *Resurrection Hope*, 82.

in Exodus.) Knowing this, the Jefferson School African American Heritage Center in Charlottesville named the Lee statue "an international lightning rod of white supremacy . . . a singular source of harm to our community," and won the right to melt down the Lee statue and turn it into public art. Recognizing an idol when they see one, they named their effort after the anti-weapon visions of the prophets Micah and Isaiah: "Swords into Plowshares."[29]

FIGURE 4

Swords into Plowshares, Bunmi Collins of StickyNote Creative and Claire Payton

A biblical hope shouts: *Swords into plowshares, Confederate statues into art!* We can't let these statues tell lies about history, our ancestors, or the present anymore. To convert them into instruments of healing, tilling, or nourishing is their only use in a loving society. If they cannot be used to uplift the community, they are fit only for destruction.

29. To support and learn more about the effort, see https://sipcville.com.

Among the George Floyd makeshift memorials on the column below Richmond's Robert E. Lee are two words: I LOVE. Perhaps there was once a third word that has since been painted over. Maybe the message was meant to stand as it appears. Given Daniel's story, either way seems a fitting pair with what's written on the other side of Lee's column, BLOOD ON YOUR HANDS and STOP BEING RACIST. Black paint nearby paraphrased what God once ominously said on Belshazzar's wall: WE WILL STAND UNTIL THE STATUE FALLS. These anti-idol activists understood what felon Father Daniel Berrigan wrote of Daniel's fifth chapter: "The gods of wood and stone stand in our public spaces, icons raised in dubious honor of robber barons and warriors. Only connect! American history is a vast diorama of idolatry in action."[30] Dwelling with the art and revelatory words on any number of these idols can aid those seeking modern garb for ancient stories.

Sixty feet beneath Lee, at the base of six steps leading up to his pillar, appears the phrase END THE RULING CLASS, surrounded by BLM and anti-Trump graffiti. High above these words rests a peace sign. The powerful might find these messages mutually incompatible. But if Daniel 5 conveys anything, it's that the ruling class can't read the writing on the wall.

These words that seem illegible to kings and courts are not so much theology as theograffiti, God's Word tagged onto state property, left in complete disregard for whether it's permissible to write on the royal wall. In the book of Daniel, God did not so much mar the wall as sacralize it, convert it to revelation, etch into it a harsh and dreadful love.

That was true then, it is true now. I see analogous theograffiti in every Confederate statue that gets tagged. When unknown hands wrote NATIVE LAND or 1619 on Lee's statue in Charlottesville, that too was not defacing but turning the site into epiphanic space. When the grandiose foundation of Richmond's Lee statue was sprayed, when it became the canvas for images of Frederick Douglass and George Floyd projected by light, that too was God's graffiti, a language unintelligible to the sovereigns but perfectly legible to those below. In doing so, they redeemed the material, transfiguring it

30. Berrigan, *Daniel*, 84.

from untruth to a revelation that foretells the doom of rulers as rulers, just as God's own hand once did on King Belshazzar's wall.

The hands of Maya Little and those as unknown as the writers on the Red Posters in Vichy France and the inscriber of Daniel 5 remind us that God too is a vandal, no respecter of kings or their things. They free the legal imagination to glimpse something of God's hand in those that redeem the bronze and stone celebrations of slavery. To paint "Black Lives Matter" on an exaltation of someone whose legacy was the destruction of Black lives is more than poetic justice. It is sacred scrawl, echoing the One who protested against an ancient king on behalf of the oppressed.

It's no surprise to see Bible references among the graffiti. That's just citing one's sources.

An Interview with Rabbi Mordechai Liebling

Rabbi Mordechai Liebling is a community organizer, writer, and longtime activist. He served as president of the Shalom Center, executive director of the Jewish Reconstructionist Federation, and director of the Social Justice Organizing Program at the Reconstructionist Rabbinical College. When Congregate Charlottesville put out a call in 2017 for clergy to converge in opposition to Unite the Right, he answered the summons. I spoke with him four years later to understand what motivated him to say yes.

Why did you come to Charlottesville to protest Unite the Right?

What compelled me to go is that both of my parents were Holocaust survivors. So it was kind of a no-brainer for me. As soon as I heard about it I knew I had to go. Both of my parents were the sole survivors in their family. All my grandparents and uncles and aunts were murdered in the Holocaust. They were from the southwestern part of Poland that is now the Ukraine. So it was a moral imperative. There was no choice really.

You know, I organized a rally in Boston in 1978 when the Nazis planned to march in Skokie, Illinois. I had my mother speak at the rally, which was cool. I organized something at that point called the Boston Committee to Challenge Anti-Semitism because that was also the time of the Boston bussing crisis. Right-wing groups and neo-Nazis, Klan folk were organizing in and around Boston. So it felt important to organize against the right wing then too.

How did you get drawn into these movement circles?

[Laughing.] It was my first or second night in college. I was in the dorms and outside were these seniors who put up a tent city protesting the lack of housing on campus. I didn't know anything, you know, this is my first or second night. I just went outside to check out what's going on here. And I met these two seniors who I talked with and they ended up basically mentoring me for a while and by the spring I remember collecting anti-war signatures. It was back during the Vietnam War.

I was at Cornell from the fall of '65 to '69. Dan Berrigan [a Catholic priest and prominent anti-war activist] was on campus as "faculty advisor" to Students for a Democratic Society. Cornell was one of the more active SDS chapters in the country—we shut down the campus for the last three months of my senior year!—and one of the few where nobody became Weathermen or went into that violent tangent, I think in part because of Berrigan's influence. When Rabbi Arthur Waskow published his freedom seder around '69, with quotes from Black Panthers and others, Bread and Puppet Theater put on a seder with him. They had these huge heads, and all of a sudden Berrigan shows up while he's on the run from the FBI and disappears in one of these huge-headed puppets. The FBI was running around but couldn't find him. So his presence was important for us, for me.

Let's fast-forward a bit. You went to both Ferguson in 2014 and Standing Rock in 2016. When you were in Charlottesville, did you feel more prepared because you had been with those communities? How were you influenced by them?

You know, Ferguson was intense because of the militarization of the police. I had been in "police riots." Some of the police in the late sixties, early seventies, you know they would just club people. That was like Ferguson, they'd go in and they had their shields on and batons and full riot gear. But in Ferguson you really saw the militarization of police at a new level. That was striking. I had been tear-gassed a while back in Israel, but there was a level of militarization that hadn't been present before, at least that I'd seen. And that was repeated at Standing Rock. And I couldn't believe at Standing Rock, you had Army personnel carriers and tanks and snipers all over the place. Man, it was unbelievable. The militarization of the cops that I saw between Ferguson and Standing Rock is such an escalation of tactics. You could see the authoritarian state and its ability to clamp down as I had never seen before.

And from what I noticed, so many people felt accepted in Standing Rock. There was a beautiful atmosphere of acceptance and community. I saw that for many people it was very transformational. And Standing Rock was such an example of faith in action. The elders really insisted that every time there's any demonstration that it be treated as ceremony. You know, they'd be very clear about that and were able to do it for public actions, which was a powerful piece for sure.

You said you were arrested in Israel? Or was it tear-gassed?

Yeah, I was both. As part of rabbinical school you're required to spend a year in Israel, so I lived there from the fall of '81 to the fall of '82. And that was during one of the wars on Lebanon. And it was of course during the occupation, and I was part of a demonstration of mostly, pretty much all, Israelis protesting the occupation. And they told us to disperse, and the folks I was with chose not to disperse. And I was brought up with an ethic of solidarity [laughing], so I just hung out, you know, and eventually the police came and arrested us. And a different time I was tear-gassed. We were on the West Bank protesting the occupation, and we landed up getting gassed. That time I was arrested in Jerusalem for protesting the occupation, though.

So, in Ferguson you have clergy out there. In Charlottesville there was a kind of liturgical confrontation with the alt-right, through song and placing of bodies in the park. And there was a very strong overlap with Standing Rock, though it was Indigenous-led ceremony rather than Jewish or Christian liturgy. I'm curious how you experienced that ceremonial and liturgical confrontation of police and tanks and the KKK. A mode of being a people of faith, as a body, in confrontation with evil, not as a remote people worshiping in a building but bringing their ceremoniality out into public to confront evil. Did you experience it as something sacred or was it just pure protest?

Standing Rock was clearly prayerful. Ferguson at times was too. I spent six days or so there when they issued a clergy call. It was organized mostly by PICO, which is now called Faith in Action. I don't know how many clergy, fifty or something, marched down to the police station. The intention was to go into the police station and get arrested. Cornel West and [Rev. Osagyefo] Sekou were there too. And our goal was to try to talk to the police and do a quasi-confessional thing with them. It was structured as a prayerful—liturgical even—event. The idea was to engage with individual police in a human, spiritual way at the same time as we were trying to get into the building. It was an interesting thing. And we chanted and we prayed, so that particular day at least was framed as clearly a moment for people of faith engaging with the powers of the state. And I think those are powerful moments. I think those are important moments.

There's a Jewish organization called Bend the Arc, and about three years ago [in 2018] they organized a day supporting immigration reform and protesting the Trump administration. There was a whole series of actions in the Capitol rotunda with different groups, and this was the Jewish moment. There were maybe fifty or sixty of us. The intent was to go to the rotunda, sit down, pray, and get arrested. And we managed—unusual for Jews [laughing]—we managed to do it in a pretty serious and liturgical way. And we sang songs, and most people wore a tallit, a prayer shawl. And you know, we did it in a very prayerful way, it was very powerful, with singing. We got arrested in a pretty ceremonial way. And in the balcony of the rotunda were lots of DREAMers, we did a lot of support work with them. And the next day when we did a debrief of the action, a bunch of the DREAMers were there and they were in tears, very moved. Those were mostly men in their twenties who probably don't cry in public very often. But they were touched by a public expression of faith, that we would really pray and sing, it touched them, and that in turn moved me.

We don't have that many instances in the progressive world of people of faith using our faith in those moments and lifting it up. We're shy about it for a variety of reasons. A lot of it is because of the way the Christian Right does things around abortion, obviously, and we don't do that. But I think it's a loss, we really need to learn more how to bring out faith into the public square.

Going back to the Ferguson action, how did the police respond to this liturgical entry of their station?

You know, they didn't respond well. They're pretty much under strict orders not to talk to you. We each tried to find one police officer and talk to him, as they were all men, about his parents, his kids. I don't know if any of us got a response. They're told not to interact. They pretty much observed discipline and did not interact with us.

I'm curious, when it comes to police, or in Charlottesville when it comes to the alt-right, the KKK, and the neo-Nazis, how do you approach them? I hear you talk about appealing to the humanity of the police. How do you understand the idea of solidarity with a group who might disagree with that approach?

Well, the Lakota made sure we didn't dehumanize the police. I think that's part of their being in ceremony. I also spent a good amount of time with veterans of the civil rights movement. I was privileged to meet John Lewis several times and folks like him. Jim Lawson. They absolutely refused to dehumanize anybody they encountered. Lewis obviously was beaten badly, but wouldn't dehumanize the folks that did it to him. Their Christian faith was very strong. They were pretty clear that they couldn't fall into the same evil that the oppressor exhibited. Hate the sin love the sinner. That's not me, necessarily, but there is a big nonviolent legacy in the southern freedom movement based on not dehumanizing the other.

I think we have to oppose people when they're in a certain role, recognize the role they're playing and oppose that. But let's not confuse the person with the role. One of the things that was striking to me in Charlottesville was when we were standing in the middle of those two groups, arm's length from Antifa and arm's length from the neofascists. The spiritual work is having compassion. Just because I have compassion doesn't mean I'm not going to oppose you, though. I'm not going to justify what you're saying or doing. I'm going to absolutely oppose it but I'm still going to have compassion on you as a person. There's a difference between compassion and justification, between excusing and compassion. They're not the same thing. That's one of the things I sat with at Auschwitz. We've got to sit with that.

You mentioned standing between two groups. Did you come to Charlottesville as a branch of the anti-fascists or did you come unaffiliated with either side to act as peacekeeper between them?

Oh, I came as a branch of one side, but with an understanding of a way to oppose fascists differently than some had.

What can compassion mean when your enemies want to commit genocide against your neighbors? What does it mean to love in this situation?

Well, if you love someone about to commit a crime, you stop them. Right? I mean that's what love means. You don't allow someone you love to commit a crime.

Since we're on love and liturgy and protest, was your experience in Charlottesville prayerful? And if so, in what sense?

[Long silence.] It's an interesting question. It was prayerful in the sense that bearing witness is prayerful. Right? I think there's a piece of spiritual life that means we have to bear witness to suffering. And we have to bear witness to evil. And I think a piece of what our work was there was bearing witness. [More silent thinking.] Yes, it's about bearing witness.

The clergy were at the murder scene right after the attack, which was horrific. And after the ambulances took everyone away, which seemed an eternity, we regrouped in an alley, we circled up, and you led us in meditation. How did that come about?

Well, I've been in violent demonstrations before, so I figured I felt centered enough for something like that, and it was clear people were a little frazzled. So I may have volunteered or been asked by [Reverend] Smash, I don't remember. I lead a fair amount of guided meditations, so I knew we needed grounding then. Whatever came to me in that moment that would ground us and connect us to each other, I said that. I don't remember what it was.

I have to ask the obvious question: were you not worried about coming to a huge neo-Nazi gathering as a Jew, wearing a yarmulke, being visibly Jewish?

Yeah, I was. You know, three or four days before we got there I got an email from the organizers saying we expect violence and the violence could be life-threatening. They were very clear about the possibility that existed. Umm, yeah I was frightened! I mean, how could I not be? [Laughter.] I mean, I was frightened as a Jew, as a visible Jew going doing there, yeah. It was still my ethical obligation, but I was frightened, for sure.

Were you at the evening service the night before at the church?

You mean the one where we couldn't get out because the Nazis and stuff were nearby? Yes. I didn't go to the sunrise service the next morning, but I was at that one. I was at a different service in the morning.

Then how did our groups meet up before the riot?

We met you at the park [where Unite the Right was amassing] after the service. We actually passed the synagogue and we saw these armed folk

[Redneck Revolt] in military fatigues. They were around the synagogue and we thought, who are these guys with guns at the synagogue?! We had to talk with them and finally figure out they were on our side. Then we met all you clergy in front of the park.

So we were lined up together then in the street with the militia, who was not on our side, facing us with their guns. What happened then? One group of clergy branched off to go block the park and another didn't. Which group were you with?

Well, I was on the far other side of the line from you all on the right, far from the steps that you blocked, so the invite to block the park took a while to get to me. And when me and my friend were on the way, you know, I turned to my friend and said, "This is about to turn very violent and we need to think about getting out of here." And literally as soon as I finish saying that we hear that we have to leave, it's time to move. The Right had attacked, so we actually walked towards you folks who were trying to block the park, but it looked like as we were approaching that you had gotten pushed off the steps or something, and we just had to get out of there. It was a melee. Things were just ugly. What was that like for you all?

Well, I can't speak for everyone but some of us felt like we failed to stop them from attacking, to stop the them from getting into the park. It obviously wasn't great.

Well, we had—we did the best we could. When you have a couple dozen people with hundreds and hundreds of neo-Nazis we're trying to stop, there was no way we could do anything. You know, we would have needed three hundred of us to have an impact on the situation. We were just so totally dwarfed by their size. Of course you're going to feel bad, but it's literally the heat of battle and you're outnumbered. We needed hundreds and hundreds but we just didn't have them.

So, as you know there were Catholic Workers out there but no Catholic clergy, even though they had a church just steps away. What does this mean to you?

Well, you know, in the bigger picture, as a Jewish person with roots in Eastern Europe, I don't feel the Catholic Church has ever really done the full level of repentance, self-examination that it needed to do post-Holocaust, and in the same line I don't think the Catholic Church has done the level of repentance, certainly reparations, when it comes to the doctrine of discovery and imperialism.

One of the things I do for Faith and Action and others is help lead trainings on racism, anti-Semitism, and Christian hegemony, so we teach about the doctrine of discovery and the Catholic Church and imperialism and slavery. And to this very day, I mean, there are delegations going to Pope Francis, who is the best of the best, to rescind the doctrine of discovery and he hasn't done it. The church still won't do that. So I just feel that the church as an institution hasn't done the work, the spiritual work that it needs to do around the Holocaust, around the doctrine of discovery, etc. There's a lot of work for the church to do that it hasn't done.

II. Considering Ivory Virtues: Civility & Nonviolence

Mary Punching Beast, Ben Wildflower

4

Of Middle Fingers, Biblical Beheadings, and Anti-Civility

The scene, a Charlottesville auditorium at night. The cast, the county school board and those hoping to squeeze their comments into three-minute windows, including the untiring Hate-Free Schools Coalition. The issue, whether Confederate imagery would continue to be allowed in schools. The protocols handed down from the meeting's chair, "Disruptive behavior will not be tolerated." No clapping or snapping, we are told, "no audible forms of support." (Town functionaries held a special, somewhat perplexing antipathy for snapping. Jail board meetings commonly began with grave warnings that there would under no circumstances be any snapping tolerated, and the chair once removed time for community comments on whether they should continue handing some inmates to ICE upon their release for deportation because "multiple snappers" had "disrupted proceedings.") We would be allowed, however, to stand or raise our hands. We were not to overlap on topics. A curious rule, given the issue at hand.

But there was more to this scene. The last meeting on August 30, 2018, had been punctuated by a plainclothes police officer attacking a community member. When the school board removed the opportunity for public comments, the community decided it would get its message across outside the meeting. Police sprang into action when the board ordered them to stop making comments even outside. Since the assailant never identified himself as an officer, the victim had no clue who was laying hands on him. He didn't strike back, but he did struggle to get out of the officer's grip as onlookers watched his face "turn purple" and get hurled over a row of chairs.[1]

The supposed crime committed by the man who was assaulted and battered by an officer? Felony assault and battery of an officer. He made it to jail only after being released from the hospital. Police arrested five other concerned citizens. The trust further deteriorated between police and community, the school board and disturbed parents. (They were frayed enough when one school board member wore a tie decorated with Confederate flags in a naked attempt to rile caring community members at the previous meeting.) Emotions were pronounced, heels dug in.

The school board chair released a public statement that conjured the notion of civility in its defense. "The School Board as a group was committed to getting through the business it was elected to do," she stated falsely, as their business was not to prevent students, parents, and residents from providing input into how their own schools function. "Fortunately, with the help from the county attorney and county police, we were able to do that. We strive to hold meetings in a civilized manner."

The following meeting, the first few commenters made clear their stance: no white nationalist imagery on clothing in schools, remove police from these meetings, especially plainclothes officers, "let us make human noises of approval without the threat of police brutality," and apologize for what happened on August 30. Several board members seemed engaged, several not. I wondered if the conversation would be different if the roles were flipped. Would schools allow Black students to wear shirts reading, "I want a culture that enslaves whites"? And if not, why would they allow that student to wear a symbol that meant the exact same thing for Black people?

The next speaker, carrying a gun, requested an *increased* police presence. A known local and outspoken racist, he complained that people called him racist.

"Racist," answered a clear voice from the crowd on cue. A lone snapper's fingers echoed through the rows. The police officer to my right stopped leaning against the wall and craned his neck to find the offender.

"You are out of order," the chair reprimanded the lawless snapper. A university librarian countered, "He can carry a gun and we can't snap our fingers?"

The infraction, asking an incisive question, at an educational meeting no less. The librarian was summarily kicked out, and four others left with

1. Baars, "Activists Arrested," 10–12. The later quote from the school board chair also appears in this article.

him, some with middle fingers raised all the way down the aisle and out the door. Many in the crowd joined in, perhaps realizing this silent language had not technically been explicitly prohibited.

FIGURE 6

Photo taken by author. Many thanks for his permission to use.

The raised fingers were seen as impolite. But I wondered what it would take to realize that a symbol celebrating centuries of murder, rape, kidnapping, enslavement is less acceptable than a middle finger issued at a bureaucracy protecting its presence among our youth. How did we arrive at a cultural place when the wrong one was seen as an evil?

Shortly after, a community member brought forward the words of a mother who was banned from the premises. "Every time you shut us down, we grow," she declared. "By any means necessary we will stop you from destroying this community." At this, the board member who previously wore a Confederate flag turned his head to the speaker for the first time and raised his eyebrows, paying far more attention than when people made well-mannered requests for banning pro-slavery images from schools.

This scene is one example among many showing how the idea of civility gets abused, leveraged to shrink the permissible space for reforming systems until the only options available are ineffective. This leaves people with a choice between accepting harm or something more drastic than reform.

Which is to say, civility doesn't work for just causes. Every significant social gain—voting rights, ending monarchy's rule in the colonies, the five-day work week and eight-hour work day, school desegregation, lower taxes, the abolition of slavery—was achieved by means considered less than civil by CEOs, politicians, or police. The concept is designed to serve those in power and act as an obstacle to social progress. Only by transgressing it does our nation even exist.

Journalist Karen Grigsby Bates points out that civility inevitably gets used as a "cudgel against People of Color" since it has historically been tethered to delusions of white superiority. "Pushing back against the status quo will be seen as inherently uncivil by the people who want to maintain it," she observes.[2] The concept is steeped in histories of "killing the Indian," taming the African, and assimilating the Central and South American.[3] It's seen as something white people have gifted to others through the process of slavery, missionizing, forced schooling, and other violent processes.

The saga of Colin Kaepernick most clearly displays the moving fenceposts of civility. He collaborated with a Green Beret about how best to protest police violence against Black people in a respectful manner, deciding to silently kneel out of everyone's way once a week. It was so unintrusive that no one noticed at first but when people caught on, part of the nation went into a frenzy. They accused him of being hateful. They said he was disrespecting the military and the American flag. (Which, given his cause, raises questions about who they did and did not understand the flag to represent.) The NFL had to pay an estimated $10 million to settle his case that they colluded against him. The president, who said "we love you" to the January 6 rioters that bludgeoned police and caused multiple deaths, called him a "son of a bitch." People followed his lead, demeaning the quarterback and even sending death threats.[4]

2. Bates, "When Civility Is Used as a Cudgel."

3. "Kill the Indian and save the man" was the mantra (from the mouth of US military officer Richard H. Pratt) for stealing Indigenous children from their parents and forcing them into the colonists' boarding school systems, where they were forbidden to speak their language and faced cultural isolation, rape, and early death in an attempt to assimilate them to "civilized culture." For an examination of this process, see Trafzer, Keller, and Sisquoc, *Boarding School Blues*, 176.

4. For a more in-depth analysis of Kaepernick's influence, see Zirin, *Kaepernick Effect*.

When protesters damage property, march in streets, sit in a politician's office, camp in a public space, or even yell, they are invariably told to find a better way to protest. But the furor over Kaepernick's kneel, which could have hardly been more innocuous or less disruptive to any individual or social life, shows how disingenuous these concerns are. (Reverend Seth Wispelwey of Charlottesville explains this by claiming he had upset the liturgy around the NFL's "worship song" in the national anthem.[5]) As theologian Bryan Massingale observed in 2020:

> People always say that there are better, more effective, more ethical ways of people making their point. I hear that, but I want to press them on that. If there are better, more effective, more ethical ways of people making their point, I wish they would tell me what they are. Because people of color, black Americans, have marched. We have demonstrated. We have organized. We have protested. We have voted. We have studied. We have taught. We have begged. We have pleaded. We have cried out. We have wept—for years, for decades, even centuries. And still we are being killed while jogging. Or poor Tamir Rice, a twelve-year-old kid killed for just sitting in a park. If there are better and more effective ways to do this, then don't just homilize about that. Tell me what they are.[6]

The same people gravely wagging their fingers at protestors for being "uncivil" would find the Bible downright scandalous. It's populated by beheaders like Judith and David, a Christ that yells insults at religious authorities in the streets, a divinely appointed prophet who kills an enslaver, a God who tags state property and slays kings, a divinely chosen people revolting against the government, multiple anti-imperial apocalypses, a messiah on death row, a disciple who cuts a cop's ear off, and plenty of other people in God's favor who commit acts that would upset civil sensibilities.

Their appearance in the Bible does not prescribe these actions in the present but establishes their space in the ancient and ongoing drama of God with the world, upsetting any notion that religious responses to injustice need to fit within the confines of respectability discourses manufactured by those in power. When theologian and philosopher David Bentley Hart reflected on his deeper biblical understandings after two-and-a-half years

5. Wispelwey, "NFL Is a Fundamentalist Church."
6. Munch, "Interview with Bryan Massingale."

translating the Christian Testament, he replied, "most of us would find Christians truly cast in the New Testament mold fairly obnoxious: civically reprobate, ideologically unsound, economically destructive, politically irresponsible, socially discreditable, and really just a bit indecent."[7]

Reverend Smash centered this insight in her christological claims after Unite the Right in 2017. "Many folks here continue to critique activists and tell people harmed by a white supremacist terror attack to calm down, be patient, let the courts handle it and be civil," she wrote. Charlottesville at the time became inundated with signs, playing on the town's name, calling for "C-villity" as the antidote for people planning genocide. (Satirical stickers appeared downtown spelling out the tone behind the slogan: "I ♥ C-villity: ca. 1619.") This fit the national mood, Smash noted, as "conservatives, moderates, and liberals alike claim we just need to be nicer to one another" while fascists openly plot in public spaces and immigration courts force unaccompanied three-year-olds to testify on their own behalf in a foreign language.[8] But this, the reverend asserted, is antithetical to the gospels. "Jesus was a threat to civility," she titled her article.[9] He so upset the status quo and threatened the religious and political structures of the day that the state executed him. The insidiousness of that civility Jesus opposed becomes clear, she said, when "There are a lot of white folks in Charlottesville who I believe are more comfortable with quiet white supremacists than with loud anti-racists."[10]

On the night of August 11, 2017, people of faith came together at the Episcopal St. Paul's Memorial Church to celebrate, reject white supremacy, and prepare to oppose Unite the Right the following day. Hundreds of people gathered and filled even the standing room, many of them probably drawn by the chance to hear Cornel West preach. But it was Reverend Traci Blackmon, a United Church of Christ preacher from the St. Louis metro area, who delivered the talk most remembered from that night.

Blackmon, like West, had been active in the Ferguson uprisings of 2014. The first female preacher in the history of her church in Florissant,

7. Hart, "On Christ's Rabble."
8. Jewett and Luthra, "Immigrant Toddlers Ordered to Appear in Court Alone."
9. Caine-Conley, "Jesus Was a Threat to Civility."
10. Beckett, "Charlottesville a Year On."

Missouri, she had been drawn more deeply into social engagement when an officer killed Michael Brown and police left his body on the streets for four hours. Angry neighbors were met by militarized police and tanks. Later asked why she took the side of the protesters in Ferguson, she replied, "We're not antipolice, but in that confrontation, there was an unequal balance of power, and we stand on the side of those who do not have power."[11]

It was her recognition of power, paired with an unwillingness to pretend that a hazy "Christian love" dissolves its reality or importance, that helped set the stage for an electrifying sermon in Charlottesville. Instead of hovering over the concrete world when she invoked the central importance of dreams, she brought it down to the pavement and the present situation. "Prophetic resistance is only possible with those who can still dream," she said. But this dream and this resistance "is only possible with the courage to speak love in the face of hatred."[12] Only here, in view of hatred's face, meaning one is close enough to see it eye to eye, could dreams lead to prophetic resistance.

Blackmon had in mind biblical tales. Joseph, Deborah, and Solomon were all dreamers, she said. Yet again she refused to let things lie in a more remote and unconnected past, linking these dreamers with those of modern history, like civil rights activists Sister Antona Ebo and Rabbi Abraham Joshua Heschel. Blackmon included figures often ignored in religious conversations like Huey Newton of the Black Panthers and Stokely Carmichael, who coined the phrase "Black Power." Those resisting in Ferguson too, she said, were dreamers of a similar kind. "When dreamers rise up, giants fall," she asserted, invoking another dreamer, David, and his foe Goliath.

David and Goliath is not a story for placid times, she said, turning to the text as "preparation for the battleground." (The story had previous relevance in the fight against white supremacy. When Bree Newsome was arrested for scaling the pole in front of the South Carolina statehouse in 2015 and removing the Confederate flag, she read the story of David and Goliath as spiritual preparation.[13]) The way Blackmon interpreted the tale helped shape the theological imagination of the clergy witness in Charlottesville.

> David knew who he was and David knew *whose* he was. David
> says to the Goliath, "You are coming against me with the sword

11. Jenkins, *American Prophets*, 105.

12. Footage of the sermon can be viewed at Editors, "Faith-Led Counterprotest to White Nationalism in Charlottesville."

13. DeConto, "Activist Who Took Down Confederate Flag Drew on Her Faith."

and the spear and the javelin but I come against you in the name
of the Lord almighty God" . . . We don't come this weekend simply
as individuals. We come as the army of God, equipped with the
spiritual weapons of warfare . . .

You see the raising of the confederate monuments and the
shiftiness of our administration is exposing once again this nation's racist roots. And they come with the same weapons that have
been used for generations. But we come in the name of the Lord.
What does it mean to come in the name of the Lord? What are the
weapons of spiritual warfare? Well, where there is hatred, we will
wield love. Where there is violence we will wield peace. Where
there is dehumanization we will reclaim the divine, where there is
vitriol we will plant prayer.

Blackmon's interpretation of the story had daunting implications for
those in the church that night, with the largest gathering of white supremacists in recent US history set to begin the next morning just down the road.
Instead of simply a church or congregation, the assembled were in fact
God's makeshift army. This suggested of course that they were on call for
battle against the ungodly, which here meant the neo-Nazis, KKK, and alt-
right groups who came not with javelins but guns and cars to ram people
with. It reconceptualized what has been reduced to a fight on the streets
between "antifa" and the alt-right, glimpsing instead a biblical struggle in
which God takes a side against oppressors through (importantly) human
hands. To oppose Unite the Right was, in fact, holy, an echo of what David
did against Goliath. To "both-sides" it, to ascribe equal amounts of blame
to each group as the president and local bishop would do, would be to dismiss the God of Scripture's stance for the vulnerable and against those who
threaten them.

Everybody is terrified to talk about violence at all . . .
Everybody has to make that disclaimer. I'm not making that
disclaimer. We're gonna have to fucking kill these people.

—CHRIS "THE CRYING NAZI" CANTWELL,
UNITE THE RIGHT LEADER, IN COURT EVIDENCE[14]

14. As reflected in court documents, as well as Charlottesville journalist Molly Conger's
court coverage, https://twitter.com/socialistdogmom/status/1460333996680921091.

And yet according to Blackmon, this army of God summoned to oppose white supremacists is to counter the sticks, shields, guns, and cars with love and prayer. This love in the face of hatred, this prayer in the face of evil, is deeply unsafe. It involves getting into the messiness of street confrontation and, without policing how others resist fascism, refusing to come armed with physical weapons. It is materially disarming while spiritually stockpiling. Her military imagery underscored the severity of the situation. This was not a time for confusing biblical faith with ease, nonviolence with passivity, church worship as secure. One must, according to Blackmon, face the guns with prayer and love—but actually *face* the guns.

Rather than offer up theological platitudes in a concrete emergency, Blackmon made the story's relevance to the coming terrorism plain:

> Until we close the camp, there will always be another Goliath. David understood that . . . You know the thing I get upset about in church is that when we tell this story as soon as David slings that stone, everybody starts dancing. But that's not the end of the story. The text says that David doesn't just knock him down and kill him, but David takes his head off.
>
> I know that makes some of you uncomfortable . . . But the fact that David takes his head off was a message to the camp, that what Goliath has brought will no longer be tolerated . . . You see, I believe that we've been celebrating victories too soon. I can remember as a little girl—I'm 54 years old now—as a little girl in Birmingham, Alabama, I can still remember standing on the street of the sidewalk and watching the Klan rally go by. I can still remember the flags, the American flags . . . and the hoods passing me by. I can still see it in my mind's eye. And here I am at 54 years old, coming back because the Klan is still rising. The Klan is rising because we never cut the head off! . . . *We must not relent until we cut the head off!*

The reverend's words may sound discordant, even abhorrent, to many ears. What can it actually mean to cut the head off with love and prayer? How could such a violent image be reconciled with the Christian virtues she espouses? Surely the story of David and Goliath can be useful because it's a story of an underdog succeeding, but is the specific detail of the beheading prescriptive in any way for a church?

Reverend Blackmon issued a resounding *yes*. The beheading is more than helpful; it is essential. In a Christian culture that urges forgiveness and service as a response to racism, as *Open Wide Our Hearts* did, her sermon provides an inbreaking of biblical imagination that addresses white supremacy directly. When Goliaths come promising violence against people who are already vulnerable, churches should aggressively help decapitate them. "God is more powerful than every Goliath," Blackmon reminded the congregation, but this only became evident when a person bodily opposed the giant. The time is already overdue, her sermon asserts, for churches to fuse their commitments to love and justice with the kind of bodily hostility to white supremacy as David had for Goliath.

We are penned in! We are surrounded on all sides by hundreds
of Nazis, hundreds of fascists on all sides surrounding us,
surrounding the statue. We have no way out. They are four
deep, five deep all around the statue. And there's more coming.

—EMILY GORCENSKI, MOMENTS BEFORE NAZIS
ASSAULTED HER SMALL GROUP, AUGUST 11, 2017[15]

Reverend Blackmon's message became all too relevant before the church service ended, when those of us inside the church heard the rumbling chants of what we now know to be Nazis yelling "Blood and Soil!" and "Jews will not replace us!" grow louder. Hundreds from the Unite the Right crowd marched with torches in the night across the street, on University of Virginia's campus, straight to the Thomas Jefferson statue where a small group of anti-racist students and community members had gathered, linking arms, singing songs, and chanting "No Nazis, no KKK, no fascist USA!" At their march's end, they completely surrounded the group at the statue, screamed anti-trans and white supremacist vitriol in their faces, and

15. Lengthy footage can be found on Gorcenski's Twitter page at https://twitter.com/ EmilyGorcenski/status/896184638804119552. This quote begins at the 31:58 mark. Gorcenski is a central leader in the fight against fascism in Charlottesville and beyond.

attacked them with mace, fists, and flaming torches. Repeatedly screaming "White lives matter!" many of them raised celebratory Hitler salutes.[16]

The gathering of thirty or so people, small and defenseless against the mob attack, absorbed the violence alone. A few had run across the street to the church where Reverend Blackmon had just preached about David cutting the head off of white supremacy. The feeling inside was empowering, with many hundreds of people singing in preparation to battle today's Goliaths. Bonnie Gordon, a professor of music who was in the pews, wrote of that moment, "when cell phones exploded with news of the alt-right torch parade, [Reverend Sekou] led the entire congregation singing and stomping 'This Little Light of Mine.' It made the building shake. 'We have some company,' he called to us, as we were singing. 'Let's show them love conquers hate.'"[17]

We sang as loudly as we could, with feet and hands and voices. "In that moment, the song became a weapon and training," Gordon said, "it fueled the courage that would become our armor in the hard phase ahead." But we didn't know that right then desperate people were on our very church steps, pleading with our security to get these people across the street to help protect the small group from the marching Nazis. They were told no, and had to go back and face it all alone.

In a video taken by Emily Gorcenski, a leading community member, just seconds before the fascists began throwing punches and swinging flames into the faces of her small group at the Thomas Jefferson statue, one of the men screaming and cursing at her yelled, "Where are your friends at?!?"

As a trans woman, she was targeted for special abuse. They shouted horrible things at her that night, faces full of sweat, and have continued harassing and trying to intimidate her ever since. Like everyone, the belligerent Nazi closing in on her could see that what was about to happen was made possible because there were so few who had banded together against Unite the Right in that moment.

---

16. Reporting and video footage from another angle can be found in Lind, "Nazi Slogans and Violence at a Right-Wing March." The video's framing, not written by Lind, includes the kind of unhelpful phraseology that equates the attackers and the attacked, such as "massive brawl breaks out" while the video clearly shows one side entrapping the other and initiating violence.

17. Gordon, "On Listening," 155.

And where were her friends? So many citizens had, in the name of keeping the peace and acting civilly, left them on their own. Too many faith communities hadn't cultivated the spiritual will to stand by them. And even when all the religious people who were committed to fighting white supremacists were concentrated just across the street, hearing about cutting the head off of the Klan and turning their songs to weapons, they didn't come to the aid of this group that was already putting into action what the faithful were preparing for. Where were their friends?

I reflect on what Gorcenski must have thought of that church, part of a religion that has taken the lead in creating a deadly culture for trans people. I think of the pain and rage in my friend's voice when they later described their experience on those church steps, begging the men at the door to summon those of us inside to stand with them. What can church possibly mean to someone after it turns them away to face an inflamed, fascist brutality in the night while singing in the comfort of its walls?

That scene is a microcosm of much in Christian culture. To the extent that Christians lean towards civil disapproval of Nazism rather than joining and embracing those already struggling against genocidal fascists, they outsource the inevitable violence to others. That is, quite literally, anti-Christ behavior, antithetical to the messiah who took violence upon himself. "Go and do likewise," Matthew's Jesus says, but too many churches seem to hear "Stay put and do what Caesars tell you."

When I look back on Reverend Blackmon's sermon, an image comes to mind, made by anti-fascist artist N. O. Bonzo. A young femme, among the foliage, as if growing amid the vines and flowers, holds a dagger upright with a strong forearm. Roses bless the hilt of the blade while growth curls up to its tip as if in embrace. The other hand, covering what the viewer assumes would otherwise be a bare breast, holds the hair of a male head, severed from its body. His close-cut hair and mustache suggest a military man, and on his collar appear a swastika and SS logo.

FIGURE 7

Against the Fascist Creep, N. O. Bonzo

The head seems about to be placed in a metallic bowl atop a Roman-esque pillar, both of which seem out of place in the flora. If its dead eyes could open, it would see three arrows in front of his nose, an anti-fascist symbol. Nearby rests another bowl with three skulls in it, all bearing differ-ent Nazi logos. Curled around the skulls is a large snake, whose face looks at the assumed beheader with what might be approval, even collaboration. The wielder of the dagger's eyes are nearly closed, the face calm, assured.

Is this in line with what Reverend Blackmon meant with the David and Goliath analogy? What else would cutting off the head of white supremacy be than decapitating Nazism? What may strike some as acceptable, proper, prescriptive in the words of the reverend may push the same people away when seen in graphic form. If there is something Christian, biblical about Reverend Blackmon's sermon, is there something Christian, biblical too in this piece of art?

A second glance suggests so. Something of Eden comes through in the garden-like setting, the otherwise naked femme covered by greenery, and the presence of a serpent. A halo arcs over the young victor's head, indicating something sanctified among the growth. Intended by the creator or not, this piece drips of the Genesis garden story.

What then can we make of it? Is the fulfillment of Reverend Blackmon's preaching a way back into the garden, a kind of communal second innocence without myths of a master race, genocide, imperial Roman structures? Or is it a sign that what our society's childlike ignorance clings to, a pseudo-Eden, is finally crumbling? Was it that the snake was right all along, that we should insist that we *do* know good and evil, that we can judge white supremacy, Nazism, and their adherents as conduits of evil?

The snake approves, what may be the enlightened Eve is no longer naked—is in fact clothed with the vegetation of creation as well as the fruits of anti-fascist resistance—and the halo blesses it all as holy, inspired, even Godly. This is the knowledge of the gods, and Eve is no longer the scapegoat but the hero, the symbolic escapee from the death of faux-innocence in the midst of horror. Eve is the one comfortable enough in the knowledge of good and evil to act on the threat to vulnerable people. Turning to the background we see what may be storm clouds, perhaps indicating the coming fascist creep. But they also might be clouds of smoke, the aftermath of whatever battle led to this scene. In either case, there is no going back to the initial Eden.

Like David with the head of Goliath in his hands, like Judith with the head of Holofernes in her hands, we must ask if this Eve for fascist times does not reveal something of how the Bible looks when things get specific, when we refuse the abstractions of the first innocence and turn to the discomfort of biblical beheadings as the vines do the dagger and the one who wields it.

Not pictured, of course, are the skulls of so many Jews, so many Romani and Sinti, so many queer folk collected by this Nazi and his fellow murderers, nor the heads of those who will get to live because this one has been gathered in first. All of this, the seen and unseen, demand of the beholder, demand of disciples, to wrestle with what it will take to assure this depiction remains an allegory. Those who demand civility in their opposition to fascism must grapple with what happens when it actually becomes a matter of whose bones are taken first. The longer Christians stay in the Eden of courteous disagreement while the Proud Boys and Nazis organize, the more we bear responsibility for the ensuing bloodshed. If Christians don't heed Reverend Blackmon's wisdom, others will reap the whirlwind when Nazis force the symbolic into the fleshly. Which kind of weapons get used, spiritual or steel, remains unknown only to those not already collected by the SS and its progeny.

The most common calls for civility in the fascist creep around the nation have been statements of unqualified faith in the first amendment. *We must let Nazis speak*, the argument goes, *because we believe in freedom of speech*. This view holds that hindering their ability to recruit at universities and invite others to join their genocidal plans breaches civil conduct. Unsavory as it might be, it says, society must allow people who worship Hitler to discuss the best way of killing all Jews, annihilating LGBTQ folks, and hastening "the day of the rope" when white people will murder Black people and immigrants—all because of the first amendment.[18] The ACLU even filed a motion on behalf of Unite the Right's organizer with this rationale when Charlottesville tried to move the "rally" just one mile away from the Lee statue. "Plaintiff's views are highly controversial," they say in the memorandum, minimizing the goal of white mastery to a mere controversy, but "this case is about viewpoint discrimination" because the city "denied him a permit to exercise his freedom of speech."[19]

The argument is morally horrific and politically obtuse. It prioritizes an intangible privilege of overt fascists over the flesh and blood of people vulnerable to their violence, a violence that becomes all the more likely because of the space afforded by these supposed free speech maximalists. Denying genocidalists the ability to organize is of course discrimination, of an ethical and intelligent kind. Had Germans exercised this kind of discrimination before 1933, six million Jews might not have been killed in camps and ghettoes. Yet time and again when people try to stop those like the Unite the Right rioters, major news outlets publish sensational screeds about "the thuggish mobs of the left killing free speech," as *The Chicago*

18. For a brief analysis of "The Day of the Rope" in *The Turner Diaries*, an inspirational book for white supremacists that has become distressingly mainstreamed lately, see Pineda, "Kathleen Bellew on the Turner Diaries and the Capitol Riots."

19. Sincere, on behalf of the ACLU, "Memorandum in Support of Motion."

Tribune did in 2017, or how anti-fascism really means "anti-First Amendment" as *Fox News* did in 2019.[20]

This accompanies the common refrain that anti-fascists simply want to strip rights from people they "don't agree with." The accusation, lazy as it is absurd, neglects all the many public speech acts that anti-fascists disagree with yet don't interrupt. It asserts that anti-fascism is rooted in an infantile desire that everyone must agree with their political views or be silenced, rather than a principled option for the right of vulnerable people to live free of fascist threats, a serious embrace of the phrase "Never Again" that arose out of the Holocaust. DC-based policy thinktank American Enterprise Institute, for example, wrote less than a month after Unite the Right that "Antifa is a domestic terrorist movement . . . which uses unlawful violence to intimidate those who disagree with their totalitarian worldview."[21]

As Mark Bray writes in his exploration of anti-fascism, freedom of speech in the US has always been qualified.[22] Speech is restricted according to location (no political sloganeering in certain condominiums or holding signs on the Pentagon's steps), content (no threatening to kill the president or yell fire in a crowded theater), and government interest (no whistleblowing when classified information is in the public interest), among other reasons. So the matter is not whether anti-fascists believe in diluting an absolutist interpretation of free speech rights, as the US government has long done that already. The issue is whether it is moral to protect speech that is used to organize murder or oppression based on white supremacist, homophobic, misogynistic, nationalist, or Christo-fascist logics.

Anti-fascists insist that risking the life of one person by allowing fascists to enlist others in a group organized for violence is obviously unacceptable. Further, despite the insistence of progressives like Elizabeth Warren shortly after Unite the Right that evil speech deserves a platform,[23] to even debate this topic in "the marketplace of ideas" is egregious. Dr. Mimi Arbeit, who co-founded Charlottesville Anti-Racist Media Liaisons, points out the category mistake most succinctly: "We're not debating. We're

20. Kass, "Lies We Were Told," and Zhao, "Kellyanne Conway Falsely Claims."

21. Thiessen, "Antifa are Domestic Terrorists."

22. For Brays' treatment of anti-fascism and free speech issues, see *Antifa*, 143–65.

23. Warren insinuates that trying to shut down fascist speech is cowardice, rooted in a fear that they might be smarter than those who oppose them. Jilani, "Elizabeth Warren Says Campus Free Speech Means No Censorship."

fighting against a genocidal agenda."[24] Advancing liberal Enlightenment principles that, when pushed to their logical conclusion, would allow public discussions about whether the rest of the Jews should be gassed or let Richard Spencer float his ideas on ethnic cleansing in front of the media is morally monstrous. And philosopher Jason Stanley writes that it's tactically unintelligent as well, arguing that "attempting to counter such rhetoric with reason is akin to using a pamphlet against a pistol."[25] Yet that has been the dominant move of media heads, city officials, and university boards these last years of fascist acceleration.

Anti-fascists also get accused of being the *real* fascists because they want to shut down the speech of others. "There is no distinction between these protesters and the fascists they claim to be resisting," claimed law professor Jonathan Turley in one of seemingly innumerable examples of this argument.[26] (Recall that even in the clergy group assembled on the morning of Unite the Right in Charlottesville, a nominally radical reverend lobbed this criticism at Reverends Smash and Wispelwey for planning to stop fascists from assembling.) But as Bray says, "If your main objection to Nazism is its suppression of the meetings of the opposition, then that says more about your politics than about those you are critiquing. Anti-fascists don't oppose fascism because it is illiberal in the abstract, but because it promotes white supremacy, hetero-patriarchy, ultra-nationalism, authoritarianism, and genocide."[27] And the notion of civility, of being courteous to others' unfettered free speech, acts as a bulwark for the movements based on these ideologies by protecting them from those that would disrupt their planning.

Charlottesville community leader and professor of religious studies Jalane Schmidt explained why some people acted in ways that authorities saw as rude and ill-mannered when they noticed Proud Boys and white supremacists organizing for Unite the Right in public. Her stance, combining experience on the ground with white supremacist terrorism and rigorous academic scholarship, redirects the "debate" about anti-fascism's anti-civility to the heart of the issue and its historical stakes:

24. Branigin, "Year after Unite the Right." For more from Arbeit and others on the history behind Charlottesville Anti-Racist Media Liaisons, its rationale, and how it fits into civility discourses, see Campbell, "Charlottesville Isn't Playing the Media's 'Both Sides' Game Anymore."

25. Stanley, *How Fascism Works*, 69.

26. Turley, "Hypocrisy of Antifa."

27. Bray, *Antifa*, 162.

The logic behind that is this: I did a lot of digging, I did a lot of research and writing about the history of the Klan locally here in the 1920s here in Charlottesville and at UVA. And in all my research . . . I couldn't find any instance of any white people who objected to these Klansmen. That, combined with the post-World War II mantra of "never again" and the importance of nipping fascism in the bud—do not give them a platform, so they can't even gain traction to organize—that was the point of showing up. Every time they show up in the park or on the downtown mall, we're going to be there. Why? Because we will not allow them to gather in our public spaces unopposed as if this is okay. They will not have a flattering sightline between them and an iconic statue. There will always be an expression of dissent somewhere there, so they can't do this. Because "never again."[28]

28. Hemmer, "Episode 1: The Summer of Hate."

5

Of Nazi-Slaying, Nonviolence, and the Mad Messiah

*The ghetto was a closed-off society—no radios allowed—but
Renia sleuthed for information. Hundreds of women were
taken to unknown locations, never to be heard from again.
A candid soldier revealed to her that these women were sent
to the front to serve as prostitutes. They contracted sexually
transmitted diseases and were burnt alive or shot to death. She
listened raptly as he told her that one time, he saw hundreds
of young women revolt. They attacked the Nazis, stealing their
bayonets, wounding them, gouging out their eyes, and then
killing themselves, screaming that they would never be made
into prostitutes. The girls who remained alive were eventually
subdued and raped.*

What was a fifteen-year-old to do?[1]

TWO MISTAKES OFTEN MIS-FRAME issues surrounding the rise of fascism
today. First, conversations about violence and fascism typically begin with
Richard Spencer, one-time leader of the alt-right referred to as "my liege" in
the movement, getting punched in the face during an interview while wearing his fashionable suit the media liked to talk about.[2] Rather than discuss

1. Batalion, *Light of Days*, 64.

2. For the organizer of Unite the Right calling Spencer "my liege" and planning
explicit violence, see Unicorn Riot, "Charlottesville Lawsuit Defendants Implicated in
Premeditated Violence."

the ethnic cleansing he openly organized for, a flood of articles appeared asking if we really want a society in which Nazis get punched. On the other hand, Alain Brossat and Sylvia Klingberg note in their oral history of Jewish radicalism that the story of the Jews in the Holocaust usually gets reduced to "their figures, bent, humiliated and starving, and the piles of their dead bodies."[3] Our collective understanding of Jews under Nazi rule then becomes pure victim, passive and acted-upon. Dora Horn captured this in the title of her book, *People Love Dead Jews.*

Let us avoid both pitfalls and begin our conversation with young Jewish women killing Nazis during the Holocaust. Consider Niuta Teitelbaum, known as "Little Wanda with the braids" by the Gestapo, walking into a Warsaw apartment in 1943 with three Nazis inside. "She blushed, smiled meekly and then pulled out a gun and shot each one." Two died and one survived, so she donned a physician's coat, found his hospital room, and killed the recovering Nazi and the policeman guarding him.[4] Vladka Meed ran dynamite into the Warsaw Ghetto bit by bit. Hela Schupper bombed a Christmas gathering at a Nazi café, killing seven. Vitka Kemper started a Jewish revenge group after the war, managing to poison two thousand SS soldiers by putting arsenic in their bread.

Judy Batalion's *Light of Days* tells the story of these and many other women, among the thirty thousand European Jews who joined partisans in more than ninety European ghettos with armed Jewish resistance groups. They kept Jews alive by smuggling food and keeping them warm, but also by killing those who were trying to annihilate them. They did this by donning Catholic-looking disguises that enabled them to traffic grenades and ammunition across ghetto walls, seducing Nazis only to stab them when they dropped their guards, hiding weapons in teddy bears or their underwear, bombing German trains, and any other means they could conjure.

To paraphrase the media's question after a concerned citizen punched Richard Spencer, do we really want a society that accepts young Jewish women attacking Nazis?

3. Brossat and Klingberg, *Revolutionary Yiddishland,* 142.
4. Batalion, "Nazi-Fighting Women of the Jewish Resistance."

Fanciful thought experiment on violence #1:

The year is 1941. You find yourself in Vilna, capital of Lithuania. Nazis have occupied the city for six months, during which time Jews were stripped of employment, stuffed in inhumane ghettoes, suffered under anti-Jewish legal codes, and tortured any time a Nazi soldier felt so inclined. You are one of many people gathered in a "damp, candlelit room," pretending to have a New Year's party but in fact receiving vital information to all those present. A young man named Abba Kovner, who summoned the crowd of 150 youths, makes an announcement in Yiddish that you cannot understand. He asks Tosia Altman, a twenty-three-year-old Polish leader of the Jewish youth resistance group called the Young Guard, to translate into Hebrew. Now the message meets your ears.

A local girl was shipped to a popular vacation site nearby and shot, you learn. Surprised to awaken some amount of time later, she found herself in a frozen ditch of corpses, "staring into the eyes of her dead mother." Waiting for dark, she climbed out and hid in the forest for two days until she could escape. She arrived near the building you are in, naked, wounded, and having fits. Local political representation for Jews did not believe her story, but Abba Kovner did, and is now relaying the critical message that the Nazis are filling mass graves with Jewish bodies. Everyone in this room could be next. (In fact, sevety-five thousand Jews would be stripped naked and killed at the site she had escaped from in the coming years.) Hitler's threats are not "the hollow phrases of an arrogant madman" that many had assumed them to be. They are real and they are being put into practice with the force of a military behind them. "The only answer: self-defense," Abba said. All Jews everywhere must be prepared with this knowledge, ready to take up arms and fight.

Tosia, a woman of plans, never sat in one place for long. Now she needed to travel to ghettos to deliver not comforting words of the movement but this horrific, urgent message. The Nazis planned to Kill all Jews. All.

It was time to resist.[5]

5. Batalion, *Light of Days*, 80–81.

Along with everyone else in the room, you are shocked and aghast. But you are also well-versed in theories of nonviolence, and find the plan of armed resistance understandable yet misguided. Seeing that Tosia is already walking out the snowy door to spread the news of the mass execution and encouraging Jews in other towns to resist by using violence, you track her down in the dark of night and convey how terribly you feel for her and her people. That being done, you get to your point:

"I respect and honor the situation you're in, and I'm in complete solidarity with you," you say. "But these plans to kill Nazis simply aren't right. Despite everything, they're humans and their lives matter. Many of them have children who depend on them. You wouldn't rob those children of their parents, would you? It seems to me there's much more decency in responding nonviolently. In fact, the integrity of your people and your cause hinges on whether you adopt this approach or not."

"Do you have any food," she asks, "that I can pass to those being starved by the Germans?"

"Not at the moment," you reply, slightly ashamed, "but I can get some in the morning."

"Good. Any and all aid will literally help save lives. We are being slaughtered—and also hunted, so please keep your voice down and stay low."

"Right. Back to nonviolence. It's a way of life expressed most fully in our times by Mohandas Gandhi. In response to oppression, persecution, or any kind of violence, he turns to *satyagraha*, meaning 'to be grasped by Truth.' He calls it 'Truth force' or 'soul force,' and it demands of the satyagrahi total devotion to living in that Truth, which refuses to cause harm. He calls that absence of creating suffering *ahimsa*. Responding to violence with more violence only furthers the cycle, ensuring that violence will keep rippling out into the future. So, he says that a people working with *ahimsa* will take that violence upon themselves willingly to appeal to the humanity in those inflicting it. This creates the conditions to *redeem* that person, in this case the Nazi soldier, which plucks out the root cause of violence rather than simply staving off one form of it for the moment."

"This sounds noble," Tosia says in hushed tones, breathing hard in the frigid winter wind. "I hope Gandhi comes to lead this nonviolent movement against the Nazis while we do what we must to avoid landing up in a mass grave."

"Well, he's busy resisting the British Empire himself, fighting for Indian liberation with nothing but nonviolent means," you explain. "It looks like it will actually work, and somewhat soon."

"I am glad for him and his people," she responds genuinely. "Since he is busy with important work, why don't you and your friends who believe in nonviolence come and embody it here on our behalf?"

You ponder for a moment, listening to the two of your footsteps rhythmically crunch in the hardened snow.

"I don't think many of my people will leave their homes to do that," you say bluntly. "Certainly not enough to stop the Nazi war machine. But there are plenty of Jews here! Imagine if a hundred thousand Jews decided to fight the Nazis by fasting or refusing to work or showing subversive love that may so disorient the Germans that they could see your dignity. Certainly, you could slow and even help dismantle the machinery of killing with only the force of Truth. Gandhi says this is all possible. You can even redeem your supposed enemy in the process, saving their lives as well as yours."

Half-amused, half-impatient, Tosia observes, "I don't think this man Gandhi understands that the circumstances we are in are very different from the ones he is in, hard as it must be there too. All this would never work here, and he doesn't grasp the Jewish situation so far from India."

"Ah," you say, ready with your copy of Gandhi's *Non-violent Resistance*, "but he has already written his advice directly to Jews in Europe. Despite the differences in circumstance, violence everywhere can be resisted by nonviolence. He says that if he were Jewish, he would simply refuse to be removed from his country or submit to degradation." You flip to the correct page and read, "'And suffering voluntarily undergone will bring [Jews] an inner strength and joy' even greater than hearing that Britain or France had defeated the Nazis. Dying nonviolently is simply better than surviving violently, in this view," you plead. "Even if Hitler massacres you all, Gandhi says, it 'could be turned into a day of thanksgiving and joy that [God] had wrought deliverance of the race even at the hands of the tyrant. For to the God-fearing, death has no terror.'"[6]

Tosia, leaning forward into the crisp gale and picking up her pace, responds, "Are you saying that the little girl who was in terror waking up next

---

6. Gandhi, *Non-Violent Resistance*, 349.

to her murdered mother in a huge tomb of Jews is insufficiently faithful to God because she doesn't want to die? That's extremely—"

"That's not my aim at all," you cut in truthfully, though you realize you might have implied it. "I'm just saying . . . look, at the heart of all this is courage. It takes extra bravery not to pick up weapons in your struggle. See this page? It asks, 'Wherein is courage required—in blowing others to pieces from behind a cannon, or with a smiling face to approach a cannon and be blown to pieces?'"[7]

Tosia frowned in the dark. "So Gandhi didn't say that courage is in telling someone *else* to march towards a cannon to be blasted apart?"

"Hey," you say defensively, "if my people were under threat—"

"Listen," she interrupts, "the Nazis have been torturing people here for six months. We have reason to believe Hitler wants to exterminate us all. This nonviolence you are talking about is simply an unacceptable thing for you to expect us to perform. If you think it's so important, *you* do it. The fact that you aren't putting your body between us and the Nazis' bullets means you don't actually have faith in your 'Truth-force,' it seems to me. Hearing all this from Gandhi is one thing, but hearing it from someone like you, someone not physically committed to risking your life according to this philosophy, is angering. Do you understand that the more you sit at home wishing we behaved better instead of embodying what you claim is so important, the more you make it likely we are killed because you have failed to act? Is that nonviolent of *you*?"

The silence that falls as you consider how to better explain breaks when she mutters in hushed but clear tones, "I have no relationship with you except for you telling me how I can and cannot behave as I try not to get murdered and save my people from genocide. What kind of human relationship is this? Is this your embodiment of Truth? Is bossing us around your 'soul-force?'"

Grasping to regain your momentum, you try again: "I see what you're saying, but even if all your plans succeed and you kill all the Nazis, saving the millions of Jews in Europe from annihilation, what then? You have saved yourselves through physical force. That's no peace. Your ends and means must cohere, according to Gandhi. You can't sow violence and expect to reap joy or harmony or utopia, just as you can't plant a weed and expect it to grow into a rose. The means you use will inevitably produce the end you receive. Though it seems dire now, to die in a refusal to do harm

7. Gandhi, *Non-Violent Resistance*, 52.

even to your oppressor will be far better for you all and for the humans who survive your ordeal than if you were to save even one life by harming one hair on the head of a German soldier. Weeds can only become weeds, and violence can only beget violence. Unfair as it seems, you must break the cycle."

Tosia, eyeing you in the dark and trying not to cough in the cold, says, "I'm sorry, but my fingers are going numb and the next town is still far off. Can I borrow one of the coats you're wearing?"

"Yes, of course!" you say with feelings of charity, taking off your warmest coat and handing it to her. "I'm heading back to my home, but you keep it. Give it to someone in most need when you arrive. And please, consider what I said about nonviolence. The root of it all is God, as the *sat* of *satyagraha* means 'being,' and nothing has being apart from God, which Gandhi says is the form Truth takes.[8] If you would cling to God, then, it's better to walk toward a tank with a willingness to let it blow your face off than to do harm to those inside it. Your faith in your God is at stake. My thoughts and prayers are with you all. Good bye!"

You part ways, unsure if you heard Tosia respond.

Now, do you know or do you not know, Mahatma, what a concentration camp is like and what goes on there? Do you know of the torments in the concentration camp, of its methods of slow and quick slaughter? . . .

In the five years which I myself spent under the present regime, I observed many instances of genuine satyagraha among the Jews, instances showing a strength of spirit wherein there was no question of bartering their rights or of being bowed down, and where neither force nor cunning was used to escape the consequences of their behavior. Such actions, however, apparently exerted not the slightest influence on their opponents. All honour indeed to those who displayed such strength of soul! But I cannot recognize herein a watchword for the general behaviour of German Jews that might seem suited to exert an influence on the oppressed or on the world.

8. Gandhi, *Non-Violent Resistance*, 3.

An effective stand in the form of non-violence may be taken against unfeeling human beings in the hope of gradually bringing them to their senses; but a diabolic universal steamroller cannot thus be withstood. There is a certain situation in which no "satyagraha" of the power of the truth can result from the "satyagraha" of the strength of the spirit. The word satyagraha signifies testimony. Testimony without acknowledgment, ineffective, unobserved martyrdom, a martyrdom cast to the winds—that is the fate of innumerable Jews in Germany. God alone accepts their testimony. God "seals" it, as is said in our prayers. But no maxim for suitable behaviour can be deduced from that. Such martyrdom is a deed—but who would venture to demand it?

—MARTIN BUBER, "LETTER TO GANDHI," 1939[9]

If there is an obvious incompatibility between a historian of nonviolence's claim that "practitioners of nonviolence are always seen as a threat, a direct menace, to the state," and an anarchist writer's claim that "nonviolence protects the state," it's because of the way the word gets misunderstood in mainstream discourses.[10] Much of this has to do with Christianity. Though the modern notion of nonviolence comes from Gandhi, the civil rights movement in the US studied and applied his philosophy and thereby imbued it with Christian overtones and content. (The word *agape*, for example, a word in biblical Greek for love, usually stands in for *satyagraha* in Dr. King's speeches.) Gandhi's understanding was itself partly anchored in Christianity, due to his strong appreciation for Jesus and the way Matthew's gospel depicts his Sermon on the Mount. Other movements like the United Farm Workers and the Catholic Worker added weight to the assumption that faithful Christianity implied nonviolence, not merely as a strategic tactic but as a mode of being.

The presumed divide between radical activists and Christianity strengthens this misunderstanding of what nonviolence is. Christianity

9. Buber, *Pointing the Way*, 140.

10. Kurlansky, *Non-Violence*, 23; and Peter Gelderloos, *How Nonviolence Protects the State*.

gets too easily associated with nonviolence, and revolutionary politics get too easily painted as (secular) "violence." I only aim here to complicate the first notion in highly unsystematic form, leaving readers to connect the dots about the second. In doing so I hope to extend the above thought experiment. The advanced stages of Nazi fascism should always be in the forefront of contemporary conversations about violence and nonviolence in the fascist creep. The issue is not Richard Spencer needing a Band-Aid. The stakes are genocide. And since Christianity influences the conversation about how to respond to this threat, and Jesus is its central figure that gets marshalled forth as its basis for nonviolence, I want to trouble the notion that Jesus fits that description without complication, or suggest that if he is the exemplar of nonviolence then it is of a different kind than often assumed.

In 1970 when the Young Lords, a Puerto Rican liberationist group that made up part of the Rainbow Coalition with the Black Panthers and Young Patriots, occupied a church in Spanish Harlem that was refusing to serve the people in the neighborhood, they defended themselves in part by drawing on the gospel stories of Jesus driving money lenders out of the temple. New York State Chairman Felipe Luciano gave a speech to the church's congregants—or at least the ones who were willing to remain present when he interrupted a church service to speak—saying that they had refused to open space to run a food program and teach Puerto Ricans about their land's history. He acknowledged that some people were frustrated by their requests, but then turned to Jesus dealing with hypocrites, saying, "Man, he didn't have as much patience as the Young Lords are having. He actually went into a church and beat them! And you talk about us being violent! He told them, get out of here you moneylenders, you are filth! All you are thinking of is filthy lucre, you are not thinking about the spirit of the Law."[11]

The group was not an overtly religious body. (Though they did claim that "If Christ were alive today, he'd be a Young Lord."[12]) But while their exegesis may sound jarring to those who hear much about Jesus' nonviolence, it's hard to argue with their biblical evidence. They drew on the Gospel of John, who writes of Jesus seeing people selling sacrificial doves and money

11. Luciano, in Enck-Wanzer, *Young Lords*, 209.
12. Enck-Wanzer, *Young Lords*, 207.

changers at the Jerusalem temple. "Making a whip of cords, he drove all of them out of the temple, with the sheep and the cattle. He also poured out the coins of the money changers and overturned their tables" (2:15).

The story appealed to them not just because they were in a church, but also because they knew that the stories of Jesus had been weaponized, from the Christianization of the Indigenous and enslaved to the present. "The Bible is used as an instrument of oppression in the hands of the imperialists," said Pablo Yoruba Guzman, the Young Lord's Minister of Information. "They teach only the parts of the Bible that will mollify the people, keep them down, you know, turn the other cheek, be cool, be humble, slow up, wait. They don't show you the parts like when things were going bad in the temple, Christ went in and threw them out and he wasn't nonviolent—he was a pretty violent cat when he had to be."[13]

This biblical exegesis from below is bolstered by how more academic scholars have approached the temple scene, which appears in distinct but overlapping ways in all four gospel accounts. John Donahue and Daniel Harrington argue that Jesus' entrance into Jerusalem and his actions in the temple "go a long way toward explaining why the Jewish and Roman leaders acted so quickly to arrest and execute Jesus" and that one of the most common interpretations of the text is that it's a "political-revolutionary action."[14] Brendan Byrne observes that driving people out comes through as an exorcism in the original Greek, suggesting something even demonic about his enemies.[15] But it's theologian and activist Ched Myers' examination of the temple scene in Mark's gospel that accentuates both Jesus' unruliness and political precision in his actions most clearly.

Mark's account does not show Jesus using a whip as John's does. In this gospel Jesus drives away those buying and selling in the temple, overturns the tables of those exchanging money and selling doves, forbids anyone to carry anything through the temple, and then teaches those who remain, saying "Is it not written, 'My house shall be called a house of prayer for all the nations'? But you have made it a den of robbers" (11:15–17). Historians agree that Jesus would not have been surprised that people were making purchases in the temple, which was the economic center of Jerusalem.

13. "Interview with Yoruba, Minister of Information, Young Lords Organization, Regarding Confrontation at the First Spanish Methodist Church in El Barrio (Spanish Harlem)" in Enck-Wanzer, *The Young Lords*, 203–7; quotation from 206.

14. Donahue and Harrington, *Gospel of Mark*, 331–32.

15. Byrne, *Costly Freedom*, 178–79.

People from barbers to trench diggers sold their trade there, suggesting Jesus was angered by something more specific than buying and selling.

He targeted the property of the money changers and the dove sellers for a reason. Money changers exchanged Roman coins with Caesar's face on them into acceptable temple currency. Pilgrims were expected to make a yearly trek and pay their dues, including a fee for new coins. These money changers were, according to Myers, "streetlevel representatives of banking interests of considerable power . . . suitable symbols of the oppressive financial institutions [Jesus] so fiercely opposed."[16] Doves were used to purify women and lepers, both of whom were seen as ritualistically unclean. Those selling doves, then, were profiting off a system that exploited already-marginalized groups to "cleanse" themselves as part of their expected religious observation. These two kinds of tables, then, "represented the concrete mechanisms of oppression within a political economy that doubly exploited the poor and unclean. Not only were they considered second-class citizens, but the cult obligated them to make reparation, through sacrifices, for their inferior status—from which marketers profited."[17]

Jesus violates contemporary understandings of nonviolence by overturning the tables they used for selling their exploitative goods, not just physically disrupting their business (how uncivil!) but also attacking their property. The Greek word for "overturning" the tables is *katestrepsen*, which means to "destroy," indicating that the direct meaning of the biblical account is that Jesus is guilty of property destruction. He then imposes what Myers calls a "guerilla ban" on business, forbidding anyone to carry goods through the temple. Police today would have probably arrested Jesus for either of these crimes and depicted him as a lawless threat on the news, but Myers emphasizes that this wasn't aimless aggression. "It is the *ruling-class interests* in control of the commercial enterprises in the temple market that Jesus is attacking," he summarizes.

When trying to understand what Jesus rebelled against, Myers is right to say that "The point is not to try to speculate on *how* Jesus might have actually accomplished this so much as to understand the *legitimation* such a narrative lends to the practice of direct action." But when the conversation

16. Myers, *Binding the Strong Man*, 300–301.

17. This and the following quotes come from Myers, *Binding the Strong Man*, 301.

comes to tactics, as it so often does when people resist fascists, then it very much matters how Jesus carried out his action. And in this, artists can be as helpful as biblical commentators. Renaissance painters like El Greco and Caravaggio were drawn to John's account, in which Jesus fashions a whip out of cords to carry out his task. Later artists like Rembrandt, Luca Giordano, and many others followed suit. There is no way to view these paintings as presenting a nonviolent Jesus. Bernardo Mei's seventeenth-century "Cleansing of the Temple," for example, shows a temple room in chaos. On one side of Jesus is a weeping child, looking up at him in pronounced fear. On the other, an elderly woman with doves seems to cower under his violence, perhaps hoping not to catch a whip in her aged face, only inches away from where Jesus' clenched fist is about to come down. These are visual stories about a Christ attacking people with a makeshift weapon, difficult to square with a nonviolent witness.

It might seem surprising, then, that Ade Bethune, the great Catholic Worker artist, also decided to depict this scene using John's account. A close friend and associate of Dorothy Day, Bethune was so central to the movement that it turned to her for its paper's masthead. Her biography notes that "not only Ade's professional life, but her personal life as well, remain rooted in the Catholic Worker teaching of Dorothy Day and Peter Maurin."[18] Those teachings include nonviolent resistance to war and injustice as well as the works of mercy from Matthew 25, illustrated most recognizably by Bethune herself in a series of images she created for the paper. Her choice to depict Jesus driving away money changers and dove sellers in the same tradition as Renaissance painters before her, in a way that seems on the surface to contrast strongly with her movement's commitments, presents a useful resource for thinking through this issue.

"My House is a House of Prayer"[19] embodies these tensions between the Catholic Worker's nonviolent tradition and the violence of John's story. Jesus appears on the right-hand side of the image, charging, it would seem,

18. Stoughton, *Proud Donkey of Schaerbeek*, x.

19. Extra thanks to Amy Shaw for tracking down an especially inconvenient image and relaying its story. No evidence exists that any originals remain. Disappointed with the quality of illustrations in missals in the 1940s, Bethune decided to contribute some of her own, but the Catholic publisher she gave them to, Benzinger, never published the missals. When she tried to buy them back she found they had all been lost or destroyed. The only evidence this particular work exists is a small proof image with paste marks marring the middle and a small inclusion in the 1988 collection of Bethune's work, Stoughton's *Proud Donkey of Schaerbeek*, 115.

toward the left. His right leg is forward and his left behind him to capture motion, his heel upturned and the hem of his garment following behind his moving body. In his right fist raised above his head is the whip made of cords, also trailing behind him. This messiah is running in pursuit, chasing.

FIGURE 8

My House Is a House of Prayer, Ade Bethune. Image courtesy of Archives and Special Collections, St. Catherine University, St. Paul, Minnesota.

On the left of Jesus are two men fleeing him. They look like they might be on Wall Street rather than in the Jerusalem temple, dressed in business clothes of the 1940s. Bald and in collared suit jackets, Bethune has transplanted twentieth-century capitalists into the role of the ancient money lenders. One has lost control of his briefcase, which seems to have opened in the chaos of trying to escape Jesus. He struggles with his right hand to stem the flow of what appears to be cash pouring out, his ill-gotten gains. Above their heads are the first words of a phrase that stretches across the background archways to the right of the scene, on the other side of Jesus. "MY HOUSE IS A HOUSE OF PRAYER," it reads, and continues on the wall visible between their bodies and Jesus', "YOU HAVE MADE IT A DEN OF THIEVES."

As with Daniel 5, we might ask who put that writing on the wall. But more relevant to the issue of nonviolence, I am drawn to the eyes of those present. The businessmen look terrified. Their mouths are agape, their eyebrows, a simple white line of Bethune's, full of fright. And no wonder, as the eyes of the man about to strike them with a whip show unmistakable ire.

The entire depiction of Jesus, as one running after people with anger in his face and a weapon in his hand caught by the artist just before the attacking weapon makes contact, exudes violence.

Rather than obliterating the idea of a nonviolent Jesus, this passage and its visual depictions nestle themselves uneasily alongside the rest of the tradition. Making too much of the episode can lead toward hasty interpretations, like St. Bernard of Clairvaux encouraging the Knights Templar during the crusades to fight like Jesus with his whip or John Calvin justifying capital punishment with John's account. But it assures that it's also too much to say, without ambiguity or complication, that violence is wholly outside of the Jesus traditions.

Interpreting Bethune's work in the fascist creep, Jesus can look suspiciously like the false media stereotype of "antifa," needlessly turning to violence just because he doesn't agree with someone.[20] Why won't he respect their right to assembly, after all? Can't he express his disagreement by holding a sign outside the temple or writing a letter to Caesar? Why is he destroying property and chasing off good, hard-working folks? (Is he too lazy to get a job of his own, by the by?) How much money is George Soros paying this guy to disrupt the day's necessary business? Can't this Christ place his trust in the marketplace of ideas and have a civil conversation with the bankers? Can we say that since he resorts to violence to make his point, he's no better than the imperial Roman army himself? And doesn't this Jesus seem like the *real* fascist?

Bethune's Jesus might not fit the "nonviolent Jesus" image, but the exegesis from Myers and the Young Lords show that his action is a response against the source of violence he has identified in rich people getting richer by oppressing women, the poor, the infirm, and the outcast. This is still a Jesus existentially against violence, recognizing its root and attacking it aggressively, with his body.

---

20. This scene recalls Reverend Seth Wispelwey on the witness stand during *Sines v. Kessler* in 2021, peppered with questions from fascists like Richard Spencer and Chris Cantwell over his statement that "Jesus is antifa."

Fanciful thought experiment on violence #2:

Christians in the US awaken to a mysterious piece of news: Dietrich Bonhoeffer's stone image at the National Cathedral in Washington, DC has gone missing. Placed by Dr. King and Oscar Romero in the cathedral's interior, Bonhoeffer's witness was not one of pacifism but most famously of being executed by the Nazis for partaking in a plot to kill Hitler. The cathedral even included this conspiracy in their short description of his life used to explain his face's presence there.[21]

Someone resides where Bonhoeffer used to. For an hour or so, no one is quite sure who it is. A wild-haired white man with a Bible in his hand, looking down on faces trying to figure out if they recognize him. Finally, a reader of history sees a photo of the new statue shared online and breaks the news: "That's John Brown!"

Like Bonhoeffer, Brown was a devout Protestant Christian all his life who proved himself willing to fight for oppressed and enslaved people with force. Like Bonhoeffer, he was killed by the state as a result. Like Bonhoeffer, he could have lived by simply doing nothing rather than intervening. (The two are also linked in that one of the few existing statues of Brown has been vandalized multiple times, including with racist slurs and a Nazi swastika on his forehead.[22]) But unlike Bonhoeffer, no churches bear his image in the United States, even though he was a citizen and Bonhoeffer not. Unlike Bonhoeffer, he did manage to kill people in his attempt to halt unspeakable state crimes. And, significantly, unlike Bonhoeffer, he did so to oppose slavery in the United States.[23]

The cathedral had decided that the one who tried to kill Hitler as a Christian act was someone to enshrine and remember in their holy site, part of how they understood the sacred story on Earth. Could they grant the same status to Brown for trying to start an uprising against slavery as a Christian act? Is arming Black people to liberate themselves from enslavers also part of the sacred story, also to be included in a holy site? The issue promised to be especially thorny since the cathedral had only recently removed their stained-glass windows dedicated to Confederate

---

21. See the National Cathedral's page for Bonhoeffer at https://cathedral.org/what-to-see/interior/dietrich-bonhoeffer/.

22. Greenstein, "John Brown's Statues Hit Again by Vandals."

23. However, Bonhoeffer did shortly flee to the United States and was dismayed and angered at the anti-Black racism he witnessed, especially in Harlem.

generals Robert E. Lee and Stonewall Jackson, just after Unite the Right in Charlottesville.[24]

A back-and-forth at the board meeting ensues. "Brown's legacy is violent," says a member opposed to letting his statue remain. "So is Bonhoeffer's," counters another. "Yes, but Bonhoeffer's group never actually carried out their plan as Brown's did," responds the first. "Oh," says Brown's defender, "so do we only love Bonhoeffer because he failed to actually commit the violence he had planned, and reject Brown because he actually set his in motion?" (They thought it unhelpful in this situation to note that Malcolm X named John Brown as the only white person who had proved his worth in the centuries-long struggle against white supremacy, or that the John Brown Anti-Klan Committee adopted him as their inspiration for resisting the KKK.[25])

And so it went. The first said they couldn't discuss killing enslavers in a church, while the second pointed out that they may as well scrub the story of Moses out of the Bible, since he murdered an enslaver and buried him in an unmarked grave (Exodus 2:11–12). Sure, admitted the first, but nobody *celebrates* that killing. But the second, knowing their Harlem Renaissance literature, read an Israelite's response to hearing about Moses' act in Zora Neale Hurston's *Moses, Man of the Mountain*: "Well, if he did that he's a friend of the race, and that's something we ain't got too much of. When can I meet him and see him? I want to shake his hand."[26] Also a reader of the Bible, they added that Psalm 136 not only celebrated the killing of *one* enslaver but of God killing of an entire *army* of them (verse 15). Yet the first, not to be outdone with church trivia, countered that the lectionary only reads from the beginning and end of that psalm, omitting the middle part about God killing enslavers.[27]

Debates continued but the central question became: why is plotting to kill Nazis accepted as uncontroversially harmonious with Christianity, in fact celebrated in church statues from DC to London to Hamburg, while plotting to kill white enslavers is not? Would they subject Brown's image

---

24. Washington National Cathedral, "Announcement on the Future of the Lee-Jackson Windows."

25. For more on the committee, see Moore and Tracy, *No Fascist USA!*"

26. Hurston, *Moses, Man of the Mountain*, 134.

27. The only time Psalm 136 appears in the Revised Common Lectionary (Year B, Easter Vigil), churches read vv. 1–9 and 23–26. The omitted section is entirely dedicated to God acting violently against enslavers and royalty who threatened the Israelites. Further, the psalmist names those acts as examples of God's love.

to the same treatment those of Generals Lee and Jackson got by removing it? And what does the mere fact of this controversy reveal about Christian understandings of violence, nonviolence, and when they are understood as divinely inspired?

In the din of this fictitious scenario, two questions were never raised: what does it mean that the standard Christian lectionary erases the psalmist thanking God for killing enslavers to free the enslaved, and how would the cathedral conversation differ if Bonhoeffer were replaced not by Brown but another martyr driven by Christian faith in the fight against US slavery, Nat Turner?

Who is worse, a non-violent Klan member or an anti-fascist who destroys property?

—UCLA STUDENT IN A RELIGIOUS FASCISMS AND ANTI-FASCISMS COURSE, IN A NOTE TO ME

Much mainstream discourse conflates nonviolence with not-violence (i.e., someone not actively committing physical harm is embodying nonviolence), using the language that came from the tradition of *satyagraha* while really recommending that people act civilly, accepting (for example) the rise of fascism without any physical counterforce. But in the absence of personally showing up to absorb violence in love, it amounts to outsourcing the inevitability of facing fatal threats to others, elsewhere. This not-violence is then merely a capitulation to brutality, all but assuring that *someone* will bear its brunt. And with this concept of "nonviolence," which is very far from the positive embodiment of love's force, it's understandable that people struggling against the fascist creep would criticize it heavily, as one critic does by concluding that "pacifism is so vapid and counterproductive that an alternative is imperative" in order to break the "stranglehold" it holds over movement discourse.[28]

28. Gelderloos, *How Nonviolence Protects the State*, 187.

Those of us who strive for nonviolence should know it is anthropologically predictable that people will fight fascism with force. We who say we are committed to nonviolence should organize the force of truth in a politically effective manner or accept that an inevitable consequence of our failure will be that some oppressed peoples and some who love them will resist with another kind of force. These means may include ones similar to Jesus driving out money changers and dove sellers in John's gospel, attacking the source of violence without neatly adhering to the definition of nonviolence. Or, if we allow fascism to reach a later stage, it may look more like the resistance in the chapter's opening quote, with young women having to gouge out the eyes of Nazis or commit suicide to avoid becoming a sex slave.

There are no innocent bystanders on the path to this scenario. To remove ourselves from the responsibility to enflesh the Christian nonviolence we espouse is to banish ourselves to become either annoying or irrelevant, and to cede the biblical witness of Jesus taking action, even when the moment seemed to call for something more than strict Gandhian *ahimsa*. Anyone, and most especially the churches, who hopes others will act nonviolently, should model the way or quietly step aside.

I think back to the moments before white supremacists began attacking anti-fascists during Unite the Right. A very small group of clergy hoped to nonviolently prevent white supremacists from gathering in the park by the Lee statue, placing their bodies on the narrow entryway on the steps. Other anti-fascists gave us the chance, and when the first group came with shields and sticks, marching right at us, we were simply too few to stop them. We had hoped for hundreds of clergy, enough to surround the entire park. Instead we failed to even block one set of steps. The anti-fascists below on the street saw this, and while we steeled ourselves for the second round, they had already formed ranks in front of us. The incoming fascists attacked them in the streets, and the chance for a nonviolent witness that actually prevented bloodshed had passed.

It passed because too few people committed to nonviolence showed up, far fewer than would criticize us after the fact for showing up alongside "antifa," who dared to use counter-force to defend Charlottesville once the nonviolent group proved unable.

Fanciful thought experiment on violence #3:

Then again, what if John's Jesus, whip of cords in hand, depicted by Ade Bethune in hot pursuit of the bankers, *is* in fact revealing Truth-force? What if it's not just the Jesus of the Sermon on the Mount but this Christ too who has something to reveal about what embodying active love means in situations of violent oppression? What would the implications be for the present if this angry, aggressive rabbi actually is embodying soul-force in the face of the exploitative rulers?

Could it be that Bethune's messiah shows us another of her works of mercy, balancing outcast-love and enemy-love in action?

An Interview with Dr. Jalane Schmidt

Jalane Schmidt is a professor of religious studies at the University of Virginia and a central figure in Charlottesville's resistance to white supremacy and fascism. She co-founded Charlottesville's Black Lives Matter chapter, leads free and immersive public history tours around town, and co-founded the Monumental Justice Virginia campaign, which successfully lobbied the Virginia General Assembly to overturn the law that prohibited cities and counties from removing Confederate statues. She directs the Democracy Initiative's Memory Project at UVA, researching public memory, conflict, and politics in the aftermath of Unite the Right. In 2018 she led a commemoration of John Henry James, a Charlottesville resident who was lynched in 1898, and the city now holds a marker telling his story. She has recently been leading civil rights pilgrimages throughout the South. While known in town and around the nation for her activism and research, I talked with her five years after Unite the Right primarily about her religious life. As with Reverends Smash and Sekou, her words give a glimpse of what kind of theological life propelled action against fascists then and now.

What made you convert to Catholicism when you were around thirty years old?

My dad was a Mennonite pastor. We lived in an intentional Christian community that was deliberately living under the taxable income limit so that we wouldn't pay revenues toward the war machine. People were praying, trying to live a life of peace and justice. My degree was in Bible and religion from a Mennonite college, Bethel. Then I worked for Mennonite Central Committee in DC, doing economic justice work on the Hill. It was a very interreligious setting, working with reformed Jews, Quakers, Catholics, Methodists, all the mainline Protestants. We worked with the Network sisters on affordable housing. These would later become the "Nuns on the Bus." So this was the first step. I liked the more capacious vision of social teaching offered by Catholics around the common good and social justice.

At Harvard we learned more about Catholicism as an intellectual tradition. I studied the history of the Christian church in the West. Bryan Hehir was there, and he basically wrote that bishops' document on economic justice that came out a few years earlier [*Economic Justice For All*]. I'd go down the street to Weston and Boston College for classes, studying with the Jesuits. Some of my besties were Jesuits. This gave me an intellectual foundation in Catholicism.

I did my two-year practicum at St. John the Evangelist Episcopal Church on Beacon Hill in Boston. It had a very monastic character, very high church, "more Catholic than the pope" type place. It was known as "the gay church" in the early nineties. It had people living with AIDS, gay folks who felt excluded by the institutional church. Gay men in particular felt it a place where they could bring their full selves and gifts to what was often quite a flamboyant liturgy, with the thurible and all that. The monastic culture was strong. The monks were long gone but it was great.

Then I went to Latin America and found my third set of teachers, the *viejitas*, these older Catholic laywomen. So it was a three-legged stool of social teaching, intellectual tradition, and popular devotion that brought me to the church. The popular devotion especially threw into relief those behind Vatican II formulations like the church as people of God. That's all well and good of course but there were some folks in the council, even progressives, who were kind of disdainful of more popular, homespun devotions of the type I participated in and wrote about in Cuba.

Back at Harvard, I was in a class with an African American Catholic and she had her priest come talk in her class about inculturation of the liturgy and what Black Catholics were doing and had been up to since Vatican II and also the Black Power movement. It was fascinating! They asked "Are there any questions?" and I'm like, "Yeah, [laughing] what time's Mass?!"

After all that I started going to St. Francis de Sales-St. Philip parish in Roxbury. I was received into the church there and both my kids were baptized there. I was on the liturgy planning committee. I had seen all these different liturgies—high church to sacrificing a goat and that sort of thing. And now I could help plan them at my parish.

But my dissertation and eventual book [*Chachita's Streets: The Virgin of Charity, Race, and Revolution in Cuba*] came out of those travels, and they were an act of devotion to Our Lady.

I remember coming into your home for the first time and seeing images of Mary greeting me.

Yeah, she's with a bunch of *santos* [saints] on one wall. Our Lady of Charity. On the opposite is a huge and heavily framed Mary, very old. A friend got it at a secondhand store. Some old person had handwritten "Holy Mary pray for us" on it. I thought, "This is great!" Very down home and sincere. It's probably four-by-three feet. In fact, look at my shirt! [She shows me the shirt she's wearing with a large Mary on it.] Pretty cool, huh?!

Yeah! So, what's your relationship with this Mary who's on your walls and your shirt?

Well, she's *la madre que nunca me falla*, the mother who's always there. Ever-present help, a calming spirit. I need a lot of calm in my life, I'm very scattered. It's kind of like she's a family member in an economy of relationships, the saint who draws people in. Robert Orsi was on my dissertation committee. He talks about the saint knitting together relationships. By virtue of being in relationship with her I'm knit in with a lot of other people. As with many families some are quite dear and many are irritating. And when I travel I always wear a rosary. I hate flying. I was supposed to be on a plane that crashed in Cuba. She saved me on two occasions.

Okay, so you entered this church where the president of the US bishops, Archbishop Gomez, called anti-fascism and Black Lives Matter pseudo-religions in a thinly veiled statement. You're co-creator of Charlottesville BLM and an active anti-fascist. How do you reconcile all this?

[Laughs] Oh, I don't know. I mean, this is where the approach of the *viejitas* serves me well. They kept the faith, kept the devotion for many decades under a very hostile communist regime. The clerics and the hierarchy were very patronizing too. They recognized that the African-inspired versions of Marian devotion were more popular than their orthodox ones and they looked down at the "heterodox" rituals of the people. But these ladies, they kind of followed their own devotional leanings, notwithstanding what the government or Catholic hierarchy said. *Yo soy Católica a mi manera*, they'd say. I'm Catholic in my way. They'd just go to mass and sit in the back and light a candle over here, you know. So there's always been little pockets in the church, usually a minority, folks over the centuries living their own devotional life that's an implicit or sometimes explicit critique of the doctrinal norms. Go back to Benedict and the monastics, that was part of it. They were against an empire that was taking over. There are always these folks like the Catholic Workers, some of whom have influenced me along the way. There are always pockets of affirmation like that, radical folks. I don't pay a lot of attention to what you mentioned, or the anti-gay stuff. It's like, "Yeah, bishop's gonna bishop."

You once told me you don't feel called to "win" in activism. Is this mindset connected to that?

Well, the Catholic Worker movement gets this. The monastic folks I know get it too. I think we're called to be faithful and that doesn't always give you the winning hand, in this life at least. It frees up a lot of energy. It's probably not going to happen for us, but that's not why we do it. I mean we try like hell, you know, but it'd be discouraging to only focus on winning. I think that's why a lot of activists get burned out. You don't always notch a win. Or sometimes it's a very long haul to do it. It just frees up energy and we're called to be faithful, not burn ourselves out.

How do you express your views on nonviolence in light of your faith commitments as well as the political realities that people are facing fascist violence today?

For myself, I don't advocate violence. I don't think ultimately it's a viable strategy, practically. Now look at me, here I am talking about winning when I just said . . . .

I'm not a saint or anything, but it just takes too much energy to hate. Christ commanded us to love. I don't love Richard Spencer, but neither do I hate him because he doesn't deserve that much real estate in my head. Some of our comrades will say they hate someone and I just think "Oh! Too bad they have that kind of power over you." That just twists my innards, thinking about hating. I haven't thought through this systematically. Hating someone is just . . . a lot of energy.

Does the commandment to love our enemies influence how you see this?

I don't love the fascists. But I don't wish them harm. I don't pray for my enemies but maybe I should. That's probably a good spiritual practice, to pray for those who persecute you. I don't practice that but King used to talk about this. One reason he didn't want to use violence is ultimately he wanted enemies to be converted. That was part of the rationale behind not using violence and loving enemies. I don't have that kind of endless, wild energy. I don't cultivate that. There are people that do that in a healthy way, though, without some kind of martyrdom.

But all this can be used rhetorically in harmful ways. So the nonviolence thing . . . I don't begrudge some of our comrades who do use violence in self-defense. I'm not talking about that. I've fended people off in self-defense several times. To great effect, I might add! I'm glad I did it. I would have been really hurt if I hadn't. But afflicting violence or pain or damage on someone, that's not what I try to do. But I don't put down those who do in defense of others.

What's disconcerting is just the sheer amount of guns in our society, predominantly on the Right but also in some leftist circles. It just gets more and more dangerous and that increases risk of violence. Even the Catholic bishops in their letter about nuclear proliferation talked about that. When you're preparing for war, you're setting yourself up for a violent outcome. There's more chance of that spark. That's concerning to me.

Shifting gears, I was on some of your historical tours of the statues in town and the auction block site. You'd ask the crowd if they knew the name of Lee's horse he's riding and someone knew every time. Then you'd ask if they could name one slave and no one could. You said that's the power of what we celebrate in public, what gets remembered and what doesn't. As someone who cares a lot about history, what do you say to this rhetoric that removing statues is erasing history?

Well, history and memory aren't the same thing. These statues are about memory and honoring someone in a public place with this monumental representation of them. That's meant to impress itself upon people who view it. But you don't know the slave's name, just the guy and the horse. I don't want to forget General Lee! But I want him framed by those people who have been forgotten in public memorial culture, enslaved people.

I like to teach about General Lee and I do it using an account of one of his former slaves recounting being whipped. So I'm not forgetting or erasing Lee, but I'm framing him with Wesley Norris. I want to remember history through its proper lens. Especially in space maintained by the state, we should only honor people whose lives and actions were in alignment with our publicly professed values of democracy. It's a civic pedagogy, and that's what we should lift up. You teach the history of these other people too, the Lees, but those don't need a place of honor in public.

You got sued for defamation by a Confederate for doing history once. What happened there?

When the Monument Fund and Sons of Confederate Veterans sued the city over removing the statues, I noticed that on our side in court were a bunch of scruffy activists. On their side were seersucker suits and pearls and Confederate flag pins and belt buckles. And I'll be damned if I didn't see members of the League of the South who attended Unite the Right. Folks over there were pursuing means of civil litigation also pursuing uncivil violence in the streets. And one of those plaintiffs is also a descendant of the family who held one of the largest number of enslaved people in the whole state. The antebellum era was good for him. They're still living on that wealth. Intergenerational wealth.

So I said to the press, why are you talking to me? Go talk to them. That's what's interesting, that these people are so normalized, being descendants of slaveholders who have all the time and resources to pursue this litigation because they're living on the wealth of stolen labor from enslaved people. And it's not enough for some of them to pursue it in courts, but they'll show up and hurt people in the streets too. So I got a reporter to look this up, Lisa Provence. She documented it all. The guy who sued me is a descendant of the First Families of Virginia, among those who "owned" the most slaves and had a reputation for being particularly cruel, selling families away from each other, forcing slaves to *walk* from the tidewater region of Virginia all the way down to Alabama where they opened new plantations. That's eight hundred miles. Unspeakably cruel. Then they had other members of the family involved in Confederate politics and the secession movement in VA. And then after that they were in state legislature, at one point pushing for massive resistance to progress in the fifties.

Then the father of this plaintiff had been—wait for it—the chair of the Charlottesville Housing Redevelopment Association during the Vinegar

Hill episode. [In the 1960s, a thriving Black business and residential district was razed for "urban renewal," displacing hundreds of people and devastating the Black economic center in Charlottesville. A Staples, a hotel, parking lots, and other buildings stand there today.] So this is that family. I said "this family has been roiling the lives of Black people for centuries." Which is a pretty mild thing to say! It's an objective fact. And ironically this guy brought it into a new century by roiling my life for having said that.[1]

I was quoting a book published by Harvard University Press by Richard Dunn [*A Tale of Two Plantations*] where he was documenting the plantation of this guy's family. The research was informed by records that were in public archives at UVA and state archives in Richmond. Family members had donated them. They were proud of themselves! All these records, Dunn got them together and told the story in a well-documented history.

So I amplified publicly available facts. *This family has been roiling the lives of Black people for centuries*. That's objectively true. And in the wake of Unite the Right, this old dude said I had defamed him [laughing] 'cause I said he was a racist, which I didn't say. Then he said I insinuated it. It was all very sloppy. The university refused to provide me with legal counsel, but the ACLU picked it up and it was dismissed. But this is what people who take history seriously have to deal with.

Do you have spiritual ancestors you look to in times like that, people who sustain you?

There's the *viejitas*, of course. My favorite saint beside the Virgin Mary is St. Francis of Assisi. He's associated with the Orisha [manifestation of God] Orula in *la Regla de Ocha* in Cuba, otherwise known as Santería, and with the divination priests, the *Babalawos*. The priests are said to be guided by Orula, kind of the original diviner priest who reigned in present-day Nigeria. Plus, in grad school I worked at the Franciscan homeless shelter. I liked their spirit of simplicity, renunciation. I remember watching when the present pope was named and took the name Francis. He was so humble, asking the faithful, "Will you please pray for me?" I was like, this is going to be different, a Jesuit who has a Franciscan charism.

I have on my porch this very minute these two cement *santos* from a secondhand store. There's a Virgin Mary and a St. Francis, and I got them for $15 each. They're on each corner of the porch, protecting the house.

---

1. For an account of the lawsuit, see Entzminger, "Speaking Out."

"Make me an instrument of Your peace," Francis said. Good words to live by.

How this is all tied in with Afro-Cuban religions is meaningful to me. Our Lady of Charity is identified with Orisha Oshun. According to my godfather who was an Ifá priest, a *Babalawo*, now deceased, Oshun is who rules my head. I'm connected in many ways with Mary, especially Our Lady of Charity.

Your godfather was a priest?

Yes, from Havana, a son of Oshun as well as an Ifá priest. So there's a thick set of influences leading to St. Francis and Our Lady of Charity. And it has to do with these African deities to whom I also have some devotion, moreso when I'm in Cuba, where they have great devotion to the dead. The cult of saints is the Christian cult of the dead there. This is the focus of a lot of catechetical energy, let's put it that way, from the church authorities trying to corral it into orthodox manners. But the people have their own ways. The Christian cult of saints is really about staying in touch with the dead. An appeal, a supplication. They intercede for us. They see God face-to-face. Plus, the saints are more relatable. The saint of barbers, the saint of miners, of incarcerated folks. It's more relatable to human experience than abstractions about "God."

So In Cuba they have these practices overlapping Afro-Cuban and spiritist devotions, and other figures in my life that have been important for me have been spiritist mediums in Cuba, often Black, who have relation-ships to *muertos*, dead ones. Some of them were enslaved, some escaped slavery. My second book that's been stalled for six years, because I'm deal-ing with Nazis here, is about the cult to the *Cimarron*, the escaped slaves. Around the Virgin shrine, the slaves who were forced to work in the mines and who were the first devotees of the Virgin, they sometimes revolted and ran away to the mountains. Rough-hewn places. Their spirits are rebellious, bellicose, powerful, difficult to control. These *muertos*, are part of a constel-lation of relationships. It's not just these Christian saints, there's this whole panoply of spirits. The bellicosity and those *muertos* are also an important example, and then the people who serve them, these living spiritists who become their host during trance ceremonies. Those are also very powerful influences in my life, spiritually and historically. They inform what I do.

I'm like those old ladies. *Soy Católica a mi manera.* In my way.

This overlaps with the movie you made, Unveiling: The Origins of Charlottesville's Monuments.[2]

Yeah, it talks about the religious nature of Confederate devotion. I discuss it as devotion to saints, a kind of a Protestant cult of the dead. They aren't usually known for that, but in this case they bend their theology quite a bit. When it comes to accommodating white supremacy, let me tell you, they'll make room. [Stonewall] Jackson in particular came in for a lot of hagiographical treatment because he was pious, people love to point out he had Bible studies for his slaves. "See, he wasn't racist," they say, because he did that for his (ahem) *slaves.* His left arm got buried at Chancellorsville, and it's a pilgrimage site. He comes in for a lot of veneration.

You mentioned your spiritual ancestors inform what you do. So would you see your anti-racism, your anti-fascism as connected with your religious life? Creating BLM in Charlottesville, the public history tours, and everything else you do: is it part of the same religious life you're describing or do you see them as separate?

Ha! You're making me synthesize things that are kind of inchoate or floating. And my Mennonite background and being in intentional Christian community is as influential as all this other stuff. You have to take action! You can't just let white supremacy and fascism happen. We're all kind of thrown into a moment in history and it falls on us to respond.

Yeah, in terms of the not hating folks, that's an influence. And not using violence too. A lot of Christian activists have inspired me this way. People like King and of course Bayard Rustin and so many others. The Berrigans. When confronted with the moment, they all took action. They recognized the moment for what it was. Reading the signs of the times, as the Second Vatican Council said. So I'm inspired by the example of these prior generations of religious activists. I do see myself as following in that, however imperfectly.

You help lead the Swords to Plowshares project, making the Robert E. Lee statue into art. Can you briefly describe the rationale?

That project is about continuing to deal with the pain that that statue inflicted on our community. That's part of the reason for wanting to keep it

2. The movie, made by PBS, can be viewed at https://www.pbs.org/video/unveiling-the-origins-of-charlottesvilles-monuments-jfksri/.

here. No, don't send it away! Transform it and keep it right here. It's a way of dealing with it. We aren't trying to erase the past. Whatever's created out of those materials, we're going to tell its whole story. There was this statue here, put in by a bunch of rich white people, it was here for a hundred years, it became the flashpoint for brutal white violence, then we changed it. What used to glorify General Lee will now honor something more worthy. The history won't be gone but even more present. It's taking history by the horns.

Part III. To Love and to Pray in a Fascist Creep

Jonah, Sarah Fuller

6

Of Enemy-Love, Vengeance Psalms, and Flaming Nostrils

*I regard hatred as bestial and crude, and prefer that my actions
and thoughts be the product, as far as possible, of reason . . .
All the same, I would not want my abstaining from explicit
judgment to be confused with an indiscriminate pardon. No,
I have not forgiven any of the culprits, nor am I willing to
forgive a single one of them, unless he has shown (with deeds,
not words, and not too long afterwards) that he has become
conscious of the crimes and the errors, and is determined to
condemn them, to uproot them from his conscience and from
that of others, because an enemy who sees the error of his ways
ceases to be an enemy.*

—Primo Levi, Auschwitz survivor, 1986 interview[1]

When I approached the security checkpoint, the officer told me I couldn't take my book into the courtroom. "No books allowed," was the exact phrase, causing a few stray laughs. I noticed moments later that a man with a Confederate flag belt buckle wrapped across his jeans walked through undisturbed.

None of us wanted to be there. We lingered near the street corner a block away from the courthouse much longer than necessary, simply to be in each other's presence free of the mood we knew would descend when we

---

1. Levi, "Primo Levi's Heartbreaking, Heroic Answers."

127

went inside. One of the survivors who would be testifying in a short time wheeled her chair over. More than a year had passed but she still couldn't walk. Talking with her made the whole affair seem momentarily pointless. What could justice possibly mean if she wasn't healed? What set of events later that day could provide the sense that goodness had won? Standing on the sidewalk by barricaded downtown roads, I think we all knew the day wouldn't fix anything. We didn't want to be there, but we knew that we had to, not because of any obligation or pressure but because we were conjoined by circumstances that called us together. Those riots, those attacks, that murder touched us deep in the marrow, and we knew what today meant without having to coordinate.

Before entering, a friend embraced me, shaking. Something about being arm in arm, cheek to cheek, flesh pressed against flesh prepared us to go inside. Nothing would be any different, but we could carry our love into a dark day together. Maybe that was the only weapon against it all.

The crowd inside was mostly familiar. We knew who each other were by now, having been through the Summer of Hate, the jail board meetings, the school board meetings, the impromptu disruptions of neo-Nazi planning sessions, the late-night bonfires. There were a few visible white supremacists, of course, including the man who planned the Unite the Right riot and bore deep responsibility for (and celebrated) the crime that another would be on the stand for this day. My friends and I took heart when three Black activists in town walked far out of their way to sit in the empty space in his row, leaving none between their legs and his. "No safe space for Nazis," laughed the preacher to my left.

When the defendant walked in, a surreal feeling took hold. I had seen his face hundreds of times while researching. He at once seemed a cold villain and almost a child. I couldn't help but wonder how someone so young could do something so heinous. Knowing the answer would not dispel the tragic mystery of it all. The problem of evil sat there with a blank face, dressed in a suit, mostly looking at some spot on the ground ten feet in front of him.

Nothing can possibly prepare you to see an FBI agent hold up a transparent bag and hear the words, "This flesh was taken from the hood of the car." He produced a water bottle stuck at the base of the windshield, as well as sunglasses stuck under the spoiler of the grey Dodge Challenger. Photos of red splotches on the paint of the car stared cruelly at the audience from a large television so the jury could gather every detail. More and more stains appeared on the screen, each one proving nothing the last had not, each one perhaps showing the life juice of any number of people on the street the day of the attack. A juror put her hand over her mouth and shook her head in controlled terror. I peered at the defendant, who seemed determined to maintain a nondescript face, looking down.

The passenger side mirror, which was picked up on Fourth Street, rested innocuously in the expert witness's hand.

The sound of snot and tears just behind my head interrupted my gaze. A close friend had, like others present, not been able to keep hearing the words "soft tissue" and "red stains" over and over as if they were mere scientific curiosities. Many of the people present still dealt with trauma from the attack that brought us there that day, yet had to watch the litany of horrific items be submitted with no sense of weight, heartbreak, or outrage. Sometime after Item #106 a man produced the front grill of the car which completely detached after plowing through so many bodies.

The witness again uttered the word "flesh," and (perhaps because I was surrounded by ministers) I could not help but think of John's Gospel and what meaning it gives the word. The same flesh—*sarx*, in Greek—that bore forth the Word into a living body in John 1:14 ("the Word became flesh") now resided in a sealed bag, submitted as evidence, having been scraped from a death machine sped into more than twenty humans, people who live and breathe and move while cradled in the living flesh that the gospel says became the substance of divine inhabitation. This material, this sacrosanct *sarx*, the malleable abode of God's own grace, what God made covenant with after the flood,[2] became mashed in the grill of this twenty-year-old Hitler-worshipping Nazi. This was the same stuff I had hugged before coming into the building, held against my cheek and took comfort in. It was unbearably disorienting to see it disembodied and given a three-digit number in the parade of evidence, each as inhuman as the last. All I could think of was that flesh was meant to be attached to a living being. What was it doing in a baggie?

As the defendant continued to stare at the ground, I jotted in my notes, "How to love one's enemies?"

A guard walked into the center aisle, summoning my friend out of the room. Suspicious, I followed them out to the lobby and found that he was

2. *Basar* is the Hebrew counterpart to *sarx*, meaning flesh. In Genesis 9:15, God uses the word twice with Noah: "And I will remember my covenant, which is between me and you and every living creature of all flesh; and the waters shall no more become a flood to destroy all flesh."

being removed for wearing a "political shirt," in the words of the guard. He had unbuttoned his flannel in court to reveal part of the words, "United Against White Supremacy." He was henceforth barred from court and had to leave immediately. "Oh, I'll just keep it buttoned up," my friend assured them, beginning to cover up the letters with the buttons of his flannel. No, he was told. "I wasn't notified I couldn't wear a shirt like this," he tried. "This is not a conversation," the officer said. I told the officer there's a man in there with a Confederate flag on his belt, an unmistakably political piece of clothing. "That's not my concern or yours," he responded, while in the precise process of making political clothing his business, and ejected my friend for good.

I won't dwell on the unspeakable accounts given by witnesses when I went back in, or the electric jolt that shot through my body on seeing the crowd of survivors come down the aisle together and take up three full rows of seats, faces that I had not seen since I watched them get loaded into an ambulance one by one at the scene of the murder, or the brutality of forcing a survivor to comment on photos of herself getting run over by a speeding car frame by painful frame or describe her scars to the jurors, some of whom physically drew back in revulsion at seeing them. But every witness conveyed the sense of joy the crowd of community defenders exuded while they marched up Water Street, oblivious to what was coming. One witness who was completely unconnected to all the proceedings felt so drawn to the mood of the marchers that she decided to get out of her car to soak it in. Their celebratory spirit was palpable, inviting.

A slew of rapid-fire photos taken milliseconds apart flash across the screen for the jury. They show the speeding car from behind, accelerating into the festive crowd walking up a street that had been closed off to auto traffic by police earlier that day. "Photo #42," the prosecutor said, "do you see any brake lights?"

"No," said the journalist on the stand.

"Photo 43, how about now?" she asked.

"No."

"Photo 44. Now?"

"No."

The same for photo after photo, as the car grew closer and closer to the humans, the animated bodies of flesh gathered together to protect each other.

"Photo 56, do you see any brake lights?" the prosecutor asked.

"No," came the reply.

"Are bodies starting to go through the air?"

"Yes."

I gazed at the defendant, who remained unmoved behind his glasses, staring vaguely forward at the ground. Just yards away sat the group of people he accelerated into, some who walked into the courtroom, some who hobbled with a cane, some who needed wheels. I marveled at his disengagement. Surveying the room, I noticed many friends who had draped their arm around those near them, comforting loved ones, flesh comforting flesh, *sarx* to *sarx*. And I glanced back at my notepad reading, "How to love one's enemies," my mind blank as the murderer's face.

How to love well in a fascist creep? What do we do with this ancient book that commands love of God, love of neighbor, love of enemies, love of creation, and love of self, especially when those loves can seem incompatible with or transform one another? And more specifically, what do these loves look like in the context of a nation populated by vulnerable peoples resisting those that want, in the most dramatic forms, to extinguish and destroy them? How do we love literal Nazis? (Is it abominable to even consider?) And how would that love relate to loving this specific person whose existence is threatened by that particular white supremacist? James Cone wrote in 1970 that "there is no use for a God who loves white oppressors *the same as* oppressed blacks."[3] But that appears to be the god of so many who have not yet wrestled with what an enemy is, how God relates to them, and how we are to relate with them. (And, for some of us, whether we *are* them.)

Some of the prescriptions in the Bible don't provide much of a road map. "Pray for those who persecute you" offers a pernicious meaning to someone who isn't persecuted in any substantive way. The temptation is to apply the teaching to those countless "others." The reading that seems natural for someone who obliviously wields social privilege, and therefore the most dangerous reading, is that all those others simply need to pray for the alt-right, the Klansmen, the neo-Nazis, the Christian conversion therapists, the MAGA cult and its MAGAsterium. It may be unfortunate, the thought goes, that they live their life on the run or in the clutches of monsters or in various shades of political exile, but they have a Christian duty (whether

3. Cone, *A Black Theology of Liberation*, 74.

they are Christian or not) to turn the other cheek, to focus on the best in their would-be murderers or subjugators.

And suddenly, almost imperceptibly, we can begin policing people who are dying by cuffing them with Bible verses and vague images of Dr. King we do not understand and neglect to apply to ourselves. We fail to grasp Cornel West's insight that "justice is what love looks like in public." We get white suburbanites condemning Black people who are getting shot at in Ferguson by men in tanks and battle armor—for being violent. And this is no kind of love, for neighbors or enemies or ourselves.

The book of Jonah, small though it is, deserves a large space in these conversations. The story is simple enough. When God assigns Jonah to go to Nineveh (present-day Iraq) and cry out against them, the prophet instead goes elsewhere, getting on a ship to Tarshish (of unknown location, but not in Nineveh). God sends a big fish to gather Jonah, who spends three days in its belly before being vomited up and finally heading to Nineveh to deliver his message. Surprisingly, when the city hears Jonah's message—"forty days more and Nineveh shall be overthrown"—people respond by proclaiming a fast in which "everyone, great and small, put on a sackcloth," a traditional sign of repentance. The king joins in, proclaiming, "All shall turn from their evil ways and from the violence that is in their hands." Seeing this, and much to Jonah's comedic chagrin, God spares them from the punishment that had been threatened while trying to comfort Jonah and his frustrated desire to see the city burn.

The beast who swallows the fleeing prophet gets most of the attention but there is more to its relevance in a fascist creep than knowing that lurking leviathans are eating people. In *Sympathy for Jonah: Reflections on Humiliation, Terror, and the Politics of Enemy-Love,* musician and theologian David Benjamin Blower posits that Jonah may have fled God because the Ninevites were known to be the epitome of evil. "The Assyrians, who ruled Nineveh, were the Nazis of the ancient world . . . legendary for their fetishized brutality." They made towers of their enemies' heads, skinned people alive as public spectacle, buried people up to their necks and left them to slowly rot, and used other torturous methods of killing those they conquered. Jonah's situation was similar to that of a Jewish man being asked to deliver Gods message to Nazis at a Nuremberg rally, says Blower. And

Nineveh was the empire's seat of power, its king "the lord, or the tyrant, of the known world."[4]

That the book was canonized, he says, is astonishing. It magnifies the message that God loves even the most evil among us. It signifies a love of those who murder God's people that will make some readers uncomfortable, even disgusted. This is a different kind of divine treatment towards enemies than that shown in the Exodus story, where God exalts the same Moses who murdered an enslaver as his chosen prophet and then buries the entire proto-Confederate army trying to retain Egypt's slaves. It shows a different kind of concern and compassion for evildoers than in Daniel 5, when the writing on the wall spells out King Belshazzar's doom, and God seems to orchestrate his slaying. The book of Jonah's enemy-love reaches out to redeem even the most evil by giving them the opportunity to turn, repent, and convert.

This kind of divinely displayed love is also modeled in a story shared in Mark Bray's *Antifa*. Sometime in the late eighties in Minneapolis, a "young Native American skinhead graffiti artist named Gator" yelled to someone across the street, "Hey, are you part of the White Knights?" He crossed over, getting nearer to the person he suspected of being in the new white power gang that had been terrorizing local people of color. When the other admitted to being in the group, Gator stepped closer to him and said the next time they met, he'd better not be. Bray notes that the strategy successfully converted a number of young white power gang members into the Baldies crew, a collection of anti-racists that loosely prefigured today's "antifa." Rather than physically attack them, this strategy "gave teens a chance to think about their stance and let them know that it carried consequences," Gator said. "It gave them fair warning."[5] There's no way of knowing how many people were saved from racist assaults as a result of Gator's approach.

The tactic might as well be plagiarized straight from God's character in the book of Jonah. God sends Jonah in Gator's place to speak with ancient analogs for Nazis. Much like Gator, God saw fit to extend a chance for repentance. The purpose in both cases seems to have been getting the evildoer—the murderers and torturers, the white power group—to turn away from their participation in evil and repent of what they have done, signifying that they will not do it anymore. In Gator's case, he even got people to pledge to stop *others* from doing so. Both situations use the tactic

---

4. Blower, *Sympathy for Jonah*, 17, 22.

5. Bray, *Antifa*, 167.

of a threat of physical violence to encourage the betterment of an enemy that doubly functions as protection against those they threatened.

Some may read Gator's story and think he was a bully or an instigator. Close readers of the Bible would say he acted in a divine spirit, similar to the God of Jonah. Whatever the case, both Gator and God seem to know what Primo Levi said in the quote headlining this chapter, that "an enemy who sees the error of their ways ceases to be an enemy." His was a hard wisdom from inside Auschwitz, the death camp today's fascists openly aim to reinstate. I think of the rioter in a "Camp Auschwitz" sweatshirt in the MAGA mob that attacked the Capitol and its police on January 6, 2021. I think of the Proud Boys in DC, leading up to the Capitol riot, sporting a "6MWE" sign, meaning six million dead Jews wasn't enough. I think of the "First stop Charlottesville, next stop Auschwitz!" chants amid the swastikas during Unite the Right. I think of the US bishops refusing to condemn the central emblem of Auschwitz. And with all this I wonder at Levi's faith that an enemy can be converted. I wonder whether there would be no need to address this more radicalized form of fascism if there had been more Gators emulating Jonah's God.

But how to understand what Blowers calls the "radical compassion for total monsters" in this prophetic tale,[6] especially in light of a very different kind of approach to enemies and love elsewhere in the Bible? This God of Jonah sits in uneasy tension with the God of Psalm 136, for example. Not only does the psalmist here remember God's slaughter of the Egyptian army to protect Israel from slavery, but sees it as a sign of God's "steadfast love" enduring forever. God is also the one who struck down the firstborn children of Egyptians and "killed famous kings" threatening Israel, the psalmist remembers, and those too are examples of God's love, listed alongside doing great wonders, making the heavens and earth, and feeding and remembering those are low.

That is, God's destruction of enemies is seen as part of the story of creation and salvation. Biblical scholar Richard Clifford underscores the emphasis on love by observing, "Psalm 136 is unique in preserving the antiphonal reply 'for [God's] steadfast love endures forever' (repeated no less than 26 times). Though other psalms have antiphons, none has them

6. Blower, *Sympathy for Jonah*, 54.

in such number."[7] Even within the context of 150 psalms praising God, this one more than any others centers a refrain on love, and does so by invoking how God killed enemies and their children.

Mennonite pastor Melissa Florer-Bixler explores this different kind of love in her book *How to Have an Enemy*, placing it in the context of other "psalms of vengeance." Psalm 137 ends with the hope that future generations of Babylon's children die, its final words saying happy is the one who will "dash them against the rock!" While some churches respond by taking these kinds of passages out of the lectionary,[8] Florer-Bixler sees something useful and even necessary in them. Responding to a commentator who asked whether it's Christian for people to pray this way, she turns it around. "People do cry out to God for vengeance because for some, at a certain point in suffering, it is impossible to see another way to bring an end to an unimaginable situation. These psalms preserve for our corporate memory the furthest extreme of human suffering." Scripture doesn't condemn these psalms but platforms them, centering voices coming from "the deepest well of anguish, from hell itself."[9]

This is true even of the Christian Testament. If all this sounds oppositional to the spirit of Jesus, Florer-Bixler brings readers right back to the scene when Jesus drove people oppressing the poor, women, and the outcast from Jerusalem's temple. In John's Gospel, "Jesus enacts one of these psalms upon the economic engine of the temple" with his whip of cords and property destruction. John's account has Jesus' disciples witnessing the scene and remembering the words of Psalm 69:9, "Zeal for your house will consume me." Drawing a quote from a psalm was, at the time, a way of invoking the entirety of that psalm. The continuation of Psalm 69, then, signifies that John's Gospel saw Jesus as continuing the legacy of these vengeance psalms when he overturned their tables: "Let their table be a trap for them, a snare for their allies. Let their eyes be darkened so that they cannot see, and make their loins tremble continually. Pour out your indignation upon them, and let your burning anger overtake them. May their camp be a desolation; let no one live in their tents." Florer-Bixler argues that John is

7. Clifford, *Psalms 73–150*, 269.

8. All thanks to the Benincasa community in New York and their nightly Vespers prayer group, headed by Karen Gargamelli-McCreight, which *does* pray with even the middle part of Psalm 136, bringing this section's material to my attention.

9. Florer-Bixler, *How to Have an Enemy*, 52.

making clear with his gospel that "Jesus' body becomes this prayer against the system of economic exploitation on the edge of the temple."[10]

Imagining the violent destruction of one's enemies has biblical precedent, even in the gospels and the character of Jesus. Rather than mandating it of all the faithful, this acts to affirm the grief and rage of victims as part of the divine story, carving out a space for it in revelation. By comparison, these passages make comments of those whose family members were killed by police in the twenty-first century sound calm and collected. When Breonna Taylor's little sister Ju'Niyah Palmer protested the killing of her sister in the middle of the night in her own hallway during a police raid that was unconnected to her, she did so using the words "Arrest the cops who killed Breonna Taylor" on her clothes in court.[11] A sheriff's deputy made her leave due to the message, but even if she called for the slaughter of that officer's children, she would fit right in with the psalmist's tradition.

Christians would do well to grapple with these two sides of how God's love treats enemies in Scripture. The God whose love for the lowly and oppressed leads to killing enemies can stick in the throat. The God who extends a chance for even Nazis to convert can do the same. But neither should be ignored. They are the two arms of loving in the face of fascism, capable of striking, embracing, extending, opening, blocking, joining, severing, and raising. But the longer Christians let them hang at our sides in indecision or feigned neutrality, the more we bear responsibility for the bloodshed—already here and escalating—made inevitable by inaction.

The Hebrew word *oyeb* gets translated as "enemy" in English Bibles, and it suggests an adversary, a foe, or hatred. Passages sometimes associate it with angrily breathing. Picturing enemyhood in this way connects it to God's relationship to humans, recalling the Genesis creation story that depicts God breathing life into the first people through their nostrils. Breath is what animates us, distinguishes us from clay or soil in the Eden account. Breath is simply what life is. (This accentuates the unspeakable evil done to people like Eric Garner and George Floyd, who died with police on their necks while pleading, "I can't breathe," having the most primordial grace given to humans choked and stolen.) An enemy, then, can be seen as that

10. Florer-Bixler, *How to Have an Enemy*, 53.

11. Roldan, "Breonna Taylor's Family Members Say They Were Kicked Out."

which makes our participation in the breath of God livid. To snort in rage at oppression is to use God's very gift of life to protest.

God modeled this use of life-breath, appearing sometimes as almost a fire-breathing dragon in times of injustice. When David sang a song of thanksgiving to God for delivering him from Saul, he sang that "I am saved from my enemies" because God heard his cry of distress. "The earth reeled and rocked; the foundations also of the mountains trembled and quaked, because God was angry. Smoke went up from God's nostrils, and devouring fire from God's mouth; glowing coals flamed forth from God" (2 Samuel 22: 4–9). He then depicts divine rebuke as "the blast of the breath of God's nostrils" (v. 16). The song is repeated in Psalm 18, validated as a worthy image of God for prayer. When Job's friend Eliphaz envisions what happens to those who create injustice, he says "by the breath of God they perish, and by the blast of God's anger are they consumed" (Job 4:9). And on the other side, when God is said to be "slow to anger" in Exodus, the literal Hebrew means that God is "long of nostril." How one responds to enemies with the very substance of livingness, then, is tied to the imagery of hot and fiery noses.

Isaiah 30:31–33 best exemplifies how this image of God gets used in ways that seem to contradict the divine approach in the book of Jonah, perhaps showing what it might have looked like if Jonah got his way. "The Assyrian will be terror-stricken at the voice of the Lord when God strikes with the rod," it reads. "And every stroke of the staff of punishment that the Lord lays upon him will be to the sound of timbrels and lyres with dancing; with brandished arm God will fight with him. For his burning place has long been prepared, also for the king; its pyre is made deep and wide, with fire and wood in abundance; the breath of the Lord, like a stream of sulfur, kindles it." Rather than offer a chance for conversion and survival, here God scorches them to death with breath, with "anger burning" and "tongue like a devouring fire," says verse 27. And all the while it seems the Israelites will dance with timbrel and lyres, celebrating the destruction of their Assyrian enemies. Two biblical specialists argue that this goes further than typical violence against enemies, saying, "Depicting Yahweh as a fire-breathing creature emphasizes the fierceness of his anger and the intensity of the battle he wages against Assyria, which should be compared not with ordinary combat against political enemies but with a ferocious attack by a wild and fearsome beast whose fiery breath consumes its prey."[12]

12. Kim and Trimm, "Yahweh the Dragon," 175.

This imagery of breath helps reimagine what an enemy is. It's that which we snort at, which raises our heart rate in anger, making us breathe harder and more furiously. It is this kind of adversary that disciples are assumed to have in the Bible when Jesus tells them in his Sermon on the Mount to love their enemies. To piously assume that we are above having enemies is to place ourselves above the God who had plenty in scripture. In a time of rising anti-Semitism, what sense can Christians even make of loving our Jewish kin if we do not become enemies to Nazis? To project blistering breath at Nazis and Confederates—much in the style of Mother Mary in Ben Wildflower's "Miraculous Metal"—is to follow in the steps of the biblical God. These witnesses give Christians permission to explore a fiery discipleship as fascists rise.

This breath is part of Jesus' call to enemy-love, not something antagonistic to it. This anger, even wrath, is a saving rage that aims to devour the evil in others for the sake of their redemption. It extends the breath of life that animates humanity, reaching out with Creation's exhalation toward that which is dead and would make others dead, angrily sharing God's salvation. This is what Jesus did when he yelled at his enemies in the streets, calling them snakes and white sepulchers, or when he shouted at the money changers and cried that they had made God's house a den of thieves. It's what he did when he rebuked demon and disciple alike. Christians have been bid to go and do likewise, learning to be similarly short of nostril with the new Assyrians, the new religious authorities more concerned with dogma than the downtrodden, the new blaspheming bankers.

But the love of Jesus in the gospels shows that holy anger does not reduce a foe simply to the status of "enemy." Jesus opposed the Pharisees publicly, but when Nicodemus came to talk at night he engaged him in good will and hope for his redemption. If insulting them as a bunch of vipers was part of Christ's love, so too was Jesus sharing God's spirit in the dark with one of them, urging him to become reborn, to change ways. Even on the cross, Luke's Jesus showed concern for his murderers.

So in naming people like ICE agents and bishops who spend their energy condemning Black Lives Matter as enemies, we do not reduce their whole being to that which we oppose. We recognize them as people with potential to repent and turn. Every person carries that breath of God, every person is kin. Cain became Abel's enemy but never ceased being his brother. We oppose Nazis and their civil enablers with the same hope Jesus had for Nicodemus under the stars together. This enemy-love kills fascists and insists they be born again into a mode of existence that embraces the stranger rather than deports them, hoping in Primo Levi's insight that a fascist and enemy who repents and converts is a fascist and enemy no more.

Though this love prioritizes the vulnerable and oppressed, it eventually comes around to being brokenhearted over the tortured souls of even the Richard Spencers and Stephen Millers, the street-level Nazis and Christo-fascists, opting for the uncomfortable and dangerous work of opposing them in their pursuit of evil. It sees that they suffer immensely. It opposes them because every fascist act brutalizes someone we love but also because we care about that suffering, knowing that every sin they commit harms them, calcifies their fascist habits, creates more victims of others and a deeper one of themselves. Like David refusing to kill Saul even though Saul was hunting him, naming him as brother—*insisting* on their brotherhood while continuing to oppose him—so we must insist on our kinship with even Klansmen while we frustrate their every attempt at organizing.

This is Reverend Blackmon's "love in the face of hatred," Reverend Brittany Caine-Conley's adopted name of Smash while wearing a hat that says LOVE. This enfleshes what Rabbi Mordechai Liebling said about enemies: "if you love someone about to commit a crime, you stop them." This is what Bryan Massingale meant when he said "God's love is subversive and destructive."[13] Yes, it builds up and heals what is holy, but it undermines and obliterates what is evil, meaning Christian love in a fascist creep requires subversion and destruction.

Is there real, practical hope in loving our enemies? That is, does it do something beyond embodying saintly disposition toward others? Can it be a link in the causal chain that leads towards meaningful justice, reparation, healing, and loving community? What leads to metanoia is rarely as spectacular as Paul falling off his horse on the road to Damascus or a cannonball shredding the bones of Ignatius. There is more often Brother Lawrence encountering a barren tree in the winter or Augustine reading a random Bible verse. No experience is too mundane to potentially turn someone from one manner of life to another, to convert a sword into a plowshare.

In this we find a seed of hope for converting those who make up the fascist creep. Perhaps in the end insisting on love only changes ourselves.

13. Massingale, "The Assumptions of White Privilege."

Or perhaps it will be one among many ingredients in the nebulous recipe for human growth. Either way, we can neither depend on it "working" nor dismiss it as utopian fantasy. We love our enemies because we are called to, because we hope, because it may (even imperceptibly) turn someone from hate, because it may make a vulnerable neighbor the slightest bit freer of threat, because we ourselves refuse to sink into the bog our enemies have sunk themselves in, because it gives a small offering of beauty to the world. We do it for all these reasons at the same time, trusting in the power of One beyond ourselves to make a feast of our dregs, hoping that our love may be one of the few fish turned to five thousand. Someone, anyone, may hunger for it, and eat.

Sometime in the early morning hours of July 9, 2018, I found myself surrounded by friends and strangers, locked outside of a Charlottesville jail, mesmerized by the stamina of someone who had been holding a piece of paper high above her head since well before midnight. She held it so those on the other side of a window could read its message, but from my view all I could see was the backside of her palm pressing it against the glass.

The magistrate had locked the door to the visitor's area of the jail before we showed up, so we were stuck in the night air, stretching our necks to catch a glimpse of those we had come to support. A crowd of forty or fifty had gathered in the parking lot, many waving their phone flashlights in the air, hoping our handcuffed community mates would see people outside while they got processed, would know that we were there for them.

"Great view, though," my friend Jordan said, looking up at the crescent moon illuminating his black-and-white Dorothy Day shirt. I thought Dorothy might agree as much about the pavement gathering as the moonlit expanse.

When a local attorney showed up to see the seven who had been arrested, the magistrate walked up to the door, listened to him announce that the arrested have a legal right to representation, refused him entry, and walked away.

The seven had been arrested for the crime of "pedestrian stepping into street with poor visibility." Or in other words, jaywalking. They were protesting at the scene of a crime, where, a year earlier, a Black man named Corey Long had committed the offense of defending himself and others without touching or harming anyone amid Unite the Right. When Long warded off a group of nearby alt-righters, neo-Nazis, and neo-Confederates with a small flame that—unlike God's style of hot breath—touched no one, an imperial wizard of the KKK yelled a racist slur at Long, pulled out a gun, fired a bullet at him, and put his gun back in his pants, all on camera. He walked away calmly. The police nearby did nothing.

The judge sentenced Long to 340 days in jail, suspending 320 of them. Supporters outside the court sang songs and held signs. Members of an anti-fascist house church led the crowd in one of its hymns, blurring the boundaries between liturgy and politics, prayer and protest. People chanted the same phrase that would spread across a banner let loose downtown: Corey Long did nothing wrong.

So, seven people went to the site of Long's "crime" and protested. Among them was one of the many people hit by the same car that killed Heather Heyer. She remained in a wheelchair due to injuries from the attack and so was arrested by a combination of police and a rescue squad in an ambulance. The vehicle designed to bring people to safety, to heal them, instead brought her to jail. Her crime? Jaywalking in solidarity with a community defender who was imprisoned for harming no one while being shot at by an imperial wizard of the KKK—on a day when white lawlessness flaunted itself in a way our country hadn't seen in decades while police looked on passively.

Just feet away from the person holding up a sign pressed against the jail glass, the lawyer for the woman in a wheelchair remained locked outside of the jail by the magistrate.

But here the crowd was, refusing separation, defying walls and bars and locks, insisting on community.

Behind all the splashy news coverage about Charlottesville were people who held each other close, cooked meals for each other, comforted each other when tears flowed, showed up at each other's court dates, burned dry Christmas trees at bonfires together, stared off into the distance together, sipped drinks downtown together. The movements were held together by friendships and neighborliness, by cradling each other's fears and joys with more hands than our own. This was, as Zy Bryant put it, our "blooming in the trenches." The trench remained, but people became manna to each other at its bottom.

When I reflect on that prolonged, continuing struggle I am not only taken back to the headlining violence but also to lesser known scenes like the one that ended in that jail parking lot, where a crowd milled about, smoking cigarettes and laughing and raging and waving lights together in the early morning hours of another bad day we turned into a celebration. And when the jail would finally release them one by one, we formed a human tunnel right at the door for them to run or wheel through, cheering and thanking and high-fiving and keeping our sagging eyelids open.

But before those festivities my curiosity got the best of me. I walked up to the woman holding her sign high up against the glass doors on the off chance that someone in handcuffs could see through the magistrate's office and the locked visitor's area. I noticed, for the first time, that she was on her tiptoes.

When I read theologians talking about solidarity, I think of her, and the way she considered herself as part of a solid whole with those inside. Their suffering was also hers. It was important to her that they might see her message on the paper, that they might be reminded that they are part of a body, not disconnected, not left alone—despite the state's best efforts to separate everyone with their bars and windows and locked doors. "Hey," I said to this respected community leader, "I gotta know what you've been holding up all this time."

As far as I knew, it was the first time she'd lowered both her hands for hours. She showed me a fiercely simple, sacred text. Her tiptoes and outstretched fingers made it another kind of makeshift writing on the wall, spelling out what sustains communities resisting fascism, foretelling the downfall of oppressors as surely as God's emissary hand in Daniel 5. She held the markings in front of me, which read in underlined capital letters that filled the page, WE LOVE YOU.

7

Of Sacred Offensives, Destructive Prayer, and Our Lady of Anti-Fascism

*The church cannot seriously consider retreat as an option,
because its very existence is affirmed and reaffirmed only as
it demonstrates to all what Christian existence is all about
in the world. There is no place for sheltered piety. Who can
"pray" when all hell has broken loose and human existence
is being trampled underfoot by evil forces? Prayer takes on
new meaning. It has nothing to do with those Bible verses
that rulers utter before eating their steaks, in order to remind
themselves that they are religious and have not mistreated
anybody. Who can thank God for food when we know that our
[kin] are starving as we dine like kings?*

—JAMES CONE[1]

A SURVEY OF HOW churches behaved among anti-fascist movements in the 1930s notes that despite opposing the rise of fascism in principle, the church's discomfort with communism mostly kept them from doing anything practical about it. In a summary that helps explain how the US bishops could produce a document like *Open Wide Our Hearts*, it concluded that "Christian anti-fascism seemed to attempt to steer a course between

---

1. Cone, A Black Theology of Liberation, 133.

143

fascism and activism, and thus became caught between the two."[2] Further, a wide survey of preaching during the Third Reich from only the Confessing Church, an organization created explicitly in dissent against the Nazis trying to consolidate all Protestant churches, found that 12 percent of sermons opposed Nazism. Meaning 88 percent did not. "Most focus on a clear exposition of a biblical text and a reflection on its significance for the Christian life, without any political or social commentary whatsoever." Of the vast minority that opposed the Nazis, most did so because of the persecution of *Christians* rather than Jews. Only 2.5 percent of the sermons opposed the Nazis because of reasons having to do with the Jewish people, and of those, only half are known to have been delivered in Germany.[3]

Moreover, pastors rarely specified the political realities around them. "The sermons do not offer a sustained attack on the Nazi state, National Socialism, or the regime's policies," the studies found. "We do not find any calls for Germans to sabotage or otherwise fight against the police state. Nor are there any sermons that call for organized and united action against the state."[4] They instead offer criticism quickly during theological reflections, fitting in with the larger pattern of Confessing Church pastors failing to speak out against Hitler or the genocide against the Jews. They failed to confront the evil swallowing the world all around them when they came together to pray.

What all of this preaching missed, of course, is their Christ, who the state found such a disturbance as to kill, and who was a Jew, called rabbi in the Scriptures. These churches failed to recognize along with James Cone that "when all hell has broken loose," prayer must take on a new meaning. And because Christianity is far more visible today within fascist movements than among those fighting fascism, we must ask why most American churches have also adopted nearly total ecclesial inaction amid the fascist creep.

In the face of what Catholic theologian Shawn Copeland calls "empire's sacrilegious antiliturgy . . . standing in silence before war and death, incarceration and torture, rape and queer-bashing, pain and disease, abuse of power," Christians need to enact the kind of liturgical confrontation evident in Traci Blackmon's sermon on David and Goliath, which specifically names evils like white supremacy and the Klan and ties them to the biblical

2. Lawson, "Christian Anti-Fascism," 139.

3. Skiles, "Protests From the Pulpit," 4, 17.

4. Skiles, "Protests From the Pulpit," 21.

imagination. (Though unlike the response that night, they also need to process as church into the places that Nazism would claim, especially when summoned by vulnerable people.) The type of specificity and confrontation modeled by Reverends Blackmon, Smash, Sekou, and Wispelwey deconstructs idolatrous anti-sacraments at the center of these antiliturgies.

This avoids a kind of "sacramental consumerism," which moral theologian Marcus Mescher says "reduces liturgical participation to reception without responsibility."[5] In fusing social responsibility and liturgy, it blesses the work of justice as sacred and consecrates anti-racist work as eucharistic. By doing so in public, this kind of liturgy also destabilizes public consciousness, banishing status quo sacramentalism that functions to uphold and bless violent and idolatrous situations by proclaiming God's life in the alleys and city halls, in the face of evils. It follows the path of Jesus, who took his life with God out into the streets, answering Blackmon's question, "Where have all the prophets gone?" by offering up its own participants.

Pastor and activist Bill Wylie-Kellermann names these responses "liturgical direct actions," outgrowths of Catholic Workers resisting New York's air-raid defense drills in the late 1950s and early 1960s.[6] When the entire city's populace was mandated to seek shelter as a form of practice for getting hit with a nuclear bomb, they remained in a public park, defying the city ordinance as an act of remaining faithful to God rather than the nuclear state. They were arrested several years in a row until the movement took on such numbers that it shut down the annual exercise.

These kinds of actions—from the Catonsville Nine to the many pourings of blood at the Pentagon organized by Jonah House and the plowshares actions that began in 1980—often get interpreted as religious kinds of civil disobedience. But with today's anti-fascists rejecting civility as a virtue and naming it as a weapon that powers use to control dissent, the very idea of "civil disobedience" gets called into question. What society calls civil is said to be by definition unthreatening to power. Yet the fanatical outrage from many white communities in response to the civil rights movement's "civil disobedience," along with the state's response of encouraging Dr. King to commit suicide, discussing internally how he needs to be "neutralized,"

5. Mescher, "Liturgy as Power-Sharing," 46.

6. Wylie-Kellermann, *Seasons of Faith and Conscience*, 104.

and in all likelihood playing a role in his murder, suggests that either civil disobedience actually can be a threat to the state or that what was threatening in that movement might better be understood with different language.

Wylie-Kellermann's "liturgical direct action" helps name many of the civil rights campaigns anew, flipping the referent from whether people disobey in a manner acceptable to authorities to whether they do so in collective prayer. (In this, his phrase functions alongside Francine du Plessix Gray's 1970 use of "divine disobedience."[7]) It also describes what Congregate Charlottesville was up to in response to Unite the Right in 2017, preparing to confront both the state and fascist groups, acting directly to sabotage their riot. And it did so *as a people of faith*, singing psalms, willing to be broken to sustain others. It was too aggressive an action even for anti-racist pastors who came from out of town to join in resisting white supremacists, many of whom decided to go pray in another park rather than block and frustrate the proceedings.

Yet a different phrase is needed to describe not just religious bodies acting subversively but also holy inbreakings through people who are secular or even hostile to religion, as well as those who define their corporate rituals as ceremony rather than liturgy, a word laden with Christian overtones. How to talk inclusively about anti-racists doing godly work by tagging Confederate statues, Lakota-led ceremonial resistance to the Dakota Access Pipeline, as well as Christian actions like the Catonsville Nine or illegal church processions during the civil rights movement?

Rather than civil disobedience, these actions ring as *sacred offensives*. Disobedience indicates a saying "no," a reacting negatively or refusing to do something. Yet these actions embodied more, displaying an aggressive seizing of initiatives. They were offensive in the same way of the garbage offensive of the Young Lords, who responded to white sanitation workers refusing to collect trash in Puerto Rican Harlem by bringing it to their neighborhoods and burning it in the streets.[8] But they're also offensive in the way of something that breaks social mores, that offends "respectable" people, that breaches the boundaries of civility, like the Kings Bay Plowshares pouring blood at a naval base. (Many Americans don't much mind the presence of nuclear weapons, but take offense if someone pours blood to signify what they are constructed for.) Sacred offensives are attacks from

7. Gray, *Divine Disobedience.*
8. For a full account of the trash offensive, see Fernández, *Young Lords.*

a holy space, whether performed in the name of religious assumptions or not.

Our problem is civil obedience. Our problem is the numbers of people all over the world who have obeyed the dictates of the leaders of their government and have gone to war, and millions have been killed because of this obedience . . . Our problem is that people are obedient all over the world, in the face of poverty and starvation and stupidity, and war and cruelty. Our problem is that people are obedient while the jails are full of petty thieves, and all the while the grand thieves are running the country. That's our problem.

—Howard Zinn[9]

In Lewis Perry's history of civil disobedience in the US, he finds the draft-board raids an instructive transgression of this kind of civility. Picketing with signs and fliers, marching, and sit-ins were legible to a nonviolent standard that stretched back to Gandhi's *satyagraha* campaigns, even if met with rage, incarceration, and violence. But breaking into (usually) the state's space, stealing its property while (if necessary) preventing its workers from stopping the theft, and destroying it seemed to be of another category altogether. Some members of the Catonsville Nine, like Mary Moylan and the Berrigan brothers, went underground rather than report for prison, violating another standard practice of submitting to legal ramifications. Not only did the act itself breach "the line between civil-respectable and violent-illegitimate forms of protest," Perry said, but "taking flight violated traditional definitions of civil disobedience in which willingness to accept punishment signifies respect for the civil order."[10] Dorothy Day, who once summarized the Catholic Worker approach as "we plead guilty and we don't take bail," wouldn't embrace the action (which included a public court defense) for these reasons. Thomas Merton, another luminary of the

9. Zinn, *Zinn Reader*, 405.

10. Perry, *Civil Disobedience*, 311, 269.

Catholic Left, expressed concern that its violence towards property would soon turn to violence against people.

Despite their differences, sacred offensive names what the Catonsville Nine (and draft-board raids more generally) and civil disobedience in the Gandhian and Catholic Worker traditions share in common. Looking to Scripture, killing the Egyptian enslavers when they pursued the Israelites was understood by biblical authors to be a sacred act of God, one that was most certainly an offensive that would likewise be interpreted as an *offensive* political model today. Yet in its aftermath it was celebrated in song by Moses and the prophet Miriam, who added instruments and dancing to the festivities. Exodus says she "took a tambourine in her hand, and all the women went out after her with tambourines and with dancing. And Miriam sang to them: 'Sing to God, who has triumphed gloriously; horse and rider God has thrown into the sea'" (15:21). This song thanking God for salvation by drowning the army would probably rankle many contemporaries if it were sung in response to a smaller-scale uprising of a similar kind, performed centuries later by Nat Turner. The assurance of livid responses are part of what makes these too sacred offensives.

Wylie-Kellermann sees in Miriam's song not just an individual prayer but corporate worship. "In its oldest form the exodus is already liturgy, a doxology on the lips of liberated slave women," he wrote. "It is a refrain to be danced, tambourines in hand. By it the God-given realm of freedom is celebrated and sung again to life in joy. The new 'world' is suggested, announced, envisioned, in the same refrain with the demise, God's unmaking, of the old."[11] And this unmaking of the old world, what Bryan Massingale called "destructive love," is inherent in all prayer, Wylie-Kellermann asserts, hoping with and to God for a transformation. Prayer inherently hopes for the ruin of present systems and ways of life in order to welcome the encroaching reign of God.

In a fascist creep Christians can learn from these traditions, from the exodus to the uprisings after George Floyd's murder, to understand what forms communal prayer can take. They can find, as Reverend Smash had, that the anti-fascist phrase ¡No pasaran!—that fascists cannot pass—is a Christian one too, and can be prayerfully enacted. Worship can take the offense, and offend, in a sacred manner. Recall that when Jesus drove the money lenders out of the temple, the synoptic gospels have him quoting Jeremiah on prayer to rebuke them. He asserts that the action was done

11. Wylie-Kellerman, *Seasons of Faith and Conscience*, 8.

in part to re-establish the right kind of prayer, one that doesn't exploit or oppress the outcast. The authorities responded, they tell us, by wanting to kill Jesus. His kind of prayer was, in both meanings, plentifully offensive.

When Sekou led the procession from the sunrise service to Unite the Right in 2017, many of the white supremacists had already arrived with their shields, helmets, sticks, and guns. The clergy countered their chants of "commie scum" and much uglier phrases by clapping and singing "Oh, Freedom," and "This Little Light of Mine." For half an hour or so, the Nazis and friends were too few to overpower our voices, so thrown off-balance by Sekou's ceremonial theatrics and being opposed by song that when we began praying aloud one by one down the line, they actually grew quiet and listened to those invoking the God of the oppressed to denounce their cause. This prayer was destabilizing, the sacred offensive had taken hold. They were ready to fight people but had no clue how to assault prayers and hymns. What good is a shield when, as Reverend Blackmon said, your enemy comes at you with love?

This was evident to anti-fascists who weren't with the clergy or wed to nonviolence. When an anonymous community defender that day was asked how they actually held their own against the fascists while vastly outnumbered and basically broke the alt-right for good that day, they answered, "The presence of counterprotestors with a personal commitment to nonviolence was important, I think." Because the fascist's aims were to look like victims of antifa, appear as friends of the police, and let the world see them win a physical battle, "all those wires got crossed in Charlottesville because of the diversity of their opposition." How to cultivate the image of a victim when unarmed clergy are singing across from you while you beat your armor for war? "By the time they figured out how to deal with one kind of counterprotestor, the situation had changed and they had to go back to square one. They had to think too hard. They didn't know if they were going to get punched or prayed at."[12]

This kind of prayer is quite literally a weapon, something to wield for a kind of attack. This is what distinguishes a sacred offensive from many contemporary (and false) interpretations of nonviolence or civil disobedience. "This isn't about violence versus nonviolence," the anonymous anti-fascist continued. "Some of the most courageous people I saw in Charlottesville were not throwing punches; they were dressing wounds, or praying, or standing solitary in front of a line of advancing riot cops. Those people

12. CrimethInc., "Squaring Off Against Fascism."

were all using the weapons at their disposal." That's how the clergy joined the community in trying to cut off the head of white supremacy. They acted nonviolently, with what Sekou for four weeks of training called "deep, abiding love." But it was part of a larger project with others, and the clergy didn't demand nonviolence from them as the price of collaboration in the offensive.

But what of private prayer, not performed on the streets? The times do not seem to call for private or contemplative approaches. Violence escalates, nights bring police tear gas and kettling of protestors, and increasingly unpredictable militia activity. But prayer of contemplative or hesychastic kinds are of utmost importance at this juncture, precisely because things are moving at such a frantic pace. This is partly for practical aims: it simply is helpful to be of clear mind, to root oneself deeply, to act and move in these chaotic times with the conscious awareness of being in communion with God and others, to walk with the knowledge that all people, no matter what boundaries they have crossed, are our dear kin, scientifically and theologically. But the value of prayer is not contained by whether it is "useful." Sacred consciousness is not just a means but a way of being Christians are called to cultivate, neither separable from nor collapsible into its social engagement.

The problem is that the most common understandings of prayer don't seem to be equipped to hold together both our relationship with God and the political emergencies around us. Apart from surveilling bedrooms and women's bodies, we appear to collectively lack the imagination to link what happens within the church to what happens outside of it. This can lead to an impatience with or even hostility to "traditional" forms of prayer. Consider this description from a writer in the process of converting to Catholicism, stunned by what she sees in a church:

> I stop and stare, never having studied a person deep in prayer
> before. She's down on the kneeler and her eyes are closed, and in
> the diffuse light with her head tipped slightly that way she looks
> beautiful, but I am impatient with this purely aesthetic judgment
> for it doesn't begin to capture what she seems. Then I see what
> makes her so unusual: her utter stillness. She has gone somewhere
> with someone she loves and they are conversing in private and she
> will have to haul herself back into this world when she is done.

If I leave right now, I think, I will have gotten what I came for, which is proof that people really do this, really live this way, with one foot in two realms. And the secret path is prayer, its worldly fruits the love and the goodness I so crave. Later, I will see this explained by the famous Indian Christian, Sadhu Sundar Singh: "Prayer is as important as breathing." Later, I will find the writings of Saint John Chrysostom: "Nothing is equal to prayer; for what is impossible it makes possible, what is difficult, easy." Now, however, I'm simply arrested by this stolen glimpse of a woman talking with God.[13]

This kind of prayer can seem utterly unproductive and entirely beside the point amid organized efforts to accelerate "racial holy war." But the need today is not to banish the kind of mystical prayer this saintly church figure has entered into but to connect her kneeler to the fascist creep. That kind of prayer is innately valuable, evidently beautiful and contagious according to the above description, but more Christians "will have to haul themselves back into this world" and bring that sacred realm they encounter in prayer into the terrible arena of increasing fascist violence. We can neither ignore that political reality nor Paul's call in 1 Thessalonians to "pray without ceasing." Engaging the world does not get in the way of contemplative prayer. Rather, it's the space from which praying people enter into contemplation. This means people will have to experiment with new forms for new times, changing with a changing world. And in this time of murderous orthodoxies, prayer must become adamantly unorthodox. In an era of rising fascism, prayer must become unabashedly anti-fascist. Every uprising against imperial ambitions and genocidal dreams looks back at us like the eyes of Christ on an icon, penetrating, challenging, inviting us not just to stare back but to commune, to partake, to taste and see.

Welcome to our worship series! Whether you're a Jesus freak or a recovering bishop or of no faith background at all, we invite you into this space. We locate ourselves within the Christian tradition of prophetic witness and radical resistance, discipling to the way of Jesus. Stand up, sit down, sing loudly, hum, engage silently, play with children, sleep—however you feel called to participate today is the way we embrace your presence.

13. Huston, "Matrimony," 151.

This was the message atop each liturgy booklet of the Advent and Lent series put on by a Charlottesville house church called Charis, Greek for "grace." Dissatisfied with how most local Christian communities failed to respond to the Summer of Hate in 2017, the group put on its own services in the church situated on its eight acres out in the woods. They had started only a few years before as a community of ecological discipleship, but quickly became a praying side of the town's anti-fascist movement.

While its founder, Grace Aheron, has been called an "Episcopal powerhouse" by media and a "people weaver" by friends, she describes herself as a multiracial queer femme from Roanoke, Virginia.[14] She graduated from University of Virginia and worked as a youth minister, organizing for environmental and gender justice through the Episcopal Church. In 2014, she got in touch with a local reverend acting as vicar to two church properties that had combined congregations, leaving one vacant. Grace saw in the empty structure an opportunity for starting "communities of resistance and prayer, akin to Catholic Worker houses, for young people." Already home to deer, foxes, bears, poplar and hickory trees, a graveyard, remnants of stone walls from time past, and all types of birds, the vicarage became host to people looking to work with and for the land from within the Christian tradition. "We wrote a rule of life together and settled on the centerpiece," she recounted: "What might it mean in this place and in this time together to follow Jesus with our whole lives? Our ministry together took shape around this question."[15]

After helping to start a feminary that connected people seeking "a radical feminist space where we could study scripture, history, and bible,"[16] by early 2016 Grace had helped found the local chapter of Showing Up for Racial Justice, a group dedicated to organizing white people in antiracist work, and they began holding leadership meetings at Charis. Activists in town had started getting used to these kinds of Christians, and people in the pews on Sundays were warming up to Charis' invites to protest or contribute toward groups they otherwise wouldn't have known about. "The more we opened our doors to events, people, and organizations, the more demand appeared," Grace said. "A vocation of hospitality began to emerge." Not only were they doing eco-liturgies each solstice and equinox in their

14. Sowder, "Episcopal-Supported Intentional Community;" Lindsey Leahy, https://creativemornings.com/talks/grace-aheron/1.

15. Aheron, "Listening to the Land," 188–89.

16. Aheron, "Introducing: The Feminary."

surrounding woods, but the vicarage and its church became host to anti-fascists planning to oppose a more visible form of white supremacy in town after Zy Bryant brought the issue of Confederate statues to the fore. Grace describes how Charis had developed by that time:

> We were regularly worshipping with other Christian leaning activists in town. We had learned to plan and lead actions of civil disobedience with love and rigor. We were building friendships and community in the streets and on front porches. We got feedback about whatever ways our different privileges showed up, had moments of fear and recoil, and regrounded and recommitted to our work. We learned and called on the names of ancestors who came before us—Dan and Phil Berrigan, Dorothy Day, Anne Braden, Bayard Rustin. It was all very new. Oftentimes we looked around saying, "Who are we to be doing these things?" but the question then turned to, "Who, if not us?" We read the prophets who were also afraid, yet convicted. We found comfort in words from our elders, like those from Dan Berrigan writing to his brother: "I am being led in the damnedest directions; as usual, without any roadmap except that of good friends."
>
> One evening during a community meeting, after opening our time together with silence, Taizé chants, and cracking a six-pack of beers, I looked at the meeting agenda: "1) Garden watering rota, 2) Grant application for basement hospitality expansion, 3) Maundy Thursday vigil at the police station—ask the church, 4) Ice cream—grocery staple or no?" And I thought, *I think this is it. I think this is who this place wanted us to be.*[17]

As the Summer of Hate approached in 2017, Charis played the role of organizing hub, refuge for people in need of physical safety or emotional respite, space for creative liturgy, weekly prayer, or pot-lucks, playground for children, late-night communal firepit, and connective tissue for a town under extreme stress. Sensing that many felt the need to do something—anything—in the palpable dread building up with the summer heat, Grace turned to a tradition from her ancestors, some of whom survived America's Japanese internment camps during World War II. That tradition said if you fold a thousand paper cranes, you are granted a wish. She invited people to fold origami cranes under the wish of eradicating white supremacy. They

17. Aheron, "Listening to the Land," 190.

made rainbow garlands with over 1,400 of them to fly over the July 8th KKK rally. (They later hung over their prayer spaces where they lived as well as around town during events.) When people would see them and say, "Oh, this is about peace right?" she would answer, "No, it's about fighting white supremacy," and each individual crane had inscribed on it one way its creator pledged to carry out that fight.

This action is typical of Grace, who insists that while she's not a standard artist she counts herself among "the creatives" because community building is an act of creation. The way she understands that work informs the kind of prayer that suffused the movement in Charlottesville. "An integral and completely necessary and complementary part of the creative act is a tearing down," she said in 2018, as Charlottesville braced for more violence two days before the anniversary of Unite the Right. "The creative act of building community is a tearing down . . . a destruction of the structures and the world that keep people from being free."[18] Like a volcano—a metaphor she used in honor of her ancestors in Hawaii—that simultaneously creates and eviscerates as two necessary parts of the same act, so with the eruption of flourishing community.

This "creative-destructive work," much in line with Reverend Smash's notion of deconstruction, took many forms with Charis. They dropped banners in public spaces and held them in public officials' faces. They sang outside courthouses, the police station, and city hall. Sometimes it was centering meditation for those under duress, sometimes building giant puppets for protests and street theater. It even manifested as a pop-up sparkly nail section at protests, "because sometimes people just need a little razzle-dazzle while you're out there chanting and singing," she observed. But all these forms held in common a "creative disturbance" that is central to protest. Because all direct action is about power and refusing to wait for a middle party to come along and save everyone, it insists on attacking unjust power as community. She held up the example of the Lakota in Standing Rock, where Grace and others in Charis (including Reverend Smash) had gone to join the movement against the Dakota Access Pipeline in 2016. She said the Lakota modeled how direct action crystalizes what needs creating and what needs destroying.

As with the biblical stories of exodus, Jesus driving out the money lenders, and the writing on the wall, Grace knew that sacred offensives entailed

18. This quote and those following from the talk can all be found at https://creativemornings.com/talks/grace-aheron/1.

deconstructing, razing, and (as her friend's name indicated) smashing. The prayers of Charis were inseparable from both contemplation and their opposition to the Klan and Nazis, to the civil status quo that upheld more overt white supremacy. They knew that to disrupt a politician's event with a banner is to help destroy the illusion that civil proceedings must be left to work their violence, whether it be a jail board meeting or a Nazi "rally." They knew that what Shawn Copeland called anti-liturgies couldn't be left alone to do their damage. They engaged in the labor of negating evil as part and parcel of planting peace, and the land of Charis itself stood as a contrast to what they fought. Grace called it "a demonstration plot for the world we want to live in," as well as "a community-building offering on the other side of what we're destroying." They held free herbalism classes, taught children to gather eggs from the chickens, and gave space and resources for collective art. People of all kinds, including very un-religious types, found themselves gravitating toward and embraced by the community. "When you build irresistible communities," Grace summarized, "that's how you draw people into this creative-destructive work."

I can feel the world asking me:
Do you see this, woman?

And me back:
Do you see this woman?

—Grace Aheron[19]

Charis responded to Unite the Right in various ways. Liturgically, they hosted a series of Advent services in their church, open to the public, called "Dwelling in the Darkness," followed by a Lenten series called "Comfort into Discomfort." Some biblical readings from the lectionary were kept, some substituted out for poems of mentors or readings from ancestors like Grace Lee Boggs or Howard Thurman. They listed the usual names in the litany of prophets but also invited into the space people like Berta Cáceres,

19. Aheron, "Collecting Healing."

Sylvia Rivera, Malcolm X, Crazy Horse, and Marsha P. Johnson. Unlike many churches in town, they brought obvious political conversations right into the sanctuary.

When they prepared the space they took the dusty American flag away from the altar (and deep into a closet), replacing it with a ribboned web to weave their written prayers into a physical structure. They rearranged the pews so people could face each other and meditated on questions like, *What standard did Jesus set regarding comfort in the garden of Gethsemane? When was the last time you grew spiritually, physically, mentally, or morally without discomfort? How does your comfort appear from the perspective of those, as Thurman says, with their backs against the wall?* Children, young adults, and community elders sang together to harp, guitar, or percussions, and prayers were tailored to grappling with what had happened that summer and what lay ahead. To the refrain of "God, hear us repent," for example, they offered Advent admissions like: *God of liberation, you abhor racial oppression from Standing Rock and Palestine to Flint and Charlottesville—we repent of white supremacy and its pacifying privilege; Sophia God, men have fashioned idols of themselves—we repent of patriarchy and its wreckage;* and *God who was rejected by the darkness, you came queerly among us and defied social standards—we repent of straight and cis hegemony, and its need for normativity.*

Charis also responded by becoming host to trans women from the Central American caravan that had wound its way up through Mexico. Grace fundraised to secure their release from ICE detention, transport them to Charlottesville, and renovate the vicarage to double its residency while they waited for asylum. It had already served as a makeshift home for people in need of short-term (and sometimes extended) housing for whatever reason, and now the wider community pulled together to arrange for a host of medical, immigration, and social appointments for its new *amigas.* These newly needed works of mercy drew the house church even closer to the vision Grace initially had of a Catholic Worker for young folks, nurtured by its close and constant relationships to Casa Alma and Little Flower, the two Catholic Worker communities nearby.

The fusion of prayer fit for a kneeler, mystical consciousness, and antifascist political commitment that Grace herself and Charis more broadly embodied can be glimpsed in their garden-planting process the month after Unite the Right, in September 2017. They prepared an area just outside their front door, at the top of a grassy slope framed by forest on both sides.

They ordered 450 pounds of burlap-wrapped mulch, soil, and compost to create a medicinal garden that imitated the local woodland ecosystem. For several weekends, community friends still traumatized from the summer's brutality came to sink their fingers into dirt and start a physical growth they hoped would mirror the spiritual and emotional work ahead. It became a site of singing, of morning walks, ritualistic processions, even a Catholic confirmation ceremony under the light of the moon and the song of the crickets, toes wet with dew and crawling with bugs. Grace recalls stepping among the plants some mornings, naming them as she went, "willing them to grow, to live." And the way she recounts their planting ceremony and its meaning for that space shows one way this anti-fascist brand of prayer arose in Charlottesville:

> After hours of shoveling compost into mounds and nestling tiny plants into their new homes, we gathered together around the garden's central bed. Into it, we dug a deep hole through the layers of burlap, grass, and earth below, preparing to plant an Asian-American hybrid persimmon tree to be the garden's central presence. Standing in a circle, we paused, listening to the muttering of our hens down the hill, the rush of the highway farther away, the gentle cracking and creaking of the second-growth poplar forest around us. We pulled old newspapers from our back pockets and one by one placed them into the hole. The headlines—future soil for our garden—shouted up at us from their resting place: *one dead, nineteen injured after car plows into protesters. Trump condemns hatred "on many sides" in Charlottesville. Deadly Charlottesville car attack. Three dead, dozens hurt after Virginia white nationalist rally . . .* We sang and held each other and wondered if this was sacrament . . .
>
> Though the community lives on in new iterations, I still wonder if that first seed was planted with the intended purpose of building a place that could hold us through that traumatic summer. Charis was our little boat that carried us through those months of turmoil and fear, a sanctuary that offered itself to activists from not only Charlottesville but across the country. And that could be enough. The community was not a temporary project or a task force, but a spiritual being who we came to know and who became our ally for a season. We laid the headlines down into the earth, awaiting the compost resurrection that would come in the spring, enacting the call that death would not have the last word over us either, so that we could be free to let the angel of Charis compost too, to be reborn again in some new way.[20]

20. Aheron, "Listening to the Land," 187–88, 193.

In 2018, anti-racists in Charlottesville reported seeing Marian apparitions. Amid the mass uprisings in the aftermath of George Floyd's murder, a curious kind of Mary revealed herself downtown. She looked suspiciously political, radical, even anti-fascist as she watched over their rage and love. Over time, she appeared elsewhere, overseeing a living room meeting of subversives, adorning a little girl's bedroom wall, blessing the typewriter on an adult's desk—who knows where else?

She came to be known as Our Lady of Anti-fascism, made manifest through the hands of local musician, writer, and artist Ramona Martinez. Since her image seemed dense with meaning for faith and prayer in the fascist creep, I set out to learn a bit more about this mysterious Madonna.

FIGURE 10

Our Lady of Anti-fascism, Ramona Martinez

A MICRO-INTERVIEW WITH MUSICIAN AND ARTIST RAMONA MARTINEZ

Mary's halo incorporates the three arrows signifying anti-fascism. Why?

The whole thing has various symbols in it. The red, white, and black color scheme signifies anti-fascism. The halo is the symbol for the Iron Front, such a well-known anti-fascist symbol that I thought it was obvious. The black mask. The roses are there for "bread and roses," socialism. Also, Mystical Rose is one of her titles, and there's often the smell of roses in apparitions. I think also of the folk saint Teresa Urrea in Mexico, who smelled like roses.

I didn't really think about it too much, she kind of popped into my head fully formed. I thought, "Oh my God, I have been given a divine transmission."

You mentioned this Mary is masked. Is she black bloc?

Yeah! It's a nod to that, at least. Her hands being open is very important, because the black mask might make you think she's a violent anti-fascist—and no shade to them at all. But her arms are open because anti-fascism is about love and openness and acceptance at the end of the day. It's the ideology of non-oppression. There's something important to me about how there are so many iterations of Mary where she's an out-and-out warrior. The Virgin of Guadalupe, some say she carries a machete. Our Lady of Sorrows has knives, and she's protective because of what Christ went through. I think it's good to have her as an icon of resistance.

Maybe she's ready for black bloc action and ready to open her arms to whoever needs help or aid. Maybe anti-fascist Mary has openness to both kinds of resistance. It's hard—I don't want to come down necessarily one way or the other. I don't want to put words in Mary's mouth. Here's the thing, everything in the universe is paradox. It's not this or that, it's this and that. Even the Virgin Mary, she's not one-dimensional. She holds multitudes. She's more of a paradox than people give her credit for. Virginal purity, yet the strength of a woman who truly lived and suffered, and in that sense no virgin at all.

Exorcists have said that demons fear the name of Mary above all else. Her name makes them run for the hills. She's known as the Empress of Hell, and demons are terrified of her.

So what has this Mary been up to, and where has she been?

The original painting is in my living room, done with acrylic and black ink. I came up with the image around December of 2019, and finished the following March. Mary of Anti-fascism was put up downtown that June. Just around the time when Trump was talking about antifa, after George Floyd was killed. I knew there would be big protests, and I wanted to get her out into the community in a prominent way. A talisman of protection, really, to watch over the people on the street. Also to show people that Mary was on our side. That we had her blessing, that we were righteous in our cause, as anti-fascists. Even the people who didn't know what it meant, it was for them too. I thought it would be up for two days, maybe. But it was up for two weeks! Miraculous. It was on Water St. and Second [two blocks from the scene of the car attack at Unite the Right]. I projected it into a big piece of butcher paper and did it with sharpies.

FIGURE 11

**Our Lady of Anti-fascism graces downtown Charlottesville, June 2020
(Photo by Ramona Martinez)**

What it did for my journey as an artist was as pressing, to me. That transmission came in so strong that I think, in retrospect, that Mary in all her different forms became my artistic inspiration for the next two years. I pretty much just made iconography.[21]

You know, you mentioned that in Daniel 5, only the oppressed could read the writing on the wall. Mary is also for the downtrodden. In her apparitions, she appears to the most humble of us. The only people who can see her are the people she chooses to show herself to. Like with Our Lady of Lourdes and Fatima, she appears to children. Sometimes outside observers think they're basically talking to nobody because they can't see her. They just can't see her.

When Rabbi Abraham Joshua Heschel was asked if he had time to pray while marching with the civil rights movement, he famously said he was praying with his feet. Charlottesville drew on that quote in smoky, late-night porch planning sessions as well as public speeches at a university.[22] The town had learned what it meant to pray with their feet, their crossed arms, their hands held as a barrier against white supremacists, their dancing legs, even their butts that sometimes sat and refused to move when ordered to stand and make room for Nazis.

Heschel also had a lesser-known saying on prayer taken up in town. Shortly before he died, he declared passionately in a televised interview that "The primary purpose of prayer is not to make requests. The primary purpose of prayer is to praise! To sing! To chant! Because the essence of prayer is a song, and [people] cannot live without a song."[23] If Charis instilled in the wider movement a pulse of prayer, they did so primarily through song. None of their events, whether as spontaneous as a two-person bonfire or scheduled as a public church service, seemed to pass without singing. Hymns, resistance songs, prayers, guitar sing-alongs accompanied with incense, round-robins, Taizé chants, call-and-responses, and other impromptu musical surprises blessed the sonic space regularly.

21. Martinez's works can be found at http://ramonamartinez.net.

22. See, for example, University of Virginia's Religion, Race, & Democracy Lab, "Praying With Our Feet: Religious Activists Remember the Unite the Right Rally in Charlottesville," August 12, 2020, https://religionlab.virginia.edu/events/praying-with-our-feet-religious-activists-remember-the-unite-the-right-rally-in-charlottesville/. The phrase was also a recurring invocation of Reverend Seth Wispelwey.

23. Heschel, *NBC* interview from 1972, https://www.youtube.com/watch?v=FEXK9xcRCho.

They brought these songs to protests, vigils, and celebrations. I remember emerging from court once after a community member had just been sentenced to jail. No one was surprised but those of us exiting the doors felt deflated. Between the sound of passing cars, though, I recognized the voice of professional musician and beloved Charis resident Claire Hitchins. She and Grace were standing in the street, leading a crowd on the sidewalk in a song anti-apartheid activists sang in South Africa when someone was sent to jail. Crossing that metal detector and seeing all kinds of friends and strangers singing together, despite everything, the occasional car honking in support, was stepping into a festival of hope that had no legal or logical right to exist. The scene combined both of Heschel's insights on prayer, and what felt moments ago like defeat gave way as we lifted our voices, singing:

> Courage, my friend, you do not walk alone
> We will walk with you and sing your spirit home
> Courage, Charlottesville, you do not walk alone
> We will walk with you and sing your spirit home

FIGURE 12

Photo by Lindsey Leahy

Existence is Resistance

—*Writing on the wall, 2018*

After Unite the Right, people across nations made their own makeshift walls and wrote on them, expressing their solidarity with us. Like the woman outside the jail, standing on her tiptoes in case those inside could see her message that she loved them, so too these people worlds away created huge banners in case we could see them through the walls that pretended they could separate us. Many of them were dedicated to Heather Heyer, murdered because she refused to let her kin struggle against would-be killers alone. "From Greece to America," read a message with Heather's face in Athens, "crush the fascists." "Destroy White Supremacy," it said above Alberta Street in Portland, Oregon, "Rest in Power Heather." In a display rich with symbolism, projected letters on the side of DC's Newseum covered the large, etched text of the First Amendment with "HEATHER HEYER 1985–2017." Deep, crimson spray paint on a Paris wall read, "Heather Heyer Dans nos cœurs [in our hearts]." Signs to Charlottesville popped up in Bern, Switzerland; Bure, France; Copenhagen; Helsinki; Berlin; and elsewhere around the world.

Back home in Charlottesville, writings have taken up permanent residence on the very walls of Fourth and Water, where chalk messages spell out words today's Belshezzars do not understand. "It can happen again," "Love one another," "Hope is love + action," "Take down hate," "Love heals," "Black Lives Matter," and hundreds of other messages have stood on the walls, physical embodiments of the refusal to forget fascism, forget one another, forget our capacity to say yes to community in the face of everything.

These little resurrections don't wipe away history or absolve injustices, murder, or bloodshed. Heather is here but still gone, dead and yet alive. "Gone but not forgotten," the chalk on the brick reads. Those same walls that absorbed blood are now laden with love, brought by hands like the one in the book of Daniel, spelling out at once the doom of imperial power and its many idolatries as well as the refusal to be separated from their victims and survivors.

FIGURE 13

Photo by Lindsey Leahy

Fascists tried to reduce Heather to a corpse. But her mother, Susan Bro, told the fascists, "you just magnified her." Likewise, the Mothers of Murdered Anti-Fascists in France saw in her "this shining face, this strong and at the same time calm determination to refuse the unacceptable. Too much light, too much determination."[1] Neither reality can negate the other. Here, at what has since been renamed Heather Heyer Way and Water, death and life must, in a maddeningly inconclusive cycle, forever co-mingle.

But all this insistence on memory, on life amid death, on community amid horror, on various kinds of faith in the face of fascism and too much light in Heather's face—it all brings me back to Merton's epiphany at Fourth and Walnut in Louisville, the place where he saw everyone shining like the sun. I felt it had nothing to say amid the wreckage of Fourth and Water, but I still find myself returning to it, wrestling with its words. Beyond Merton's initial recognition of a human unity thicker than monastic enclosures, he continued exploring his connection with the strangers before him:

> At the center of our being is a point of nothingness which is untouched by sin and by illusion, a point of pure truth, a point or spark which belongs entirely to God, which is never at our disposal, from which God disposes of our lives, which is inaccessible to the fantasies of our own mind or the brutalities of our own will . . . It is like a pure diamond, blazing with the invisible light of heaven. It is in everybody, and if we could see it we would see these billions of points of light coming together in the face and blaze of a sun that would make all the . . . cruelty of life vanish completely . . . I have no program for this seeing. It is only given. But the gate of heaven is everywhere.[2]

Merton had people on errands in mind, not genocidal fascists. But his insistence that everyone has an untaintable truth in them draws me out from my Manichean hideaway, where we are good and they are bad in a fixed and final way. And yet. The graves of so many who have been murdered by fascists demand we fight cheap reconciliations, that we never skip straight to a vision of cruelty vanishing completely. I don't know what it means for these graveyards, for this intersection here with *this* particular

1. CrimethInc., "To the Charlottesville Anti-Fascists."
2. Merton, *Conjectures of a Guilty Bystander*, 158.

history, to be a gate to heaven. I am stretched between a hope that Merton is right—that there must be humanity beneath all the swastikas, must be pure diamonds blazing in everyone's core, however hidden—and a fierce fidelity to the slain as well as the living who really are in danger of being tortured or murdered by fascists who really are planning for it. Can we truly hold both at once?

It seems impossible to talk about heaven in a place where hell has broken in, so I find relief in the words of Emily Gorcenski. Speaking of the tendency to reduce Charlottesville to the date of August 12, 2017 and its terrorist attack, she countered, "I do know that we are people, not numbers; communities, not moments. As long as we don't forget that, then I am certain that no matter the cost, no matter the time, that the demons of fascism will be returned to hell once again."[3]

I'm not sure if Merton and Gorcenski are in tension or harmony with one another, if this place is a gate to heaven, a site where fascist demons go to hell, or both. But I don't want to let go of either vision. If that intersection is a national crossroads, it includes not just a terrorist attack but also the shrine of love and memory and resistance people have made of it since.

I have no program for this seeing, and we as a church and nation certainly don't either. But we have each other in this muddiness. From here, maybe, we can turn to communities bearing, in the words of Mothers of Murdered Anti-Fascists, too much light, too much determination, creating a society in which fascist violence is unimaginable instead of predictable. Maybe here we can learn from the new Daniels to read the writing on the wall or, as Grace and Smash and Sekou and so many from Portland to Charlottesville and everywhere between have done, to become it ourselves.

3. Gorcenski, "Did We Win?"

FIGURE 14

Photo by Lindsey Leahy

Acknowledgments

Inexpressible thanks to everyone in Charlottesville and elsewhere building a better world, often at extraordinary costs. Sometimes it's better not to name everyone, so I trust that you know my deep gratitude better than I could express by printing it here.

Thanks also to everyone who gave feedback on all or parts of this book, no matter how little, including Mimi Arbeit, Marjorie Corbman, Amanda Daloisio, Leah Donnella, Lisa Holsberg, and Anna Markowitz. And to the artists who made their work available: Ramona Martinez, Lindsey Leahy, Sarah Fuller, N. O. Bonzo, Ben Wildflower, Bunmi Collins, and Claire Payton.

To Jalane Schmidt for telling me to write this. To Jim Douglass, who helped convince me writing is part of my vocation; Bill Frankel-Streit, who has been more adamant than anyone that I keep writing; Sue Frankel-Streit, whose boundless hospitality helped sustain the writing; Meg Linehan, who kept me duty bound to finish; and Brandy Daniels & Bill Wylie-Kellermann, who helped make sure the writing got seen. And to Anna, who gave me an old typewriter, Fritz, so I could do this thing right.

To Rose Marie Berger for inviting me to write the original piece this book grew from, and Da'Shawn Mosley for enhancing it. To everyone who supported the *Sojourners* editors when it was proclaimed "inflammatory," "offensive," a source of "outrage," and something that "should not have been published" while briefly removed from the internet, especially Nichole Flores, who reached into the updo. And to Charlie Collier for editing this much longer version.

To all Catholics making the church less of a home to fascists by struggling against its patriarchy, white supremacy, and persecution of queer communities, especially Bryan Massingale and Jamie Manson.

To friends who accompanied this book while it materialized, including Jim Robinson, Marjorie Corbman, Vanessa Williams, Mary Kate Holman, Gregory Tucker, Jason Steidl, Eileen Markey, Amelia Marini, Paul McCullough, Heidi Kallen, Álvaro Rodriguez, Michael Avery, Geoff Gusoff, Jim Fisher, Martha Hennessy, and Carmen Trotta. And to the Catholic Worker communities who have been home to me along the way, including Little Flower, Casa Alma, Maryhouse, St. Joe's, and DC's Dorothy Day House, as well as Benincasa, Agape, Kings Bay Plowshares, and Green Willow Farm.

To Curtis Leighton, an undeserved pilgrimage partner across countries and decades, and Ina Yurena Zerr, for poking at old orthodoxies with me.

To all the students I've been in class with, especially those in UCLA's Religious Fascisms and Antifascisms, who helped refine these ideas and supported the book to the end—especially Zy.

To family, and to Anna for encouraging me throughout the whole process, and more.

Of course: to Reverends Smash, Seth Wispelwey, and Osagyefo Sekou, for making gospel specificity & goodness happen. And to all my Charis folks, for a hundred thousand things. What a ride so far.

Bibliography

Aheron, Grace. "Collecting Healing." *Radical Discipleship*, February 29, 2016. https://radicaldiscipleship.net/2016/02/29/collecting-healing/#more-4100.

———. "Introducing: The Feminary." *Radical Discipleship*, December 9, 2015. https://radicaldiscipleship.net/2015/12/09/introducing-the-feminary/.

———. "Listening to the Land: Eco-rooted Activism at the Charis Community in Charlottesville, Virginia." *Anglican Theological Review* 103.2 (2021) 186–95.

Alter, Robert. *The Hebrew Bible: A Translation with Commentary—Volume III, Ketuvim.* New York: Norton, 2018.

Antifa Nebraska. "Bennett Bressman, Nebraska Governor's Field Director." *Anti-Fascist Action Nebraska*, March 11, 2019. https://antifaneb.noblogs.org/post/2019/03/11/bennett-bressman-governors-state-field-director/.

Atwood, Sara. "'This List is Not Complete': Minnesota's Jewish Resistance to the Silver Legion of America, 1936–1940." *Minnesota History* 66.4 (2018/2019) 142–45.

Baars, Samantha. "Activists Arrested: Violence Erupts Outside Albemarle School Board Meeting." *C-Ville*, September 5–11, 2018, 10–12.

Batalion, Judy. *The Light of Days The Untold Story of Women Resistance Fighters in Hitler's Ghettos.* New York: HarperCollins, 2020.

———. "The Nazi-Fighting Women of the Jewish Resistance." *New York Times*, March 18, 2021. https://www.nytimes.com/2021/03/18/opinion/sunday/Jewish-women-Nazi-fighters.html.

Bates, Karen Grigsby. "When Civility Is Used as a Cudgel Against People of Color." *National Public Radio*, March 14, 2019. https://www.npr.org/sections/codeswitch/2019/03/14/700897826/when-civility-is-used-as-a-cudgel-against-people-of-color.

Beckett, Lois. "Charlottesville a Year On: 'We Can't Fix the Whole Nation. Hopefully We Can Fix Ourselves.'" *The Guardian*, August 4, 2018. https://www.theguardian.com/usnews/2018/aug/04/charlottesville-virginia-one-year-on-violence-far-right.

Bellew, Kathleen. *Bring the War Home: The White Power Movement and Paramilitary America.* Cambridge: Harvard University Press, 2019.

Berrigan, Daniel. *Daniel: Under the Siege of the Divine.* Farmington, PA: Plough, 1998.

Biko, Steve. *I Write What I Like: A Selection of His Writings.* London: Bowerdean, 1997.

Black Catholic Clergy Caucus. "A Statement of the Black Catholic Clergy Caucus, April 18, 1968." In *Black Theology: A Documentary History, 1966–1979,* edited by Gayraud S. Wilmore and James H. Cone, 322–32. Maryknoll, NY: Orbis, 1993.

Blassingame, John. *Slave Testimony: Two Centuries of Letters, Speeches, Interviews, and Autobiographies*. New Orleans: Louisiana State University Press, 1977.

Blower, David Benjamin. *Sympathy for Jonah: Reflections on Humiliation, Terror and the Politics of Enemy-Love*. Eugene, OR: Wipf & Stock, 2016.

Boorstein, Michelle. "A Horn-Wearing 'Shaman.' A Cowboy Evangelist. For Some, the Capitol Attack Was a Kind of Christian Revolt." *Washington Post*, July 6, 2021. https://www.washingtonpost.com/religion/2021/07/06/capitol-insurrection-trump-christian-nationalism-shaman/.

Branigin, Anne. "A Year After Unite the Right, Charlottesville Is Taking a Stand Against Media and 'Allies' Who Implicitly Support White Supremacy." *The Root*, August 9, 2018. https://www.theroot.com/a-year-after-unite-the-right-charlottesville-is-taking-1828223168.

Bray, Mark. *Antifa: The Anti-fascist Handbook*. Brooklyn: Melville, 2017.

Brossat, Alain, and Sylvia Klingberg. *Revolutionary Yiddishland: A History of Jewish Radicalism*. New York: Verso, 2016.

Brown, Emma. "Two Teens Charged with Hate Crime for Video Threatening Black Classmate with Noose, Gun." *The Washington Post*, April 11, 2016. https://www.washingtonpost.com/news/education/wp/2016/04/11/two-teens-charged-with-hate-crime-for-video-threatening-black-classmate-with-noose-gun/.

Bryant, Zyahna. *Reclaim. A Collection of Poetry and Essays*. Independently published, 2019.

Buber, Martin. *Pointing the Way: Collected Essays*. London: Humanities, 1990.

Byrne, Brendan. *A Costly Freedom: A Theological Reading of Mark's Gospel*. Collegeville, MN: Liturgical, 2008.

Caine-Conley, Britany. "God's Insistence: Responding to the Call and Call and Call, The Ordination Papers of Brittany Caine-Conley." June 2017. Unpublished.

———. "Jesus Was a Threat to Civility," *Sojourners*, June 29, 2018. https://sojo.net/articles/jesus-was-threat-civility.

———. "Procession of Protest." Sermon, April 9, 2017. Unpublished.

Caine-Conley, Brittany, and Seth Wispelwey. "Call to Clergy and Faith Leaders—Summer 2017." Summer 2017, Congregate Charlottesville. https://congregatecville.com/home.

Campbell, Andy. "Charlottesville Isn't Playing the Media's 'Both Sides' Game Anymore." *Huffington Post*, August 7, 2018. https://www.huffpost.com/entry/charlottesville-isnt-playing-the-medias-both-sides-game-anymore_n_5b63390ce4bob15abaa0e48b.

Cardenal, Ernesto. *The Gospel in Solentiname Vol. 2*. Maryknoll, NY: Orbis, 1978.

Césaire, Aimé. *Discourse on Colonialism*. New York: Monthly Review, 2001.

Cheri, Bishop Fernand. "Let the Church Roll On." Address given to the Conference of Major Superiors of Men, August 4, 2020. https://www.mostblessedsacrament.com/08082020.

Clifford, Richard J. *Psalms 73–150*. Nashville: Abingdon, 2003.

Collins, John J. *Daniel: A Commentary on the Book of Daniel*. Minneapolis: Fortress, 1994.

Cone, James. *A Black Theology of Liberation (Twentieth Anniversary Edition)*. Maryknoll, NY: Orbis, 2007.

———. *The Cross and the Lynching Tree*. Maryknoll, NY: Orbis, 2011.

Conger, Molly. Twitter, November 15, 2021. https://twitter.com/socialistdogmom/status/1460333996680921091.

Copeland, M. Shawn. "'The African American Catholic Hymnal' and the African American Spiritual." *U.S. Catholic Historian* 19.2 (2001) 67–82.

Cordero, Jonathan. "Challenging the Conventional Narrative: Telling the Truth about the California Missions." Lecture for the Los Angeles Catholic Worker's series "Reckoning With Our Mission Histories," January 30, 2022.

Courier Journal. "See It: Protesters take to the streets again for another Breonna Taylor protest." *Courier Journal*, May 29, 2020. https://www.courier-journal.com/picture-gallery/news/local/2020/05/29/breonna-taylor-protests-demonstrators-block-6th-and-jefferson-friday/5287717002/#slide:5289945002.

Cox, Karen. "Black Protesters Have Been Rallying Against Confederate Statues for Generations." *Smithsonian Magazine*, April 12, 2021. https://smithsonianmag.com/history/black-protestors-have-been-rallying-against-statues-generations-180977484/.

CrimethInc. "Squaring Off Against Fascism." *CrimethInc.*, September 4, 2017. https://crimethinc.com/2017/09/04/squaring-off-against-fascism-critical-reflections-from-the-front-lines-an-interview.

———. "To the Charlottesville Anti-Fascists: A Message from the Mothers of Murdered Anti-Fascists in France." *CrimethInc.*, August 10, 2018. https://crimethinc.com/2018/08/10/to-the-charlottesville-anti-fascists-a-message-from-the-mothers-of-murdered-anti-fascists-in-france.

Daniels, Brandy. "The Antifa Activist as Good Samaritan?" *Religion and Its Publics*, October 29, 2020. http://relpubs.as.virginia.edu/the-antifa-activist-as-the-good-samaritan-by-brandy-daniels/.

Davis, Cyprian. *Black Catholics in the United States*. New York: Herder & Herder, 1995.

DeConto, Jesse James. "Activist Who Took Down Confederate Flag Drew on Her Faith and on New Civil Rights Awakening." *Religion News Service*, July 12, 2015. https://religionnews.com/2015/07/12/activist-who-took-down-confederate-flag-drew-on-her-faith-and-on-new-civil-rights-awakening/.

DiLorenzo, Francis X. "Statement on Events Occurring in Charlottesville." August 12, 2017. https://richmonddiocese.org/bishop-francis-x-dilorenzo-statement-on-events-occurring-in-charlottesville/.

Dockter, Jake. "The Gospel Is Not a Neutral Term: An Interview with Rev. Sekou." *Medium*, October 24, 2014. https://medium.com/theology-of-ferguson/the-gospel-is-not-a-neutral-term-an-interview-with-rev-sekou-ae7990e66fe2.

Donahue, John R., and Daniel J. Harrington. *The Gospel of Mark*. Collegeville, MN: Liturgical. 2007.

Douglas Kelly Brown. *Resurrection Hope: A Future Where Black Lives Matter*. Maryknoll, NY: Orbis, 2021.

Du Bois, W. E. B. *Writings (Library of America No. 34)*. New York: Library of America, 1987.

Dunn, Richard. *A Tale of Two Plantations: Slave Life and Labor in Jamaica and Virginia*. Cambridge: Harvard University Press, 2014.

Dye, Aldona. "Why UVA Should Rename Alderman Library." *Virginia Mercury*, July 30, 2019. https://www.virginiamercury.com/2019/07/30/uva-should-rename-alderman-library/.

Economou, Allison. "Former Newport Beach Students Nazi Salute Around Swastika at High School Party." *New University*, March 22, 2019. https://newuniversity.

org/2019/03/22/former-newport-beach-students-nazi-salute-around-swastika-at-high-school-party/.

Editors. "The Faith-Led Counterprotest to White Nationalism in Charlottesville." *Sojourners*, August 12, 2017. https://sojo.net/articles/faith-led-counter-protest-white-nationalism-charlottesville.

Enck-Wanzer, Darrell. *The Young Lords: A Reader*. New York: NYU Press, 2010.

Entzminger, Brielle. "Speaking Out: UVA Prof Jalane Schmidt Offers Thoughts on Public Engagement, Defamation Lawsuit." *C'ville*, November 27, 2019. https://www.c-ville.com/speaking-out-uva-prof-jalane-schmidt-offers-thoughts-on-public-engagement-defamation-lawsuit.

Evans, Robert. "Woman Accused of Stealing Nancy Pelosi's Laptop Appears in Video Making Nazi Salute." *Bellingcat*, February 24, 2021. https://www.bellingcat.com/news/americas/2021/02/24/woman-accused-of-stealing-nancy-pelosis-laptop-appears-in-video-making-nazi-salute/.

Fernández, Johanna. *The Young Lords: A Radical History*. Chapel Hill: University of North Carolina Press, 2019.

Florer-Bixler, Melissa. *How to Have an Enemy: Righteous Anger & the Work of Peace*. Harissonburg, VA: Herald, 2021.

Fraga, Brian. "Thousands Call for Gomez to Apologize After Calling Protests Pseudo-Religions." *National Catholic Reporter*, November 12, 2021. https://www.ncronline.org/news/people/thousands-call-gomez-apologize-after-calling-protests-pseudo-religions.

Gafney, Wilda C. *Womanist Midrash: A Reintroduction to the Women of the Torah and the Throne*. Louisville: Westminster John Knox, 2017.

Gallagher, Charles R. *Nazis of Copley Square: The Forgotten Story of the Christian Front*. Cambridge: Harvard University Press, 2021.

Gandhi, M. K. *Non-Violent Resistance (Satyagraha)*. Mineola, NY: Dover, 2001.

Gelderloos, Peter. *How Nonviolence Protects the State*. Olympia: Detritus, 2018.

Gorcenski, Emily. "Did We Win?" August 9, 2022. https://emilygorcenski.com/post/did-we-win/.

———. *How Hate Sleeps*. https://howhatesleeps.com.

———. Twitter, August 11, 2017. https://twitter.com/EmilyGorcenski/status/896184638804119552.

Gordon, Bonnie. "On Listening." In *Charlottesville 2017: The Legacy of Race and Inequity*, edited by Louis P. Nelsen and Claudrena N. Harold, 154–62. Charlottesville: University of Virginia Press, 2018.

Gordon, Linda. *The Second Coming of the Klan: The Ku Klux Klan of the 1920s and the American Political Tradition*. New York: Liveright, 2017.

Gray, Francine du Plessix. *Divine Disobedience: Profiles in Catholic Radicalism*. New York: Vintage, 1971.

Greenstein, Melissa. "Slavery Opponent John Brown's Statues Hit Again by Vandals." *KSHB 41 Kansas City*, November 20, 2019. https://www.kshb.com/news/local-news/slavery-opponent-john-browns-statue-hit-again-by-vandals.

Greve, Joan E. "FBI Chief Calls Capitol Attack 'Domestic Terrorism' and Defends US Intelligence." *The Guardian*, March 2, 2021. https://www/theguardian.com/us-news/2021/mar/02/fbi-christopher-wray-capitol-attack-domestic-terrorism.

Grimes, Katie Walker. "'But Do the Lord Care?' Tupac Shakur as Theologian of the Crucified People." *Political Theology* 15.4 (2014) 326–52.

Gutiérrez, Gustavo. *A Theology of Liberation: History, Politics, Salvation (15th Anniversary Edition)*. Maryknoll, NY: Orbis, 2004.

The Harper Collins Study Bible, New Revised Standard Version. San Francisco: Harper One, 2006.

Hart, David Bentley. "On Christ's Rabble." *Commonweal*, September 26, 2017. https://www.commonwealmagazine.org/christs-rabble.

Hemmer, Nicole. "Episode 1: The Summer of Hate." *A12: The Story of Charlottesville*, https://millercenter.org/A12.

Horan, Dan. "When Will the US Bishops Address the Evil of Systemic Racism Head-On?" *National Catholic Reporter*, June 10, 2020. https://www.ncronline.org/news/opinion/faith-seeking-understanding/when-will-us-bishops-address-evil-systemic-racism-head.

Howe, Thomas A. *Daniel in the Preterists' Den: A Critical Look at Preterists Interpretations of Daniel*. Eugene, OR: Wipf & Stock, 2008.

Hurston, Zora Neale. *Moses, Man of the Mountain*. New York: Amistad, 2010.

Huston, Paula. "Matrimony." In *Signatures of Grace: Catholic Writers on the Sacraments*, edited by Thomas Grady and Paula Huston, 131–63. New York: Dutton, 2000.

Inchausti, Robert. *Subversive Orthodoxy: Outlaws, Revolutionaries, and Other Christians in Disguise*. Grand Rapids: Brazos, 2005.

Imperatori-Lee, Natalia. *Cuéntame: Narrative in the Ecclesial Present*. Maryknoll, NY: Orbis, 2018.

Jaffe, Sarah. "Faith and Freedom on the March in Charlottesville." *Bill Moyers*, August 14, 2017. https://billmoyers.com/story/faith-freedom-march-charlottesville/.

Jenkins, Jack. *American Prophets: The Religious Roots of Progressive Politics and the Ongoing Fight for the Soul of the Country*. New York: HarperCollins, 2020.

Jewett, Christina, and Shefali Luthra. "Immigrant Toddlers Ordered to Appear in Court Alone." *The Texas Tribune*, June 27, 2018. https://www.texastribune.org/2018/06/27/immigrant-toddlers-ordered-appear-court-alone/.

Jilani, Zaid. "Elizabeth Warren Says Campus Free Speech Means No Censorship or Violence." *The Intercept*, October 27, 2017. https://theintercept.com/2017/10/27/elizabeth-warren-says-campus-free-speech-means-no-censorship-or-violence/.

Kass, John. "The Lies We Were Told about Who Would Silence Free Speech." *The Chicago Tribune*, April 28, 2017. https://www.chicagotribune.com/columns/john-kass/ct-free-speech-kass-0430-20170428-column.html.

Kelly, Mike. "From a Catholic Prep School to Nazism: The Strange Journey of Rinaldo Nizzaro." *North Jersey*, March 9, 2020. https://www.northjersey.com/story/news/columnists/mike-kelly/2020/03/09/mystery-how-catholic-prep-school-grad-turned-nazism/4977284002/.

Kim, Brittany, and Charlie Trimm. "Yahweh the Dragon: Exploring a Neglected Biblical Metaphor for the Divine Warrior and the Translation of '*Ap*." *The Bible Translator* 65.2 (2014) 165–84.

Kitts, Margo. "Proud Boys, Nationalism, and Religion." *Journal of Religion and Violence*, 9.1 (2021) 12–32.

Kotzé, Manitza. "An Interpretation of Daniel 1:8–16." In *Passion, Persecution, and Epiphany in Early Jewish Literature*, edited by Nicholas Peter Legh Allen, Pierre Jordan, and József Zsengellér, 126–38. Philadelphia: Routledge, 2020.

Kurlansky, Mark. *Non-Violence: The History of a Dangerous Idea*. New York: Modern Library, 2008.

"Lacrosse Player Didn't Know about Swastika on His Leg, School Says." *East Bay Times*, May 26, 2022, https://www.eastbaytimes.com/2022/05/26/lacrosse-player-didnt-know-about-swastika-on-his-leg-school-says-coach-resigns-after-uproar/.

Lavin, Talia. *Culture Warlords: My Journey into the Dark Web of White Supremacy*. New York: Hachette, 2020.

———. "Foreword: On the Uses and Manifestations of Antifascism." In *¡No Pasaran! Antifascist Dispatches from a World in Crisis,* edited by Shane Burley, 1–3. Chico, CA: AK, 2022.

Lawson, Tom. "Christian Anti-Fascism." In *Varieties of Anti-Fascism: Britain in the Interwar Period*, edited by Nigel Copsey and Andrzej Olechnowicz, 119–39. London: Palgrave Macmillan, 2010.

Levi, Primo. "Primo Levi's Heartbreaking, Heroic Answers to the Most Common Questions He Was Asked About 'Survival in Auschwitz." *The New Republic*, February 16, 1986. https://newrepublic.com/article/119959/interview-primo-levi-survival-auschwitz.

Lind, Dara. "Nazi Slogans and Violence at a Right-Wing March in Charlottesville on Friday Night." *Vox*, August 12, 2017. https://www.vox.com/2017/8/12/16138132/charlottesville-rally-brawl-nazi.

Marchin, Tim. "High-Ranking Republican Cheney Calls GOP Representative Steve King's Comments 'Racist' and 'Abhorrent.'" *Newsweek*, January 10, 2019. https://www.newsweek.com/high-ranking-republican-cheney-steve-king-racist-gop-abhorrent-white-1287439.

Martinez, Ramona. http://ramonamartinez.net.

Massingale, Bryan. "The Assumptions of White Privilege and What We Can Do about It." *National Catholic Reporter*, June 1, 2020. https://www.ncronline.org/news/opinion/assumptions-white-privilege-and-what-we-can-do-about-it.

———. *Racial Justice and the Catholic Church*. Maryknoll, NY: Orbis, 2010.

Mathias, Christopher, and Nick Robins-Early. "Rep. Steve King Goes Full White Nationalist in Interview with Austrian Site." *Huffington Post*, October 19, 2018. https://www.huffpost.com/entry/iowa-rep-steve-king-austria-white-nationalist_n_5bca4851e4b0a8f17eec6001.

Merton, Thomas. *Conjectures of a Guilty Bystander*. New York: Doubleday, 1989.

Mescher, Marcus. "Liturgy as Power-Sharing: Synergy for Solidarity." In *Liturgy & Power*, edited by Brian P. Flanagan and Johann M. Vento, 46–62. Maryknoll, NY: Orbis, 2017.

Moore, Hilary, and James Tracy. *No Fascist USA!: The John Brown Anti-Klan Committee and Lessons for Today's Movements*. San Francisco: City Lights, 2020.

Moxley, Elle. "St. Teresa's Alumnae Outraged after Students Pose with Swastika While Drinking." *NPR*, September 21, 2017, https://www.kcur.org/education/2017-09-21/st-teresas-alumnae-outraged-after-students-pose-with-swastika-while-drinking.

Munch, Regina. "'Worship of a False God': An Interview with Bryan Massingale." *Commonweal*, December 27, 2020. https://www.commonwealmagazine.org/worship-false-god.

Myers, Ched. *Binding the Strong Man: A Political Reading of Mark's Story of Jesus*. Maryknoll, NY: Orbis, 1988.

Nakatsu, Penny. "Speech at the United Front against Fascism Conference." In *The U.S. Anti-Fascism Reader*, edited by Bill V. Mullen and Christopher Vials, 270–72. New York: Verso, 2020.

NBC Bay Area Staff. "Modesto Police Investigate Noose, Gun Snapchat Video at Catholic High School." *NBC Bay Area*, April 11, 2016, https://www.nbcbayarea.com/news/california/modesto-police-investigate-noose-gun-video-hate-crime-catholic-snapchat/91770/.

Nelsen, Louis P., and Claudrena N. Harold, eds. *Charlottesville 2017: The Legacy of Race and Inequity*. Charlottesville: University of Virginia Press, 2018.

Obie, Brooke. "For Activist Rev. Sekou, 'The Revolution Has Come.'" *Ebony*, February 10, 2016. https://www.ebony.com/news/rev-sekou-interview/.

Orwell, George. *As I Please, 1943–1946 (The Collected Letters, Journalism, & Letters, Vol. 3)*. London: Penguin, 1970.

Osberg, Molly. "GOP Governor Pete Ricketts Allegedly Had White Nationalist on Payroll." *Splinter*, March 19, 2019. https://splinternews.com/gop-governor-pete-ricketts-allegedly-had-white-national-1833203562.

Parsons, Elaine Frantz. *Ku-Klux: The Birth of the Klan During Reconstruction*. Chapel Hill: University of North Carolina Press, 2015.

Paul, Dwayne David. "U.S. Catholic Bishops Must Choose: Black People or the Police." *Christian Socialism*, July 24, 2020. https://christiansocialism.com/us-catholic-bishops-racism-police-abolition/.

Paxton, Robert O. "American Duce." *Harper's Magazine*, May 2017. https://harpers.org/archive/2017/05/american-duce/.

———. *The Anatomy of Fascism*. New York: Vintage, 2005.

———. "The Five Stages of Fascism." *The Journal of Modern History* 70.1 (1998) 1–23.

———. "I've Hesitated to Call Donald Trump a Fascist. Until Now." *Newsweek*, June 11, 2021. https://www.newsweek.com/robert-paxton-trump-fascist-1560652.

Perry, Lewis. *Civil Disobedience: An American Tradition*. New Haven: Yale University Press, 2015.

Philadelphia Gay News. "The Rev. Osagyefo Uhuru Sekou—Ally to All." *Philadelphia Gay News*, May 9, 2017. https://epgn.com/2017/05/09/the-rev-osagyefo-uhuru-sekou-ally-to-all/.

Pineda, Dorany. "Kathleen Bellew on the Turner Diaries and the Capitol Riots." *Los Angeles Times*, January 8, 2021. https://www.latimes.com/entertainment-arts/books/story/2021-01-08/kathleen-belew-on-the-turner-diaries.

Porter, Tom. "Iowa GOP Congressman Steve King Won't Apologize for Retweeting British Neo-Nazi." *Newsweek*, June 17, 2018. https://www.newsweek.com/iowa-gop-congressman-steve-king-wont-apologise-retweeting-british-neo-nazi-996898.

Powell, Mario. "'How Long, O Lord?' Psalm 13 is the Cry of Black Americans." *America Magazine*, June 3, 2020. https://amaericamagazine.org/faith/2020/06/03/how-long-o-lord-psalm-13-cry-black-americans.

Roldan, Roberto. "Breonna Taylor's Family Members Say They Were Kicked Out of Hankison Trial for Clothing Featuring Her Face." *Metro Louisville*, February 24, 2022. https://wfpl.org/breonna-taylors-family-members-say-they-were-kicked-out-of-hankison-trial-for-clothing-featuring-her-face/.

Ross, Alexander Reid. *Against the Fascist Creep*. Chico, CA: AK, 2017.

Rowland, Christopher. "The Book of Daniel and the Radical Critique of Empire." In *The Book of Daniel, Volume 2: Composition and Reception* by John J. Collins, 447–67. Boston: Brill, 2000.

Ruland, Sam. "Student Stopped from Wearing 'Black Lives Matter' Mask at York Catholic Graduation." *York Daily Record*, August 3, 2020. https://www.ydr.com/

story/news/2020/08/03/student-pulled-york-graduation-ceremony-wearing-blm-facemask/5571478002/.

Saint-Jean, Patrick. "After George Floyd's Suffocation: A Litany for Oxygen from a Black Jesuit." *The Jesuit Post*, May 29, 2020. https://thejesuitpost.org/2020/05/after-george-floyds-suffocation-a-litany-for-oxygen-from-a-black-jesuit.

Santanam, Ramesh. "Police say Accused Synagogue Shooter Talked of Killing Jews." *AP News*, October 12, 2021. https://apnews.com/article/robert-bowers-pittsburgh-pennsylvania-pittsburgh-synagogue-massacre-massacres-369209d137a5b4e9fbcce b31d458645e.

Sarfatti, Michele. *The Jews in Mussolini's Italy: From Equality to Persecution*. Madison: University of Wisconsin Press, 2006.

Schiano, Chris. "Charlottesville Violence Planned Over Discord Servers." Unicorn Riot, September 5, 2017. https://unicornriot.ninja/2017/charlottesville-violence-planned-discord-servers-unicorn-riot-reports/.

Schmidt, Jalane. *Chachita's Streets: The Virgin of Charity, Race, and Revolution in Cuba*. Durham, NC: Duke University Press, 2015.

Schwing, Emily. "After Years of Sexual Abuse in Native Communities, Jesuits Sent Many to Retire on Gonzaga's Campus." *Northwest Public Broadcasting*, December 17, 2018. https://www.nwpb.org/2018/12/17/after-years-of-sexual-abuse-in-native-communities-jesuits-sent-many-to-retire-on-gonzagas-campus/.

Segura, Olga. *Birth of a Movement: Black Lives Matter and the Catholic Church*. Maryknoll, NY: Orbis, 2021.

———. "Do US bishops really believe black lives matter?" *National Catholic Reporter*, May 8, 2020. https://www.ncronline.org/news/coronavirus/do-us-bishops-really-believe-black-lives-matter.

———. "I Reached Out to Every U.S. Diocese. Here Are the Ones Implementing the 2018 Pastoral Letter on Racism." *America Magazine*, November 21, 2019. https://www.americamagazine.org/faith/2019/11/21/i-reached-out-every-us-diocese-here-are-ones-implementing-2018-pastoral-letter.

Segura, Olga, and Michael J. O'Loughlin. "U.S. Bishops Adopt New Anti-Racism Letter, First in Almost 40 Years." *America Magazine*, November 14, 2018. https://www.americamagazine.org/faith/2018/11/14/us-bishops-adopt-new-anti-racism-letter-first-almost-40-years.

Sekou, Osagyefo Uhuru. "Dear God." *Killing the Buddha*, February 25, 2010. https://killingthebuddha.com/mag/dispatch/dear-god/.

———. "A Prophet in Exile: A Personal Meditation on James Baldwin." *The Feminist Wire*, August 1, 2011. https://www.thefeministwire.com/2011/08/a-prophet-in-exile-a-personal-meditation-on-james-baldwin/.

———. "There Will Be At Least One Riot." *Truthout*, July 11, 2013. https://truthout.org/articles/there-will-be-at-least-one-riot/.

———. *Urbansouls: Reflections on Youth, Religion, and Hip-Hop Culture*. Nashville: Chalice, 2018.

Sharman, Jon. "Steve King: Republican Criticized by Own Party for Saying 'We Can't Restore our Civilization with Someone Else's Babies.'" *Independent*, March 13, 2017. https://independent.co.uk/news/world/americas/us-politics/steve-king-republican-iowa-congressman-restore-civilisation-babies-someone-else-geert-wilders-a7627191.html.

Shaw, Devin Zane. *Philosophy of Antifascism: Punching Nazis and Fighting White Supremacy.* London: Rowman & Littlefield, 2020.

Sincere, Richard. "Memorandum in Support of Motion for Temporary Restraining Order and/or Preliminary Injunction" *ACLU,* August 10, 2017. https://acluva.org/sites/default/files/field_documents/kessler_memoinsupportanddeclarations.pdf.

Skiles, William S. "Protests From the Pulpit: The Confessing Church and Sermons of World War II." *Sermon Studies* 1.1 (2017) 1–23.

Smith-Christopher, Daniel. "Daniel." In *The New Interpreter's Bible, Volume VII,* 38–39. Nashville: Abingdon, 1996.

Sowder, Amy. "Episcopal-Supported Intentional Community in Charlottesville Embodies Radical Discipleship—and Permaculture." *Episcopal News Service,* August 18, 2017. https://www.episcopalnewsservice.org/2017/08/18/episcopal-supported-intentional-community-in-charlottesville-embodies-radical-discipleship-and-permaculture/.

St. Félix, Doreen. "An Image of Revolutionary Fire at Charlottesville." *The New Yorker,* August 14, 2017. https://www.newyorker.com/culture/annals-of-appearances/an-image-of-revolutionary-fire-at-charlottesville.

Stanley, Jason. *How Fascism Works: The Politics of Us and Them.* New York: Random House, 2018.

Stoughton, Judith. *Proud Donkey of Schaerbeek: Ade Bethune, Catholic Worker Artist.* St. Cloud, MN: North Star, 1988.

Tabachnick, Toby. "Catholic Students Learn That Hate Can Hurt." *Pittsburgh Jewish Chronicle,* June 1, 2016, https://jewishchronicle.timesofisrael.com/catholic-students-learn-that-hate-can-hurt/.

Thiessen, Marc A. "Antifa are Domestic Terrorists. Meet Their Academic Apologist." *American Enterprise Institute,* September 5, 2017. https://www.aei.org/society-and-culture/antifa-are-domestic-terrorists-meet-their-academic-apologist/.

Trafzer, Clifford E., Jean A. Keller, and Lorene Sisquoc. *Boarding School Blues: Revisiting American Indian Educational Experiences.* Lincoln: Bison, 2006.

Turley, Jonathan. "The Hypocrisy of Antifa." *The Hill,* August 29, 2017. https://thehill.com/blogs/pundits-blog/civil-rights/348389-opinion-antifa-threatens-to-turn-america-into-an/.

Turnage, Clara. "The KKK Once Gave UVa $1,000. These Professors Want the University to Admit It." *The Chronicle of Higher Education,* August 15, 2017. https://www.chronicle.com/article/the-kkk-once-gave-uva-1-000-these-professors-want-the-university-to-admit-it/.

Uenuma, Francine. "The Massacre of Black Sharecroppers That Led the Supreme Court to Curb the Racial Disparities of the Justice System." *Smithsonian Magazine,* August 2, 2018. https://www.smithsonianmag.com/history/death-hundreds-elaine-massacre-led-supreme-court-take-major-step-toward-equal-justice-african-americans-180969863/.

Unicorn Riot. "Charlottesville Lawsuit Defendants Implicated in Premeditated Violence." *Unicorn Riot,* November 18, 2021. https://unicornriot.ninja/2021/charlottesville-lawsuit-defendants-implicated-in-premeditated-violence/.

United States Conference of Catholic Bishops. *Open Wide Our Hearts: The Enduring Call to Love—A Pastoral Letter Against Racism.* November 2018. https://www.usccb.org/resources/open-wide-our-hearts_o.pdf.

Van Gelder, Sarah. "Rev. Sekou on Today's Civil Rights Leaders." *Yes!*, July 22, 2015. https://www.yesmagazine.org/social-justice/2015/07/22/black-lives-matter-s-favorite-minister-reverend-sekou-young-queer.

Washington National Cathedral. "Announcement on the Future of the Lee-Jackson Windows." September 6, 2017. https://cathedral.org/press-room/announcement-future-lee-jackson-windows/.

White, Christopher. "Iowa Bishop Calls King's Racist Rhetoric 'Totally Inappropriate.'" *Crux*, January 16, 2019. https://cruxnow.com/church-in-the-usa/2019/01/16/iowa-bishop-calls-kings-racist-rhetoric-totally-inappropriate.

Whitman, James Q. *Hitler's American Model: The United States and the Making of Nazi Race Law*. Princeton: Princeton University Press, 2018.

Wiesenthal, Simon. *The Sunflower*. New York: Schocken, 1998.

Wildflower, Ben. "Miraculous Metal." https://benwildflower.com/products/miraculous-metal-print.

Wilkes, Andrew. "Living in the End Times: An Interview with Rev. Osagyefo Sekou." *Religious Socialism*, May 16, 2015. https://www.religioussocialism.org/_an_interview_with_rev_sekou.

Williams, Shannen Dee. "If Racial Justice and Peace Will Ever Be Attained, It Must Begin in the Church." *The Dialog*, June 10, 2020. http://thedialog.org/opinion/if-racial-justice-and-peace-will-ever-be-attained-it-must-begin-in-the-church-shannen-dee-williams/.

Wilson, Charles Reagan. *Baptized in Blood: The Religion of the Lost Cause, 1865–1920*. Athens: University of Georgia Press, 1982.

Wispelwey, Seth. "The NFL Is a Fundamentalist Church. And the Anthem Is Its Worship Song." *Sojourners*, June 1, 2018. https://sojo.net/articles/nfl-fundamentalist-church-and-anthem-its-worship-song.

Wylie-Kellermann, Bill. *Seasons of Faith and Conscience: Explorations in Liturgical Direct Action*. Maryknoll, NY: Orbis, 1991.

Zhao, Christina. "Kellyanne Conway Falsely Claims Antifa Stands for 'Anti-First Amendment' on 'Fox & Friends.'" *Newsweek*, August 19, 2019. https://www.newsweek.com/kellyanne-conway-falsely-claims-antifa-stands-anti-first-amendment-fox-friends-1455110.

Zinn, Howard. *The Zinn Reader: Writings on Disobedience and Democracy*. New York: Seven Stories, 1997.

Zirin, David. *The Kaepernick Effect: Taking a Knee, Changing the World*. New York: New 2021.